Climate Design

Climate Design

Solutions for
Buildings that Can Do More
with Less Technology

Gerhard Hausladen
Michael de Saldanha
Petra Liedl
Christina Sager

Birkhäuser

Contents

Foreword

The development of energy and room climate concepts is a multidimensional process which is carried out throughout all the various stages in planning a building – starting with the analysis of building use and local site conditions, following on into the optimisation of the building layout and facade and continuing up to the final dimensioning of the detailed design. The subject has been divided into five main chapters in order to represent the multilayered range of themes in the linear medium of a book. "Man", "Systems", "Typologies", "Technologies" and Planning" have been chosen as typical areas of planning. Some themes are dealt with in more than one chapter, each offering another point of view and having different degrees of detail.

"Man" explores people's relationships and needs, which it examines from the point of view of comfort. The most important aspects relating to design are expressed concisely. "Systems" sets out the concepts for facades, ventilation and room climatisation, their functions and interactions with the building. Comparative tables and decision charts are provided as an aid in all stages of planning and design. "Typologies" explains the relationships between use and energy and room climate concepts for administration buildings, atria, educational buildings, halls and residential buildings. Example projects create the link to practice. "Technologies" presents the most important facts for the design of facade elements, air conditioning components and energy generation systems in a compact one-page format. "Planning" summarises local site factors and their effects on building planning and design and the important legal considerations. Planning tools, their functional basis and areas of application are also introduced.

The book is founded on extensive experience in practical design and scientific knowledge. Additional calculations and simulations are set out in order to explain certain questions in more detail. The potential and consequences of current innovations are discussed. Drawing up energy and room climate concepts should not be based on technical and physical rules alone; it must also to be seen in a historical, cultural and sociological context. The introductions to each chapter take up these aspects in a thematicised way using associative elements.

The book may be used by architects, for whom comfort and low energy consumption are important in their work, and by engineers who would like to create holistic concepts by optimisation of the building layout and facade. For students, the disciplines of "Building Design" and "Building Services Technology" are brought together so that their studies may follow an interdisciplinary approach. Clients, investors and all those with an interest in building are offered the fundamental knowledge needed to competently assess concepts, designs and buildings, and from that to be able to make better decisions.

As befitting the complexity of the theme, the book has been the work of a team. The technical content of the book owes a great deal to the work of Hana Meindl, Michael Smola, Moritz Selinger, Christiane Kirschbaum and Fabian Ghazai. They deserve particular thanks for their contributions.

We wish all readers great pleasure and interesting discoveries on their journeys through the world of the senses, physics, architecture, technology and design.

Munich, Saint Tropez, Porto Corallo, 2004

Gerhard Hausladen
Michael de Saldanha
Petra Liedl
Christina Sager

Climate design

3 + X dimensions

Climate design is a planning discipline through which buildings can offer the user maximum comfort for minimum energy. Energy cost is not limited to heating energy; it is also related to all energy and material flows relevant to buildings. Comfort does not just mean thermal comfort but extends to a person's overall feeling of well-being. To achieve this goal requires an integrated approach to planning in which architecture and building services technology cannot be planned in series but must be part of a concerted overall system. By activating synergic affects in this way, we can create successful buildings that are flexible in use.

An accurate analysis of the use and comfort requirements is prerequisite to constructing a building that is fit for the purpose it is meant to serve at the lowest possible cost. Often a critical examination of the individual requirements can reveal great potential for savings. The location of a building has possibilities and requirements which have to be taken into account, in particular in the design of the building layout and facade. Many technical systems can be dispensed with provided the facade is matched to the building use and is equipped with all the required functional elements. The integration of the ventilation and the building concepts can save drive energy and ensure a comfortable supply of fresh air. Ventilation in conjunction with thermal storage mass can also improve room climate. If the constructional parameters are optimised, then that is a good basis for the installation of a regenerative energy system.

An integrated approach to planning not only considers the geometry of building but also brings in further parameters such as temperature, energy, solar radiation or time, and therefore the process requires the full involvement of a climate designer. With his approach spanning all disciplines he would enable the various specialists to work together efficiently. His skills include backing up soft facts with calculations. Ideally he contributes to all concepts from the very beginning right up to the commissioning of the building in order to be able to work out the potential for optimisation in all planning phases. This is normally done by intuition based on experience of planning and the systematic analysis of competed buildings, augmented by the targeted use of design tools. Successful buildings of the future rely on a critical examination of those of the past.

Man

Comfort in buildings is often equated with the compliance with standard, measurable limiting values, e.g. for room temperature, air velocities or illuminance. Wellbeing often involves subjective and difficult to evaluate aspects such as aesthetics, security, the ability to influence and understand one's surroundings or the spirit of the age. People do not analyse their surroundings like a physical measuring instrument. They rely on an overall impression gained from more than one of their senses. Therefore, for example, the perception of temperature and sound is connected with the colour of the surroundings, whilst sensitivity to odours is linked to air temperature and humidity. Facades and technical equipment in rooms should be so designed that the user can set the room temperature, air changes, natural and artificial light ambiance to suit his individual requirements.

In the planning of administration buildings, room air conditions in summer are becoming just as important as they are in winter. In this connection the question of what maximum room temperature would a user find unreasonable arises. In the assessment of comfort this value is important but the number of hours spent in very high room temperatures must also be taken into account. In this respect, standards give basically sensible indicatory values for the summer limits to room temperatures.

Short-term temperatures in excess of these limits are certainly acceptable, as long as the days of very high temperatures are few and far between. Excessive temperatures over several weeks are on the other hand not acceptable, especially if the employees are expected to adhere to a dress code. With a well-considered building concept and moderate heat loads, these maximum room temperatures can be accommodated even without cooling.

Nowadays it is possible to automate almost all processes of building operation. Optimising the way a building is operated can provide energy savings but it can also result in unintended overconsumption. Normally the user only becomes involved when a fault affects him. Thus an unnecessarily heated room would be noticed much later than one which was too cold. As well as this, people like to feel that they can do something about such a situation themselves. A good example of the above is the car, where manual transmissions are still as popular as ever. The car driver likes to experience the joy of driving. Transferring this into the context of buildings, people don't care so much about heating graphs and mass flows but would rather be able to set the rate of air change and room temperatures themselves there and then, and if possible be able to sense the effects of their intervention.

Buildings

Every location for a building has its own individual conditions with respect to shading, solar radiation, wind, air pollution and noise. If these external influences have been taken into account whilst the concept for the building was being drawn up, then possible problems may be avoided in the future. The costs of technical systems and energy are reduced and the user's enjoyment of the building increases. The orientation of the building should be selected to suit the desired amount of solar radiation admitted. External form and the arrangement of buildings are to be appropriate for the prevailing wind direction so that wind pressures on the facades are not too high and no areas of the building are subject to excessive wind speeds. In addition, occupied rooms should face away from busy roads. The building should be partitioned to ensure that all rooms can benefit from natural light and ventilation. The building height and circulation zones can allow thermal air movements to be used to drive ventilation. Wind forces can also improve through ventilation.

As the interface between the user in the building and the outside climate, the facade has a special significance for room climate, building functions and the costs of energy and technical content. The more effectively the building envelope can react to climatic and user-specific requirements, the less energy needs to be used. If the user has several different types of ventilation openings available, then he can select the best ventilation strategy for his needs and the outside climate. An efficiently adjustable shading system must be able to block solar radiation effectively, whilst allowing enough natural light into the room and, in ideal circumstances, provide some deflected light. Innovative facade materials can ensure a building envelope is successful. New insulation systems, such as vacuum insulation, and translucent insulation materials produce efficient facade designs. Variochromic glazing solves the fundamental problem of shading exposed to the weather.

Increased flexibility of buildings reduces the thermal storage mass considerably. The thermal dynamic is increased, especially in conjunction with the extensive transparency of the facade. This dynamic leads to higher energy demands and can only be overcome at great technical cost. In planning a building there should always be attention paid to providing adequate active thermal storage mass. Where this is not possible, latent heat storage in the form of PCM components offer an interesting alternative.

Technology

In the last decade the implementation of technology in buildings has moved between technology for its own sake and a phobia of technology. Both extremes normally have negative consequences for construction. A minimum amount of building services technology is essential as physical construction measures alone cannot achieve a comfortable internal climate. Polluted locations are only really capable of being developed by the incorporation of technical systems. If buildings are sensibly designed they will not result in increased energy consumption but will be able to effect savings. And certainly there is always the danger that the designer will abuse the building technology options to construct a building that by its very form will result in high energy and technical costs.

Optimising the building concept allows energy savings of up to 80% to be made compared with conventional buildings. To make further savings by constructional measures is only possible at unjustifiable cost. It is only with technical solutions that further savings potential may be realised. This could involve regenerative heating and cooling energy generation such as shallow geothermal energy, ground water, solar heating and photovoltaics, or the use of efficient energy generation systems such as fuel cells, combined heat and power plants and heat pumps. Renewable fuels such as wood or rape oil represent an ecologically attractive alternative.

Technical systems have always to be painstakingly integrated into the building process. This is time and cost intensive and prone to error. One solution is to reduce the complexity of the interface between building construction and services technology by designing technical systems as prefabricated modules. Another approach is to integrate technical systems into the facade. It is most important to consider the extremely different life cycles of the building structure and its technical systems. The building concept should incorporate building services in such a way that they can be maintained, modified or replaced conveniently at any time in the future.

In the design of the building the planner must have one eye on the technology that the building requires. Regenerative systems are to be preferred to fossil-fuelled systems. The designer must optimise his physical construction options before he can use this technology in the most efficient manner. In the case of the use of building services technology in buildings the following maxim applies: as much as necessary, as little as possible.

Man

It's the mass that counts

Rome, 7th August:
You stride forth from your fully air-conditioned hotel, full of enthusiasm for your journey of discovery into the bustling activity of this ancient metropolis. Highly motivated, you plan to investigate the ancient town's monuments. The blazing heat softens the asphalt. You've only reached the Colloseum and already your strength is fading. You manage to drag yourself past the Fontana di Trevi as far as the Pantheon. While your eyes are still in the process of adjusting themselves to the muted light, you feel the soothing coolness of this massive construction. Your goals change. You relax and happily while away the time until your evening Chianti.

I

Needs

We

Seeing

Hearing

Smell

A journey through the senses

Intuition

Feeling

Every person is an individual – different in all sorts of respects to all other people on the Earth. Factors such as age, sex or skin colour are external differences. People are different in terms of their cultural backgrounds, education, attitudes and behaviour. Some are mentally and physically well balanced, whilst others often appear nervous or anxious. Psychologists try to classify people's personalities by means of the "five factor model". Everyone has a particular profile of the following five characteristics: extroversion, in the sense of interests concentrated on the surrounding world, agreeableness, conscientiousness, emotional stability and openness to experiences. These factors are reflected in a person's specific personality profile. It differentiates us to a greater or lesser degree from other people. The question of how individual differences between people form and what causes them would have to consider influences from heredity and personal surroundings. Studies on twins have provided a great deal of research on this phenomenon.

The famous personality researcher Gordon Allport uses the sentence "The same fire that melts the butter hardens the egg" to explain that the same stimulus applied to different people produces different effects.

A person is not only different to other people, he or she changes and develops over time. Everyday fluctuations in mood, certain events or times of the day or seasons can also lead to one and the same person behaving differently at various times and in various situations. These fluctuations in personality are present in everyone to a varying degree. Psychologists make a distinction between relatively stable traits and transitory states. This distinction is very well illustrated by the example of anxiety. A general persistent anxiousness (trait) is different to an anxiety (state) particular to a situation. Differences between people mainly show up in traits, whereas fluctuations in mood of individual people are generally due to states.

Everyone has needs that demand to be satisfied. According to Maslow's hierarchy of needs, elementary needs come first and the needs of each higher level only become important when all the needs of the lower level have been fulfilled to a certain extent. On the first level of the hierarchy are basic physiological needs, such as food and water or oxygen. If the satisfaction of these needs is urgent, all other needs have to wait. Then come the needs for safety and belonging, which express themselves in the desire for comfort, peaceful coexistence and to give and receive love. If a person is satisfied, feels safe and a sense of social inclusion, then the urge for self-esteem and prestige becomes stronger. This level includes the wish to regard oneself as competent, capable and appreciated by others.

These four categories of need are described by Maslow as "deficit motivation". If these needs are not met, the result is a deficit, which is usually the way the person first becomes aware of the situation. At the top of the needs hierarchy, a person is satisfied, free of fear, loved, and self-loving and assured in the sense of self-respect. People who, in addition to these basic needs, also strive towards the full release of their potential or self-realization, show this through creativity, spontaneity and openness to change. The highest point of the hierarchy includes needs of transcendence, which can lead to a higher state of consciousness and to a cosmic vision of a person's place in the universe. Maslow calls these needs "growth motivation", as their satisfaction is the key to the full development of personality. The inherent need to grow and fulfil one's own potential is the driving force of mankind.

A journey through the senses

Porto Corallo Harbour, Sardinia.
A week of intensive work for this book is coming to an end. The idea of a journey through the senses is born.

Munich, two weeks later.
The stages are determined: 24 hours living without seeing, then 24 hours without hearing. Both in familiar surroundings. Interaction with others will be permitted. Then 24 hours in a meditation room, without seeing, without hearing, without outside stimulation.

Five pages in this book are planned for the description of this journey. One page for the time before, one for each stage and a page for the time after. We do not know how this will look. Perhaps they will remain blank. Because the expedition might have to be cut short. Because there is nothing to say. Because certain things are not allowed to be mentioned. But whatever is said it must be authentic. That is the only prerequisite.

I will now recount what I experienced.

One week before the start. *"Yes I'll do it."* That's the decision made. I gazed at the stars and listened to voices in the courtyard. What will it be like, days without senses? What will be different, during and afterwards?

Thursday evening. *"It will be over in a week."*

Sunday. Cycling around the lake at Starnberg. The first day off for weeks. Tomorrow is the start. Travel nerves.

Monday. I wake up. The sun is shining. Birds are chirping. It begins today at noon. *"We won't be seeing each other again until tomorrow."* Everything is prepared. Am I?

In a few minutes my eyes will be blindfolded. An uneasy feeling. I can hardly wait.

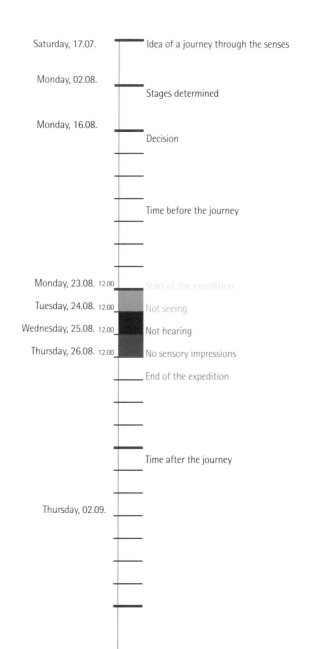

Saturday, 17.07. — Idea of a journey through the senses

Monday, 02.08. — Stages determined

Monday, 16.08. — Decision

Time before the journey

Monday, 23.08. 12.00 — Start of the expedition
Tuesday, 24.08. 12.00 — Not seeing
Wednesday, 25.08. 12.00 — Not hearing
Thursday, 26.08. 12.00 — No sensory impressions

End of the expedition

Time after the journey

Thursday, 02.09.

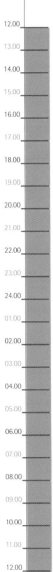

12.00
13.00
14.00
15.00
16.00
17.00
18.00
19.00
20.00
21.00
22.00
23.00
24.00
01.00
02.00
03.00
04.00
05.00
06.00
07.00
08.00
09.00
10.00
11.00
12.00

Not seeing

Leaving the house
Café

Church

Park

Eating at home

Sleeping

Monday, 12 noon.
I close my eyes. They are blindfolded. I can't see anymore. Everything is dark grey. As a consequence I hear more. The conversation stops. Silence. Amazingly: in spite of the blindfold everything seems normal to me, nothing spectacular.

Orientation inside the house is easy. I make tea. Household chores not done. I now hear and feel what I would otherwise see. I need little help.

The phone rings. I pick up the handset as usual. The caller has no idea that I cannot see anything. I too have almost forgotten.

13:30 hrs.
I leave the house. A friend's hand lends me a little security. The first few steps down are still uncertain. At the bottom at last. It is lovely and warm outside. My steps are short and my feet scrape along the ground. Slowly and carefully. I am aware of every little rise and fall in ground level. Every unplanned change in direction unsettles me. But I am not anxious.

14:00 hrs, in the café with friends.
Sunglasses conceal the eye patches. The café staff do not see through my "disguise". I hear conversations. I am not interested in what the owners of the voices look like. I imagine them in outline only. Like listening to a radio play.

16:00 hrs, in a church.
I detect the sacred space by its sounds. Intuition guides me in the direction of the exit. I fail in my attempt to orient myself by outside noises. *"I should trust my intuition more often."* Time passes more quickly than I think it does.

17:00 hrs, in a park.
I have to find my own way back home. For my safety there is always someone with me. I have to concentrate completely. At the beginning it goes unexpectedly well. The heat from the sun gives me the compass direction. My ears alert me to the traffic. I can tell the direction but not the distance. My feet probe the type of ground beneath and keep me on the paved surfaces. My outstretched arms warn me of obstructions. I am thirsty. My concentration flags and I have difficulty finding the right way. I need help. Got there. In the end.

20:00 hrs, at home.
My friends are there. My inability to see is not discussed. The outside world does not perceive it as a restriction. I take part in the conversation quite normally. I can tell the voices apart. I turn to face the people when speaking. I would prefer very much to see them.

Without colour the food does not taste as good. *"You eat with your eyes."*

I switch on the light. Out of habit.

22:00 hrs.
Everything is done deliberately. That is strenuous. I am tired. *"From tomorrow noon I will see again."*

Next day.
I wake up. What time would it be?
What's the weather like. Fresher overnight. Perhaps it will be a beautiful summer's day.

The time before the journey seems long ago.

What a joy! I can see again. How will not hearing be? How different will it be to cope with?

The human eye is often likened to a camera when explaining the process of perception. A deformable lens in the eye projects an inverted image onto the light-sensitive retina (film) attached to the back of the eye. The coloured iris has a circular opening in the middle, the pupil (shutter), which regulates the amount of light admitted. The retina converts the projected illuminance map into nerve impulses. This is done by two types of receptors, which are called rods and cones because of their shape. The cones have low sensitivity to light. They allow colours to be detected and ensure visual acuity when looking at objects. They are concentrated at the centre of the retina. The rods, with their high sensitivity to light, are simply responsible for detecting the contrast between light and dark and are effective in night vision. They are mainly concentrated on the periphery of the retina.

Considering the eye as just an optical system is not enough to describe human visual perception. The real work in perception is not in the image of the world on the retina but rather in the interpretation of this image. The eye's task is to convert the electromagnetic light waves into a pattern of nerve impulses, which are then carried along the optic nerve to the brain, where the visual cerebral cortex performs the conscious perception.

Three-dimensional vision is made possible by the different observation angles of the eyes, which cause their fields of view to partially overlap. The two viewing angles create a slightly offset image of the same object on each retina. The brain calculates the three-dimensional perception of depth.

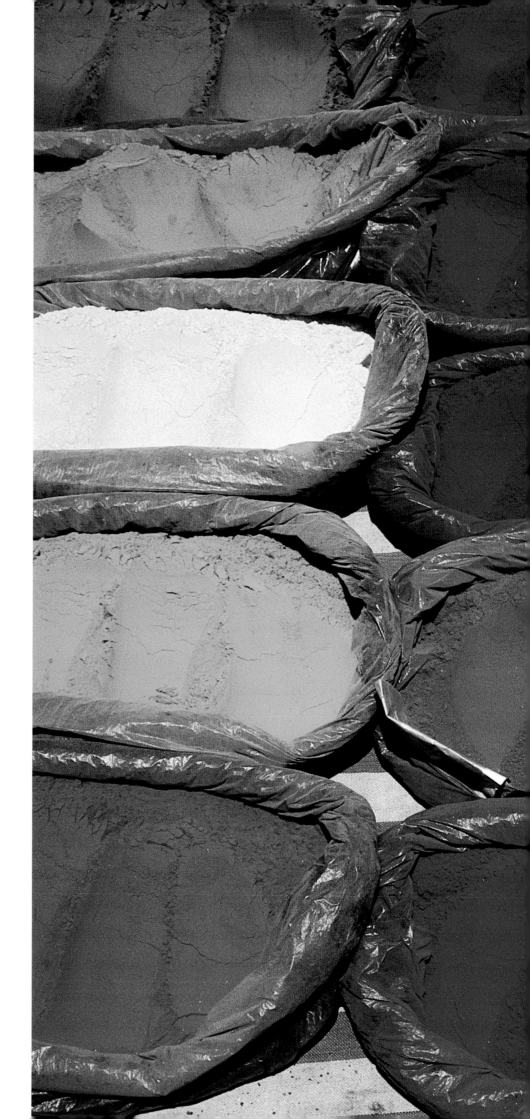

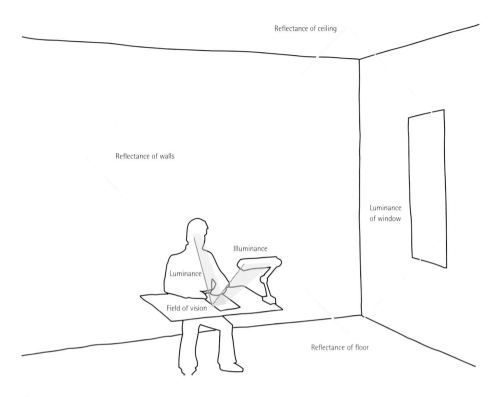

Reflectance of ceiling

Reflectance of walls

Luminance of window

Illuminance

Luminance

Field of vision

Reflectance of floor

Humans

Perceivable illuminance:
0.1 to 100,000 lx
Luminance range:
10^{-6} to 10^{5} cd/m²
Human field of view:
vertical 140°, horizontal 180°
Eyesight worsens with old age
and the sensitivity to glare rises.

Seeing

The human eye uses electromagnetic radiation from the sun in the wavelength range from 380 to 780 nm. The Earth's atmosphere is transparent to these wavelengths and this gives humans a reliable means of perceiving their surroundings. Visual comfort, safety and the state of the user's eyesight are important aspects of workplace lighting. Higher visual comfort at work promotes a feeling of wellbeing and can therefore contribute to increased productivity. This can be by means of natural light, artificial light or a combination of the two. The lighting ambience is determined by the distribution and level of illuminance, glare, light direction, light colour and colour rendering. Parts of the workplace with particularly high requirements for visual comfort are specially identified as visual task areas.

The required illuminance is calculated from the most demanding anticipated visual task and the ambient contrast. Pronounced changes of illuminance near the working area can lead to visual overload and discontentment as the distribution of illuminance in the whole field of view of the user must be able to be accommodated by the user's eyes. For the needs of eyesight and wellbeing it is also important that the colours of the surroundings are rendered as natural as possible and that there is an outside view.

Recommended illuminance

for various visual tasks (minimum values for the immediate surrounding area)
Filing room: 200 lx
Filing, copying, circulation zones, reception:
300 lx (200 lx)
Workplaces: 500 lx (300 lx) CAD workplaces: 500 lx (300 lx)
Conference and meeting rooms: 500 lx (300 lx)
Technical drawing: 750 lx (500 lx)
Colour rendering index R_a: at least 80

Recommended reflectance

Ceiling	*60–90%*
Walls	*30–80%*
Working surfaces	*20–60%*
Floors	*10–50%*

(in accordance with EN 12464-1)

Illuminance [lx], luminance [cd/m2] and colour temperature [K] of light sources

Candle	Incandescent lamp		Full moon	Sun	Overcast sky		Clear sky
			1 lx	*100,000 lx*	*10,000 lx*		*50,000 lx*
			2,500 cd/m²	*10^9 cd/m²*	*2,000 cd/m²*		*10,000 cd/m²*
			4,100 K	*5,000-6,000 K*	*6,400-6,900 K*		*10,000-26,000 K*

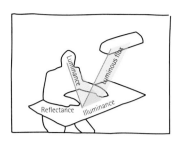

Terms

Luminous flux [lumen, lm] is the total output of light radiated by a light source. Illuminance [lx] is the amount of luminous flux falling on a surface. It is defined as 1 lm/m². Luminance [cd/m²] on the other hand is the amount of light propagating from this surface. It is the basis for the perceived brightness (luminosity) and depends on the reflectance of the surface. The actual impression of brightness is influenced by the state of adaptation of the eye, the surrounding contrast and the amount of information on the viewed surface.

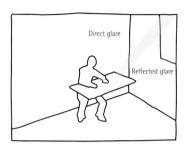

Glare

Glare is caused by bright surfaces in the viewing field and can be experienced as discomfort or as disability glare. Discomfort glare is only considered disturbing. Disability glare, on the other hand, diminishes the capacity of the visual function. Absolute glare occurs when the illuminance is greater than 10⁴ cd/m² and the adaptation of the human eye is exceeded. Direct glare is caused by too high a luminance in the viewing field. Screened luminaires and arranging the light source to be parallel to the direction of viewing of the observer can eliminate glare. Relative glare is caused by too high a luminance contrast in the viewing field. Reflected glare depends on the reflectance and the position of the reflecting surface as the glare light source is reflected by the observed object or the surroundings. A suitable arrangement of luminaires and workplaces, mat surfaces and limiting the luminance can avoid reflected glare.

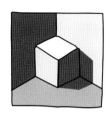

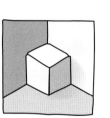

Diffused and directed light

Diffused light is emitted from large luminous surfaces. It creates an even soft light that illuminates the whole of a room and makes it visible without casting shadows or causing reflections. Directed light is emitted from a point light source. It creates shadows on objects and non-smooth surfaces and reflects off reflective surfaces. The optimum is a balanced ratio of diffused and directed light. Daylight from a clear sky has a ratio of directed to diffused light of between 5 to 1 and 10 to 1. An object or surface texture needs modelling with light and shadow for it to be perceived in three dimensions.

Brilliance effects are cause by reflection or refraction of directed light. They depend on the luminance of the light source. Glare occurs if the lighted object has no informational content. Illuminance and colour temperature must be compatible with one another in order for the effect to be pleasant. Warm light colours of up to 3,000 K are recommended for low illuminance and directed light. Neutral white to daylight white light colours from 4,000 to over 5,000 K are recommended for higher illuminance requirements.

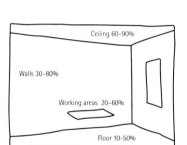

Reflectance and luminance

Glare can occur if luminance is too high. Great differences in luminance cause fatigue due to continuous adaptation of the eyes. Too low luminances or low differences in luminance on the other hand result in a less stimulating working environment. The luminance of surfaces depends on its reflectance and the illuminance on it. The luminance ratios should not exceed the limiting values of 10:3:1 in the area of the actual visual tasks, immediately adjacent area and remote surrounding area respectively.

Reflectance of materials [%]

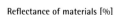

Aluminium	White paper	White interior plaster	Fresh snow		Wood	Rough concrete
80–85	*70–80*	*70–80*	*70*		*40–60*	*20–30*

12.00	Not hearing
13.00	
14.00	Going out
	Library
15.00	
16.00	
	At home
17.00	
18.00	Eating
19.00	
20.00	In the shower
21.00	
22.00	
23.00	
24.00	
01.00	
02.00	
03.00	
04.00	
05.00	
06.00	
07.00	
	Waking up
08.00	
09.00	Packing bag
10.00	Discussing stages
11.00	Walk to
	meditation room
12.00	

Tuesday, 12 noon

My ears are plugged. I open my eyes. I see in slow motion. Familiar surroundings. And yet different. Everything appears wonderfully soft. My eyes need time to get used to the light. Carry out tasks as usual.

I feel more cut off from the outside world than yesterday. That's surprising. I would have thought it was the other way around. No voices. No music. No shouting. No telephone. Just me. Seeing allows me to keep in contact with the outside world. Hearing allows the outside world to keep in contact with me.

14:00 hrs, going out.
Changed perception. My voice sounds dull and loud to me. My breathing wheezy. Insecurity on crossing the road. I must pay a lot of attention to compensate with my eyes for not being able to hear.

Leaves are moving on the trees. No rustling.

14:30 hrs, library.
Read a book. Hardly any distractions. I find it easy to concentrate. *"I must shut out sound more often in future."*

16:30 hrs, at home.
Suddenly there is someone standing in the room. No warning door bell, knocking or approaching footsteps. I feel taken by surprise. Greater insecurity than with not seeing. Hearing allows me to perceive the whole room. In front, behind and near me. Seeing is limited to a field of view.

18:00 hrs, eating.
People speaking to me. I don't react at first. Only after being touched. Lip-reading works. But cuts down eye contact. Slow clear speech and great concentration is required. Details are lacking. Sound of laughter absent.

After an initial curiosity there is less interest in speaking from the others at the table. Tiring. Communication drops off in the course of the day. I sometimes feel as if behind a glass wall. Isolated.

20:00 hrs, in the shower.
Just like standing under a waterfall, as usual. The brush has just fallen to the floor. I heard no impact.

20:15 hrs, watching TV with friends. Lip-reading is impossible. I feel excluded. I go to bed.

07:30 hrs.
I wake up. And still silence. I am thinking about the next stage at noon today. Excitement.

09:00 hrs.
Bag packing for the final 24 hours of the journey. Sleeping bag, pillow, tape recorder, toothbrush, towel, blindfold, jogging suit.

10:00 hrs.
I go over the rules for the final stage once more: no information about the time. No communication. No touching. Water, tea and food are always available. There is always someone in the vicinity of the room. Take time to consider things at low points before quitting. The exercise can be halted without failure. I will be brought out after 24 hours.

10:30 hrs.
We set off to walk to the meditation room. 20 minutes walk. I will not see the room until 12 noon. It is on the second floor next to the stairs. There will always be someone in the hall below.

11:30 hrs, in the cemetery.
Gone for a walk. Intensive perception. Strange mood.

11:55 hrs
The time has arrived. Tense. Relief to be finally underway. I say goodbye for now.

Hearing

The ear is the body's balance and hearing organ. The ear has three areas; the outer, middle and inner ear.

What we perceive as sound is transmitted to the ear by wave-like movement of air molecules caused by vibrating objects. Sound waves are conducted through the outer ear and along the auditory canal to the ear drum and are converted into vibrations. Three small bones in the middle ear (hammer, anvil and stirrup) transfer the vibrations to the fluid-filled, snail-shaped cochlea of the inner ear. Hairs lining the cochlea pick up the vibrations and convert them into electrical impulses, which are carried to the brain by the auditory nerve and are processed into a sensation. Each sound frequency is detected at different places in the cochlea and passed on to different parts of the brain so that with a little practice a person is able to distinguish individual tones from a mixture of frequencies. People differ strongly in their ability to hear and see. The hearing threshold is the lowest sound pressure at which a sound is detected by the human ear. The inner ear also acts as the body's balance organ, providing the means of perceiving "up" and "down" and acceleration.

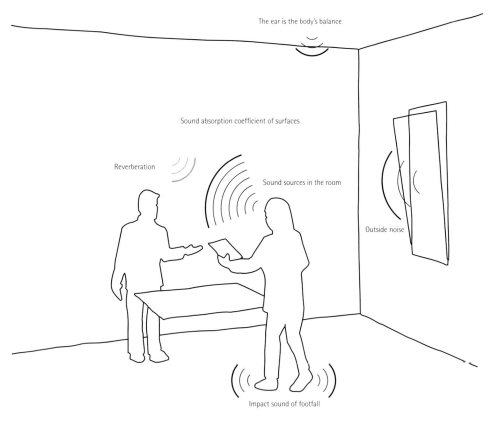

The ear is the body's balance

Sound absorption coefficient of surfaces

Reverberation

Sound sources in the room

Outside noise

Impact sound of footfall

Hearing

The acoustic behaviour of a room depends on the layout of the rooms in the building, outside noise, sound insulation of the building components enclosing the room, noise generated by in-house equipment, room size and shape, quality of the room-enclosing surfaces and furnishings. The dimensioning and positioning of sound absorbing or reflecting surfaces is important in determining acoustic behaviour.

The term room acoustics refers to the propagation of sound within rooms. The optimum reverberation time for a room depends on its size and use. Long reverberation times are not conducive to good intelligibility of speech in work rooms. Airborne sound is attenuated but not completely deadened by construction components.

Required reverberation time T (s)
Offices: 0.5 s
Conference rooms, seminar rooms: 0.6 s–0.9 s

Humans
Perceivable frequency range
16 to 20,000 Hz
Frequency range of human speech
100 to 8,000 Hz
Perceivable sound pressure level
0 to 130 dB

Sound absorption coefficient of materials in the frequency ranges 125/1,000/4,000 Hz

Absorber	*Acoustic panel, e.g. Heraklit*	*Parquet*	*Window, mirror*	*Wallpaper, plasterboard*	*Linoleum, PVC*	*Masonry*	*Carpet*
0.3 / 0.81 / 0.62	*0.13 / 0.54 / 0.71*	*0.03 / 0.05 / 0.05*	*0.12 / 0.04 / 0.02*	*0.02 / 0.05 / 0.08*	*0.02 / 0.04 / 0.05*	*0.02 / 0.04 / 0.07*	*0.03 / 0.2 / 0.4*

Loudness

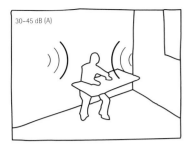

The sound level in a room must not adversely effect communication or concentration of people at work. The recommended sound level for offices is 30–45 dB(A).

Above 40 dB(A) an increase or decrease of 10 dB(A) is perceived as a doubling or halving of loudness. At less than 40 dB(A) even smaller changes in level are perceived as doubling or halving of loudness. A doubling of adjacent sound sources produces an increase in loudness of 3 dB, for ten sound sources the increase in level is 10 dB.

Weighted sound level [dB(A)]

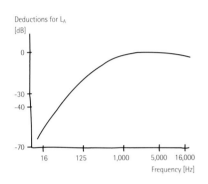

The human ear is more sensitive to certain frequencies than others and perceives them as having different levels of loudness. Sound levels are measured with weighting filters to take account of this. People hear very well in the 1,000 to 5,000 Hz frequency range but less so for the same loudness of sound with frequencies above and below this range. The index A in the unit dB(A) for expressing the weighted sound level L_A means that the various frequency ranges of a noise have been taken into account. The final result takes less account of the frequency ranges under 1,000 Hz and above 5,000 Hz.

Reverberation times

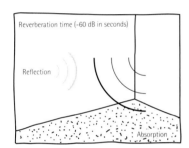

Reverberation time is the most important parameter in the characterisation of the acoustic qualities of a room and determines the duration of a sound event in a room. This is equal to the time it takes for the sound level to decay by 60 dB from the end of generation of the sound. The echo is the equivalent of reverberation in nature. The sound absorption surfaces of all materials in a room and the volume of the room affect reverberation time. Airborne sound energy is reduced by reflection off the materials enclosing a room and turning into heat. The sound absorption coefficient α is defined as the ratio of the non-reflected to the incident sound energy.

Materials absorb different frequencies of sound to different degrees. The reverberation time is long for very reflective materials (α – 0, complete reflection) such as those with hard smooth surfaces and this produces uncomfortable room acoustics. Sound absorbing materials (α = 1, complete absorption) such as those with porous rough surfaces suppress reverberation and hence deaden the noise. Doubling the sound absorption reduces the sound level by a factor of 3.

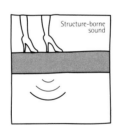

Airborne and structure-borne sound

Airborne sound is the sound vibration perpendicular to a surface. It is reduced by materials with a high mass per unit area and absorption.

Structure-borne sound is the direct vibration of a material, in most cases the floor. It is reduced by elastic and porous lightweight materials with a suitable dynamic stiffness. A material with a low dynamic stiffness provides better impact sound insulation.

If sound sources and hearers are situated in different rooms then sound reduction is mainly achieved by sound insulation, if in the same room, it can only be achieved by sound absorption.

Weighted sound level of noises [dB(A)]

Leaves rustling
20

Normal conversation
50

Inkjet printer
70

Traffic noise
80

Airplane taking off
110

Alarm siren
150

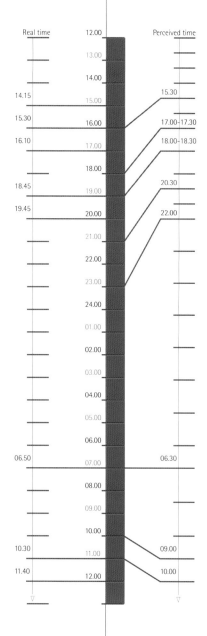

Wednesday, 12 noon, meditation room. Explore the room. I recognise it from earlier. I orientate myself. On the right; sleeping bag, pillow, bag. Left; tape recorder, drinking glass, thermosflask, cup. Two mats on the floor. I sit down in a comfortable position. Feels like taking off in a plane to an unknown country. Excitement. Breathing deeply. There is no turning back. Looking forward in anticipation to what I might discover.

"The next 24 hours belong to me." No deadlines. No telephone calls. No distractions. No impression of what's happening outside. No expectation or explanation necessary. Just me. Silence. Reflection. Meditation. Final sort out. OK.

Let's go.

I feel carried. Tired, I lie down to sleep. Wake up. I recall the situation. How long have I been asleep?

Walk to the toilet on the first floor. My hands and feet give me security. No stumbling. I close the door to my room quickly behind me. Immersion. Energy. *"I feel as if I am in another world".*

I can smell food. Rice and vegetables. Nice. I feel the human warmth in the food. Gratitude. How many hours have already passed? Impaired sense of time.

"Is anyone there?"

Concentrated attention. Clarity. Calm. Security. Feeling of wellbeing.

I feel my way to the window. Fresh air. Nothing done without thinking. I would like to move about. Physical exercise.

Prayer. Trust. Closeness. Harmony.

What time is it? Half-way through? I feel as if I am completely subjugated. *"I can give up at any time."* I miss the warmth of human company.

"Every day has 24 hours, every hour 60 minutes. But how differently the pace of time passes for me."

Oppressive. *"Is there such a thing as telepathy?"*

I lie down. Absolute silence. *"Am I still here?"* I touch myself. I sleep long, deep and solidly. Dreams.

I wake up. Is it morning already? Refreshed by sleep. I spread out and stretch. Vigorous exercise to obtain a sense of my body. I try to hold on to routine. Morning teeth brushing.

No tea or water here. *"Have they forgotten me?"* I feel dependent.

Meditation. It is still going well. Doing anything involves an effort. I try to sleep.

I become uneasy. In anticipation. How much longer will it go on?

"And what if they leave me here?"

Walk to the toilet. *"Is someone still there? You were supposed to bring me out at noon. It seems that time to me."*

Back in the room again. I'm struggling. Is anyone there? My breathing is deep and steady.

Feeling

The skin is the most versatile human sensual organ, with receptors for cold, heat, pressure and pain. The skin converts stimuli into electrical impulses, which are carried along countless nerves up the spine to the brain and then processed into what we actually feel. Cold is registered locally by cold sensors in the skin, whilst heat is detected globally by heat sensors in the brain.

Blood capillaries and sweat glands in the skin are spread over the entire body and allow highly sensitive temperature control. Touch organs are found in greater densities in the finger tips. The sense of touch is the least developed sense in humans. It can be trained to be highly discerning, for example in blind people.

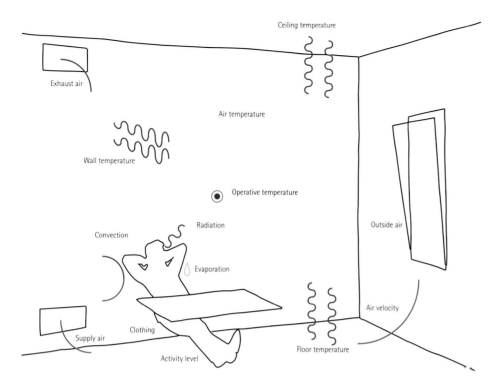

Ceiling temperature

Exhaust air

Air temperature

Wall temperature

Operative temperature

Radiation

Convection

Evaporation

Outside air

Clothing

Supply air

Air velocity

Floor temperature

Activity level

Humans
Skin temperature: average 32-34 °C
Body core temperature: 36.5-37 °C
Surface area: 1.7-1.9 m²
Volume: approx. 70 dm³
Mass: approx. 70 kg
Moisture dissipated:
approx. 60 g/h, at high air humidity (70%),
in summer 30 g/h,
during heavy work up to 150 g/h
Total heat dissipated: between 80 and 270 W
Average heat flow density: 40 W/m²,
Proportions of heat dissipated:
head 30%, hands 20%, soles of the feet 35%,
torso 15%
Humidity of exhaled breath: 95%
Temperature of exhaled breath: 35 °C

Thermal comfort
A person's sensitivity to heat is influenced by physical activity, type of clothing, age and gender, health, time spent in the room, season and room climate. It is also affected by air temperature and distribution, radiation conditions, air velocity and air humidity. Thermal comfort depends on the heat physiology of the person: A person must keep his core body temperature constant and therefore has to be able to transfer the excess heat produced by his metabolism into the surroundings. Office work has high comfort requirements as the users spend long periods in the room without being able to change location. Comfort is highly dependent on the conditions in the room. Spending long periods in rooms where the temperature is too high reduces performance, whilst too low a temperature can lead to illness. Large air movements cause local cooling of the body. In winter this can be uncomfortable, whilst in summer high air velocities can increase comfort at high room temperatures.

Air humidity has a minor effect on the perception of temperatures in the comfort zone. In this zone a 10% increase in air humidity feels like an increase in operative temperature of 0.3 °C. Air humidities of below 35% promote the build-up of electrostatic charge in plastics and dust accumulation. High air humidities in summer can make it feel uncomfortably close.

A person carrying out light office work produces 1.2 met (1 met, "metabolic rate" = 58.15 W/m²) from the heat of human metabolism. Normal office clothing in summer has a heat resistance of 0.5 clo, in winter 1 clo (1 clo, "clothing" = 0.155 m²K/W).

Room climate with average requirements for comfort
In winter:
$T_{operative}$: 22 ± 2.0 °C
Air velocity: 0.16 m/s
In summer
$T_{operative}$ 24 ± 1.5 °C
Air velocity: max. 0.19 m/s
(in accordance with DIN EN ISO 7730, Draft)

Conductivity [W/mK] and density [kg/m³] of various materials

Mineral fibre	Wood	Plastic		Glass	Brick	Concrete	Steel
0.040 W/mK	0.21 W/mK	0.25 W/mK		0.81 W/mK	1.0 W/mk	2.0 W/mK	60 W/mK
10–200 kg/m³	800 kg/m³	1,700 kg/m³		2,500 kg/m³	2,000 kg/m³	2,400 kg/m³	7,800 kg/m³

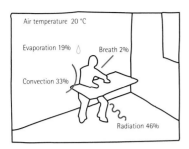

Heat dissipation

Thermal equilibrium in the human body is achieved when the heat produced in the body is equal to that dissipated by the body into the environment. Radiation from the body depends on the surface temperatures of the surrounding surfaces, convection depends on air temperatures and air movement, the amount of evaporation depends on absolute air humidity and body movement. A proportion of body heat is dissipated in moist breath.

The heat dissipated by a normally clothed person not engaged in physical activity in still air and an air temperature of 20 °C: radiation 46%, convection 33%, evaporation 19%, breathing 2%

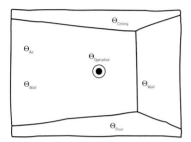

Operative room temperature

The operative room temperature is related to the average temperature of the surfaces enclosing the room and the room temperature. The difference between the air and surface temperatures should be a maximum 3 K. Within certain limits lower surface temperatures can be compensated for by higher air temperatures and vice versa.

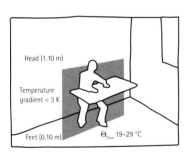

Vertical temperature distribution

Even though the head, hands and feet have small surface areas, people dissipate a large proportion of their heat from these body parts. The temperature of the floor has a decisive influence on thermal comfort. The temperature difference between the areas of the feet and head should be a maximum 3 K.

Average comfort requirements

Surface temperature of the floor: 19–29 °C
Temperature gradient: max. 3 K

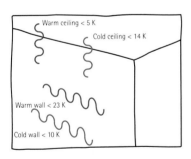

Radiation asymmetry

An asymmetric distribution of radiation temperature in a room due to opposing room enclosing surfaces being too hot or too cold can lead to discomfort.

The difference between the temperatures of opposing surfaces must be no greater than:
warm ceiling: max. 5 K
cold ceiling: max. 14 K
warm wall: max. 23 K
cold wall: max. 10 K
(in accordance with DIN EN ISO 7730, Draft)

Heat flow resistance [clo] office clothing

Skin	Shoes	Socks	Underclothes		Shirt	Trousers	Jacket
0	0.02	0.02–0.04	0.07		0.2–0.25	0.2–0.25	0.25–0.35

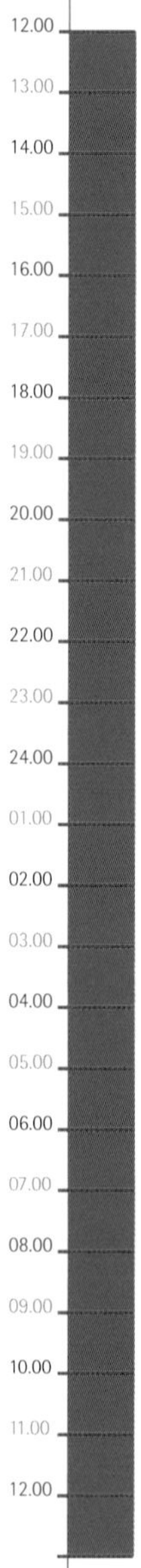

12.00	End of the journey through the senses	Thursday, 12 noon.
13.00	Excitement	I replied: *"I will be very pleased when it is*
14.00	Eating	*over."*
15.00		
		Embrace. Joy. Relief. Excitement.
16.00		I have made it.
17.00		
		I can see and hear again. And I can hardly find
18.00		words for it. This moment is indescribable.
19.00		
		Questions answered. Words often fail me. I can
20.00	Reflection	hardly assimilate the experience.

"A lot has happened."

"No, I had not wished to give up."

"There is nothing to hold on to."

"Sometimes all you had was your breathing."

"I cannot say that I would wish to do it again."

13.30 hrs.
Extreme hunger. I notice how drained I am.

20.00 hrs.
The journey is over. And now it really begins. I relive the previous few days in my mind.

Day after

Friday morning.
I have seldom felt so good. My thoughts are wide ranging and lucid. I feel as if I have returned from several weeks away in a distant land. Everything is familiar and yet completely new. Thankful for the experience. Good to have done it. In spite of doubts over the level of preparation. *"It is never the right moment - or always"*. It was one of the best experiences I have ever had.

It has changed something. Something important.

Looking at things consciously.

Present.
Concentration on an object.
"If I walk then I walk. If I stand then I stand ..."

I have discarded much that was superfluous. My mind is open. I have to be home.

I long for silence.

Smell

The original purpose of the sense of smell was to trigger rapid protective reactions subconsciously by reflex in the event of danger. The nose provides man with the quickest pathway to the emotions as every smell goes straight to the part of the brain that deals with emotions and memories, to the amygdala in the limbic system. Smells that you remember always have an emotional connection. Smells stay in our memories longer than images or noises. The sense of smell takes part much more often than we realise in the decisions we make.

Scent particles enter the nostrils, the insides of which have small stiff hairs. These hairs prevent foreign objects such as dust or small insects from being inhaled into the nasal passages. The actual organ with the sense of smell is the nasal mucous membrane, which has the odour-detecting nerves, the olfactory nerves. The cilia on the ends of approximately 10 million olfactory sensory neurons act as receptors. They are stimulated and transmit this stimulation along nerves to the brain where the complex impression of a smell is produced. There are 1,000 types of receptors to filter out certain odorants and thus distinguish between different smells. In the course of your life these odour receptors die in great numbers. A person is able to distinguish between at least 10,000 different smells using a matrix of smells stored in the brain, even at extremely low concentrations.

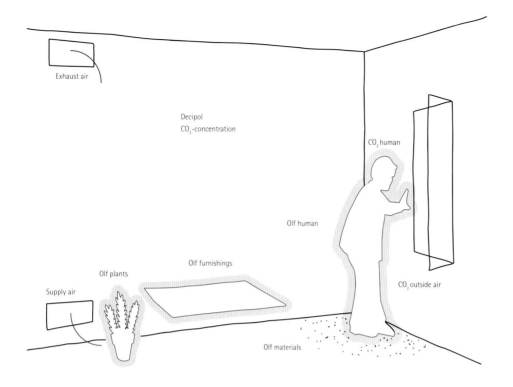

Exhaust air

Decipol
CO_2-concentration

CO_2 human

Olf human

Olf furnishings

Olf plants

Supply air

CO_2 outside air

Olf materials

Humans

1 olf
Differentiation of 10,000 different odours
16 breaths/minute
Breathing air flow: 0.5 to max. 9 m/h
CO_2 production: 10 to 20 l/h
Rule of thumb: each litre of CO_2 given off requires
$1m^3$ fresh air

Smell

The quality of room air depends on the quality of the supply air and the contaminants arising from the use and conditions in the room caused by people, plants, working processes, furnishings and building materials. The load on the air determines the required rate of air changes for the room. The fewer polluting materials used and the lower the proportion of smokers in the rooms, the lower will be the rate of air changes required for good air quality. Ventilation is important for supplying oxygen and removing CO_2, moisture and pollutants. Supply air should achieve the quality of unpolluted clean outside air. Air humidity has a significant effect on a person's sensitivity to odours: Tobacco and kitchen smells are perceived as less strong at high humidity, whilst rubber, paint and linoleum on the other hand seem stronger. The perceived air quality becomes less with increasing air humidity and air temperature.

Relating contaminant load to floor area in offices

Occupants: 0.1 olf/m²
Smokers: 0.1 olf/m² + 0.1 olf/m² for a smoker proportion of 20%
Materials and ventilation openings: 0.3 olf/m²

Contaminant load rates
Low level of contaminants in the building: 0.2 olf/m²
for a smoker proportion of 40%: 0.6 olf/m²

Air contaminants [olf/m²] from materials

Marble	*PVC/linoleum*	*Carpet, wool*	*Rubber seal Window / door*
0.01	*0.2*	*0.2*	*0.6*

Olf

One olf (olf) is equal to the air contamination caused by a person carrying out light office work, daily changed underwear and 0.7 showers per day. The strength of all sources of contaminants of the room air is given by summation.

Decipol

One decipol (dp) is equal to the perceived contamination of the room air when clean air moving at a velocity of 36 m^3/h is contaminated by one olf. The requirements for an air quality that would be perceived as acceptable on entry to the room is between 0.7 and 2.5 dp. If the outside air quality is high the outside air flow can be reduced.

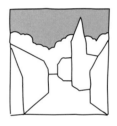

Typical outside air quality

Mountains, seaside: 0.05 dp
City with high air quality: 0.1 dp
City with average air quality: 0.2 dp
City with low air quality: 0.5 dp

Air contaminants and air changes

The Pettenkofer standard limits the CO_2 content of the room air to 1,000 ppm (equivalent to 0.1 Vol%). The CO_2 concentration should not exceed 0.15 Vol%. 20 m^3 of fresh air per hour are required to achieve this concentration. Ailments like headaches can occur when CO_2 concentrations rise above 0.04%. CO_2 concentrations of greater than 2.5% can start to have detrimental effects on health.

Minimum outside air flows per person for HVAC systems

Individual office: 40 m^3/h
Open plan office: 60 m^3/h
Conference room, circulation room: 20 m^3/h
Training room, pub: 30 m^3/h

Air contaminants [olf] from people

Human	*Smoker*	*Sportsperson*		*Flowers*	*Perfume*
1	*6-25*	*30*			

"It's great to be great, but it's greater to be human."
William Penn Adair "Will" Rogers (1879–1935)

"Music is the universal language of mankind."
Henry Wadsworth Longfellow (1807–1882)

"Faith is a function of the heart. It must be enforced
by reason. The two are not antagonistic as some think.
The more intense one's faith is, the more it whets one's
reason. When faith becomes blind it dies."
Mahatma Gandhi (1869–1948)

"Because it´s there."
George Leigh Mallory 1886-1924 on being asked why
he wanted to climb Mount Everest, New York Times
(18 March 1923)

"Music expresses that which cannot be said
and on which it is impossible to be silent."
Victor Hugo (1802–1885)

"The only real valuable thing is intuition."
Albert Einstein (1879–1955)

Systems

"*Modern elevators are strange and complex entities... This is because they operate on the curious principle of 'defocused temporal perception'. In other words they have the capacity to see dimly into the immediate future, which enables the elevator to be on the right floor to pick you up even before you knew you wanted it, thus eliminating all the tedious chatting, relaxing, and making friends that people were previously forced to do whilst waiting for elevators. Not unnaturally, many elevators imbued with intelligence and precognition became terribly frustrated with the mindless business of going up and down, up and down, experimented briefly with the notion of going sideways, as a sort of existential protest, demanded participation in the decision-making process and finally took to squatting in basements sulking.*"

Douglas Adams, The Restaurant at the End of the Universe (1980)

"'*Is there any tea on this spaceship?' he asked. (...) He had found a Nutri-Matic machine which had provided him with a plastic cup filled with a liquid that was almost, but not quite, entirely unlike tea. The way it functioned was very interesting. When the Drink button was pressed it made an instant but highly detailed examination of the subject's taste buds, a spectroscopic analysis of the subject's metabolism and then sent tiny experimental signals down the neural pathways to the taste centres of the subject's brain to see what was likely to go down well. However, no one knew quite why it did this because it invariably delivered a cupful of liquid that was almost, but not quite, entirely unlike tea.*"

Douglas Adams, The Hitchhiker's Guide to the Galaxy (1979)

Douglas Adams, The Hitchhiker's Guide to the Galaxy
© 1995 Reissue edition by Del Rey. Ballantine Books, New York
ISBN 0-345-39180-2

Douglas Adams, The Restaurant at the End of the Universe
© 1995 Reprint edition by Del Rey. Ballantine Books, New York
ISBN 0-345-39181-0

Facade systems

Ventilation systems

Room conditioning systems

Combined facade
Low Energy Office, Cologne

Single-skin facade
KPMG, Munich

Mullion and transom facade
Regional office for the environment,
Augsburg

Unsegmented double facade
Max-Planck-Institut, Munich

Mullion and transom facade
Regional office for the environment,
Augsburg

Combined facade
University of Brixen

Box window facade
Regional office for statistics and
data processing, Schweinfurt

Corridor facade
Trade Exhibition Tower, Hanover

Alternating facade
Münchener Hypothekenbank, Munich

Facade systems

The form and construction of a facade not only have great influence on the technical costs of a building, they also contribute to and are crucial for the wellbeing of building's users. They determine the internal conditions with respect to natural light, the entry of direct sunlight, glare, ventilation and sound insulation. The user should be able to intervene to take direct control. Care in formulating the facade concept and detailed design can create great potential for ecological and cost savings. The aim is to optimise the facade to provide increased user comfort with reduced energy and technical costs. Not least, aesthetic and cultural aspects must be considered in combination with technical and physical constraints and requirements to produce a worthwhile overall concept.

If facades were hermetically sealed, this would certainly result in the objective comfort parameters being fulfilled, but many subjective aspects of comfort would be ignored. The perception of the environment through odours, noises, airflow, moisture and temperature fluctuations is lost. The sense of the time of the year or day is greatly reduced.

The trend towards extensive transparency in architecture embraces the desire to eliminate the outer shell and allow the building to appear light and open. Furthermore, fully glazed architecture supplies a homogeneous appearance to the outer shell, which is associated with dynamism, precision and progress. From the outside, fully glazed buildings are, however, only transparent if they are backlit, that is to say seen in the twilight or with the sun shining through them. For the user inside, a high degree of transparency is unfavourable because of glare and possible overheating in summer.

The option of natural ventilation has become a fundamental consideration in facade design. Faced with a sudden need for fresh air, the user is able to take quick and for him immediately noticeable remedial action. In places with good air quality, a facade through which fresh air is introduced to the benefit of comfort can take the place of a ventilation system. If the type of usage means mechanical ventilation is necessary, then it should be supplemented by natural ventilation.

If facades are in direct sunlight, then they are suitable for the exploitation of electrical and thermal solar energy through integrated systems. An ideal solution would be to create constructional and economic synergic effects, e.g., where the solar system can be used to form the outer shell or solar cells be used as sun screening. For administration buildings, the exploitation of thermal energy is not advantageous, as they only have a small heat requirement.

The integration of technical systems into the plane of the facade can increase the flexibility of buildings, as the space for shafts and ducts does not have to be found internally. Technical systems can be easily fitted later if the use of the building is changed. In addition, the amount of prefabrication for decentralised concepts is higher.

Facades must be able to react dynamically to variations in climatic conditions and interior requirements. In this context, the availability of variochrome glass offers some completely new possibilities in facade design.

The facade as an interface

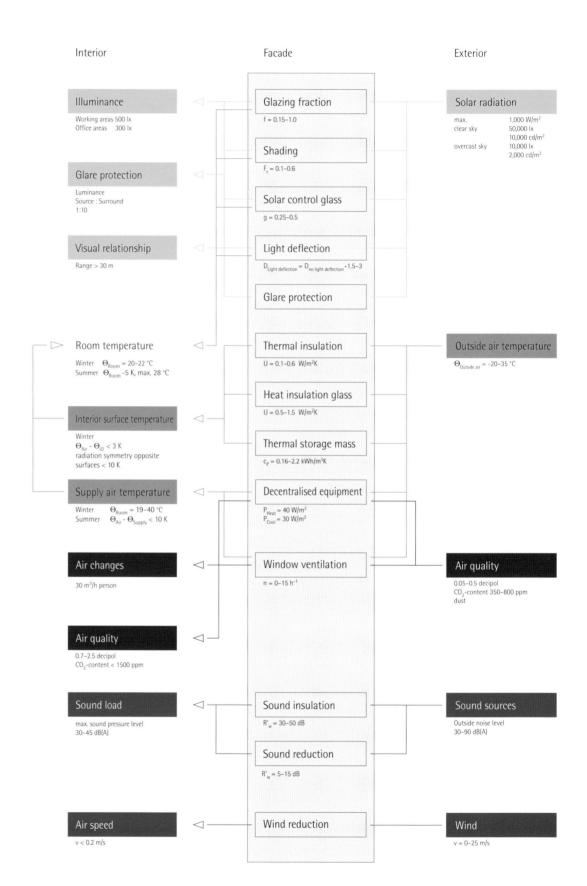

Interior

Illuminance
Working areas 500 lx
Office areas 300 lx

Glare protection
Luminance
Source : Surround
1:10

Visual relationship
Range > 30 m

Room temperature
Winter Θ_{Room} = 20–22 °C
Summer Θ_{Room} –5 K, max. 28 °C

Interior surface temperature
Winter
$\Theta_{Air} - \Theta_{iO} < 3$ K
radiation symmetry opposite
surfaces < 10 K

Supply air temperature
Winter Θ_{Room} = 19–40 °C
Summer $\Theta_{Air} - \Theta_{Supply} < 10$ K

Air changes
30 m³/h person

Air quality
0.7–2.5 decipol
CO_2-content < 1500 ppm

Sound load
max. sound pressure level
30–45 dB(A)

Air speed
v < 0.2 m/s

Facade

Glazing fraction
f = 0.15–1.0

Shading
F_c = 0.1–0.6

Solar control glass
g = 0.25–0.5

Light deflection
$D_{Light\ deflection} = D_{no\ light\ deflection} \cdot 1.5–3$

Glare protection

Thermal insulation
U = 0.1–0.6 W/m²K

Heat insulation glass
U = 0.5–1.5 W/m²K

Thermal storage mass
c_P = 0.16–2.2 kWh/m³K

Decentralised equipment
P_{Heat} = 40 W/m²
P_{Cool} = 30 W/m²

Window ventilation
n = 0–15 h⁻¹

Sound insulation
R'_w = 30–50 dB

Sound reduction
R'_w = 5–15 dB

Wind reduction

Exterior

Solar radiation
max. 1,000 W/m²
clear sky 50,000 lx
10,000 cd/m²
overcast sky 10,000 lx
2,000 cd/m²

Outside air temperature
$\Theta_{Outside\ air}$ = -20–35 °C

Air quality
0.05–0.5 decipol
CO_2-content 350–800 ppm
dust

Sound sources
Outside noise level
30–90 dB(A)

Wind
v = 0–25 m/s

Fig. 3.1.1 **The facade as an interface**
The facade of a building forms an interface between the environment outside and the user inside. In the winter it must ensure a comfortable interior climate, in summer prevent the entry of too much direct sunlight. It should provide natural light penetrating far into the building and a high degree of natural ventilation. These requirements lead to conflicts of objectives. Solar protection required for summer usually reduces the amount of natural light entering the building. Optimum use of natural light and the desired amount of direct sunlight in winter are often accompanied by glare. Predominantly natural ventilation in heavily trafficked locations is connected with undesirable entry of noise. The aim in devising a facade concept is to find for each location and intended use an optimum compromise between the various requirements

f   glazing fraction
F_c reduction factor for shading
g   total solar energy transmittance
D   daylight factor
U   thermal transmittance
c   heat storage capacity
P   output
n   air changes
R'_w weighted apparent sound reduction index
Θ_{iO} internal surface temperature

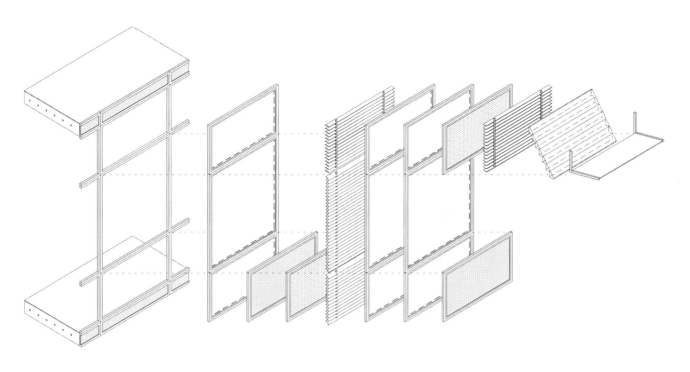

	Internal and external visibility			Shading					Light deflection		
Top area	window			lamellae	solar control glass	switchable glass	printed glass		lamellae	prismatic panel	light shelf
Middle area	window			lamellae	solar control glass	switchable glass					
Bottom area	window	opaque material	printed glass	lamellae	solar control glass		opaque material				

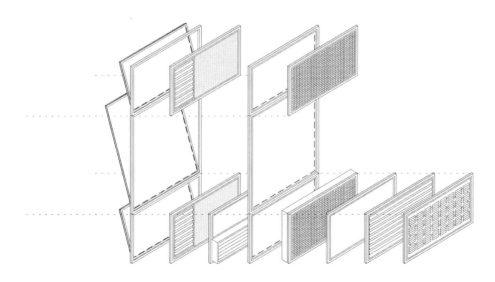

	Ventilation			Energy gain				
Top area	window	ventilation flap		passive	Tralucent thermal insulation			
Middle area	window			passive				
Bottom area	window	ventilation flap	decentralised ventilation equipment	passive	translucent thermal insulation / thermal storage	air collector	water collector	photovoltaic

Fig. 3.1.2 **Facade elements**
The facade can be divided into areas (top, middle and bottom) based on functions. Each of the three parts can perform various tasks in relation to views out and in, solar protection, light deflection, ventilation and energy gain. The various elements combine and complement one another to form the complete facade system.

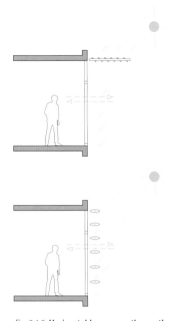

Fig. 3.1.3 **Horizontal louvres on the south facade**
The high solar altitude allows horizontal louvres at a flat angle to be used. Diffuse radiation retains the views to the outside and the provision of natural light.

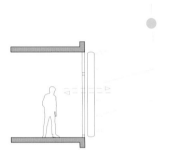

Fig. 3.1.4 **Vertical louvres on the east and west facades**
The solar radiation strikes the facade at a flat angle on east and west facades. Therefore horizontally hinged louvres have to be almost closed in order to limit the entry of solar energy. This means that visibility is lost and insufficient daylight enters the building. Artificial lighting must be switched on. A better solution is offered by vertically hinged louvres, which retain visual contact and provide the room with natural light.

The facade in summer

The thermal behaviour of buildings in summer is primarily determined by the solar radiation entering the room and the internal heat loads. Whilst the heat given off by people and equipment can be influenced only slightly, the entry of solar radiation is directly related to the orientation of the building and the energy transmittance of the facade. Optimising the facade for summer can produce unfavourable effects on the provision of natural light and undesirable solar gain in winter.

Building orientation A north-south orientation of a building means that only the south facade receives direct sunlight. In summer, at a high solar elevation, the sunlight strikes the vertical surface of the south facade at too acute an angle, causing the impinging radiation to be low and the reflection high. Sunshading louvres aligned horizontally can cut out direct sunlight with only a slight reduction in the visibility. Diffuse low-energy natural light is able to penetrate the internal space and contribute to the reduction of electricity demand and the associated internal heat loads. Fixed sunscreening features such as cantilevers, roof projections or balconies can be used on the south facade as seasonal solar protection. In winter the sun stays low in the south and can penetrate deep into the internal space, thus reducing the heating energy demand. With an east-west orientation, the surfaces of both facades receive light from a low sun. The angle of incidence is almost perpendicular and hence the amount of solar radiation entering is high and the reflection from the glass panels is low. The low position of the sun requires almost full closure of the horizontal louvres, which obstructs the view and cuts out natural light. The electricity demand for lighting and the internal loads rise and the building user loses his reference to the outside world.

The possibility to reduce the shading on the east and west facades is provided by the use of guided articulating vertical louvres. The adjustable angle of the louvres allows direct solar radiation to be cut out whilst retaining some visibility. In winter the amount of solar radiation received on the east or west facade is very little.

Glazing fraction The amount of solar radiation admitted is directly proportional to the glazing fraction. This is important to consider if large glazing fractions are proposed for facades that are exposed to solar radiation. On the north side, extensive glazing can be implemented with relatively few problems. On the south, and in particular the east or west facades, this is only possible with very good shading. In respect of daylight provision the arrangement of transparent areas is more important than their absolute size. The top edge of the window plays an important role. With glazing fractions of over 50% the additional solar gain in winter is hardly useable.

Solar radiation transmittance The solar radiation transmittance is determined by the total solar energy transmittance of the glazing and the reduction factor of the shading. The total solar energy transmittance can be influenced by coating the glass or by shading in the plane of the glazing. The reduction factor of the shading depends on whether it is internal or external. If it is external then its efficiency is higher by a factor of 3 to 5, although it has to be raised in windy weather. Internal systems are low maintenance, cost less and can be used whatever the weather. As well as having limited efficiency, their higher surface temperature and the associated heat emitted into the room can result in a feeling of discomfort. Placing them in the facade cavity of double-skin facades achieves a higher degree of independence from the weather.

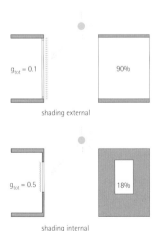

$g_{tot} = 0.1$ 90%
shading external

$g_{tot} = 0.5$ 18%
shading internal

Fig. 3.1.5 **Achievable glazing fractions**
The maximum possible glazing fraction depends on the position of the shading under conditions of constant solar energy entry and coexistent internal loads.

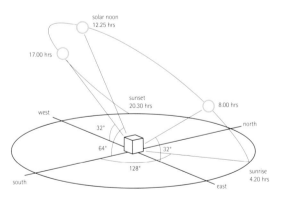

Fig. 3.1.6 **Course of the sun on 21 June (CET, Stuttgart, 48°46' N, 9°10' W)**
In summer the sun climbs to an azimuth angle of 128°. The solar load is particularly high, especially on the east and west sides, as the sun shines almost at right angles to the facade in the morning and afternoon. The direct sunlight reaches far into the interior of the room. On the south side, however, the sun stands high in the sky and therefore the amount of solar energy entering the building is much less.

external
$F_C = 0.10$

fixed 50%
d = 0.5 · window height
+ internal
$F_C = 0.40$

fixed
d = window height

internal
$F_C = 0.40$

Legend to Figs. 3.1.7 and 3.1.8
F_c = reduction factor for shading
d = depth of projection

Fig. 3.1.7 and 3.1.8 **Effect of shading on room temperatures in summer**
With an external system (yellow curve), room temperatures remain within an acceptable range even on hot days. Maximum temperatures exceed 28 °C for only approximately 15 hours per year, operative temperatures of 26 °C are exceeded for a total of 115 hours per year.

The efficiency of the fixed shading depends on the ratio of the window height to the projection depth d. If the latter equals the window height then the values on the red curve can be reached. This is however only acceptable in exceptional circumstances or with additional measures. For very small projection depths the values become worse and room temperatures rise uncomfortably. The combination of fixed projections and internal systems represents good weather-independent solar protection. Even if the depth of the projection equals half the window depth (orange curve), similar ratios can be achieved; for larger projection depths the results are much better still. Fixed systems are only viable on the south facade,and even then elevated room temperatures can arise because of the low sun.

Internal systems (green curve) and glazing fractions lead to uncomfortable temperature conditions. Room temperatures are continuously above 28 °C over a period of five weeks. Comfortable temperatures cannot normally be achieved even with passive cooling.

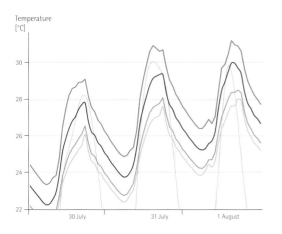

Temperature [°C]

Fig. 3.1.7 Operative room temperatures on three very warm days in relation to form of shading (south facade)

Excess temperature hours / year [h/a]

Fig. 3.1.8 **3.1.8** Excess temperature hours during hours of use in relation to shading

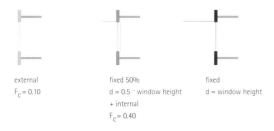

30%

50%

70%

90%

Glazing fraction 30%

Glazing fraction 50%

Glazing fraction 70%

Glazing fraction 90%

Legend to Figs. 3.1.9 and 3.1.10

Fig. 3.1.9 and 3.1.10 **Influence of glazing fraction on room temperatures in summer**
For glazing fractions of up to 50% and efficient shading, acceptable conditions can be achieved in summer even without cooling measures. If the glazing fraction is higher, temperatures rise to critical levels if no other measures are introduced. Even if extreme values are not reached, there are still long periods of time when, although it is not unbearably hot, it is too warm to feel comfortable. Improvement potential lies in further optimisation of shading and night cooling.

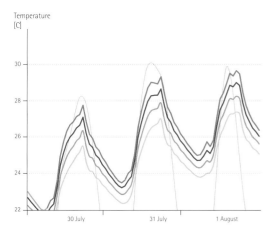

Temperature [C]

Fig. 3.1.9 Operative room temperatures on three very warm days in relation to glazing fraction (south facade)

Excess temperature hours / year [h/a]

Fig. 3.1.10 Excess temperature hours during hours of use in relation to glazing fraction

Boundary conditions applicable to Figs. 3.1.7–3.1.10 unless varied as a parameter

Orientation	south
Facade area	13.5 m² (4.5 m x 3 m)
Glazing fraction	70%
Total solar energy transmittance g = 0.6	
Shading external	$F_c = 0.20$
Office area	22.5 m² (4.5 m x 5 m)
Ceilings	solid
Wall	lightweight
Loads	2 people + 2 PCs
Ventilation 8:00 – 10:00 hrs	n = 5 h⁻¹
10:00 – 18:00 hrs	n = 2 h⁻¹
18:00 – 8:00 hrs	n = 2 h⁻¹
Lighting	none
Cooling	none
Climate	Würzburg

Insulating glazing 2 pane
$UW_{with R2}$ = 1.28 W/m²K
$UW_{with R3}$ = 1.65 W/m²K

Insulating glazing 3 pane
$UW_{with R1}$ = 0.77 W/m²K
$UW_{with R2}$ = 1.12 W/m²K
$UW_{with R3}$ = 1.49 W/m²K

Window area   0,3–1m²
Glazing fraction 35–50%

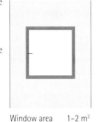

Insulating glazing 2 pane
$UW_{with R2}$ = 1.23 W/m²K
$UW_{with R3}$ = 1.49 W/m²K

Insulating glazing 3 pane
$UW_{with R1}$ = 0.75 W/m²K
$UW_{with R2}$ = 1.00 W/m²K
$UW_{with R3}$ = 1.26 W/m²K

Window area   1–2 m²
Glazing fraction 50–65%

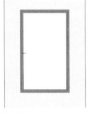

Insulating glazing 2 pane
$UW_{with R2}$ = 1.20 W/m²K
$UW_{with R3}$ = 1.39 W/m²K

Insulating glazing 3 pane
$UW_{with R1}$ = 0.74 W/m²K
$UW_{with R2}$ = 0.92 W/m²K
$UW_{with R3}$ = 1.11 W/m²K

Window area   2–4 m²
Glazing fraction 65–75%

Fig. 3.1.11 **Influence of the window frame on thermal transmittance U [W/m²K]**

Boundary conditions

Insulating glazing 2 pane		U_g = 1.1 W/m²K
Insulating glazing 3 pane		U_g = 0.7 W/m²K
R 1	Passive frame	U_f = 0.8 W/m²K
R 2	Low energy frame	U_f = 1.4 W/m²K
R 3	Timber profile frame	U_f = 2.0 W/m²K

Facades in winter

The energy balance of buildings has changed crucially over recent years. The use of materials with low U-values, increased thicknesses of insulation and enormously improved glazing is reducing the transmission of heat losses considerably. Administration buildings have internal heat gains from computer workstations and a high occupancy density. Improved thermal insulation means that solar gains are usable only to very limited degree and play a significant role only on the south side. Therefore nowadays the greatest proportion of the heating heat is required to make up for ventilation heat losses that arise from ventilation through the facade.

Insulation and surface temperature In addition to avoiding heat losses, thermal transmittance also plays a decisive role in thermal comfort; the smaller the heat flow through the external component, the higher the surface temperature on the internal wall surface. The operative temperature is made up of the surface temperatures and the air temperature. Therefore higher surface temperatures lead to improved comfort or allow a lower air temperature, which reduces ventilation heat losses. Furthermore a higher surface temperature of the external facade reduces radiation asymmetry in the room. Cold air drop at the external facade is reduced by improved insulation properties of the external skin, especially the glazing.

Window frames Over recent years improved glass characteristics have made window frames the thermal weak spot in a facade. Heat losses can be cut by reducing the proportion of frame or by improving the thermal properties of the frame. The U_g-value is a measure of the thermal transmittance of the glazing; the U_w-value is the thermal transmittance of the window, i.e. the combination of the frame and the glazing. The U_w-value must be determined for every window, typical U_w-values are between approx. 0.2 to 0.5 W/m²K greater than the U_g-values. For minor openings, e.g., for ventilation, rendering them opaque should be considered as this makes limiting the heat losses easier.

Heat bridges Improved insulation standards lead to the increased significance of the effects of heat bridges, which can be created by building geometry or by local reductions in the insulation properties of the facade. Apart from energy losses, heat bridges are typical locations where condensation or mould forms. In administration buildings with mullion and transom facades, heat bridges often occur in the area of the ceiling connection. In spandrel zones as well, large thicknesses of insulation are often only possible with some difficulty. The problem of thermal insulation at points with limited space can be overcome with vacuum panels.

Passive solar gain The reduced heating demand leads to a reduction in the useful solar gain, in particular as heating heat is generally only required on cold winter days, when, in any case, the amount of solar radiation admitted is very limited. The internal loads make the solar energy gain of hardly any use.

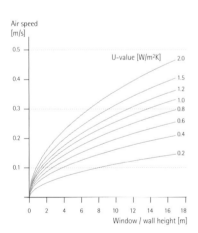

Fig. 3.1.12 **Air speeds of cold air drop at the facade in relation to the window / wall height and U-value** *(after Pültz)*

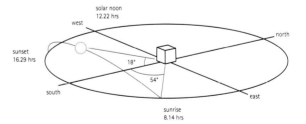

Fig. 3.1.13 **Course of the sun on 21 December (CET, Stuttgart, 48°46′ N, 9°10′ W)**
In winter the sun climbs to an azimuth angle of 54°. Solar gain is only worthwhile exploiting for a south-facing orientation.

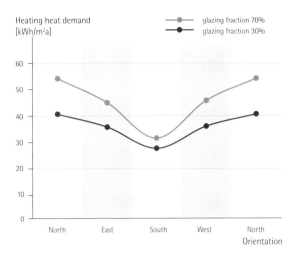

Heating heat demand
[kWh/m²a]

— glazing fraction 70%
— glazing fraction 30%

Fig. 3.1.14 **Influence of the orientation and glazing fraction on the heating energy demand**
As the glazing fraction increases, the heating heat demand rises due to the higher transmission heat losses. This effect is not compensated for by increased solar gains as they have hardly any benefit other than in residential buildings.

Variations of orientation and glazing fraction
Orientation   north, east, south, west
Glazing fraction   30%, 70%

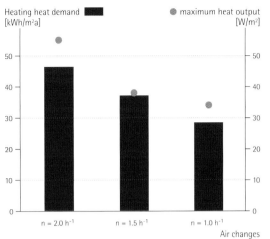

Heating heat demand
[kWh/m²a]

● maximum heat output
[W/m²]

Fig. 3.1.15 **Influence of air changes n on heating heat demand**
The rate of air change is considerably important for heating heat demand. For high air change rates, ventilation heat losses greatly exceed transmission heat losses

Variations of air change rate
$n = 2.0 \ h^{-1}$
$n = 1.5 \ h^{-1}$
$n = 1.0 \ h^{-1}$

Boundary conditions applicable to Figs. 3.1.14–3.1.17, unless varied as a parameter

Orientation	south
Facade area	13.5 m² (4.5 m x 3 m)
Glazing fraction	50%
Thermal transmittance	
Coefficient	$U_F = 1.4 \ W/m^2K$
Total solar energy	
Transmittance	g = 0,6
Shading	open
Office area	22,5 m² (4.5 m x 5 m)
External facade	lightweight, U= 0.25 W/m²K
Internal walls	lightweight, adiabatic
Ceilings	solid, adiabatic
Loads	weekdays
8:00–18:00 hrs	2 people + 2 PCs
Ventilation	weekdays
8:00–18:00 hrs	$n = 1.0 \ h^{-1}$
	at other times
	$n = 0.5 \ h^{-1}$
Lighting	weekdays
8:00–10:00 hrs	10 W/m²
10:00–16:00 hrs	off
16:00–18:00 hrs	10 W/m²
Ideal heating	winter operation only
Climate	Würzburg

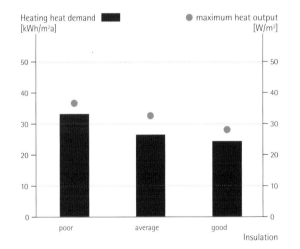

Heating heat demand
[kWh/m²a]

● maximum heat output
[W/m²]

Fig. 3.1.16 **Influence of the insulation standard of the facade on heating heat demand**
For administration buildings the heating heat demand is largely determined by the internal thermal loads and ventilation heat demand. For this reason the influence of the insulation is not as large as in residential buildings. Possible savings are around 30%. However, better insulation reduces the required heating load and improves comfort.

Insulation standards
poor U_{Wall} = 0.5 W/m²K U_{Window} = 1.5 W/m²K
average U_{Wall} = 0.3 W/m²K U_{Window} = 1.3 W/m²K
good U_{Wall} = 0.2 W/m²K U_{Window} = 1.1 W/m²K

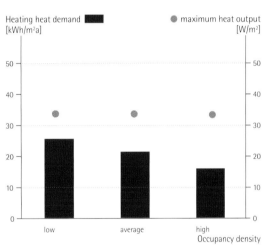

Heating heat demand
[kWh/m²a]

● maximum heat output
[W/m²]

Fig. 3.1.17 **Influence of room occupancy density on heating heat demand**
For administration buildings, the heating heat demand is largely determined by the internal heat loads and ventilation heat demand. In this respect occupancy densities play a role. The influence is somewhat attenuated as high room occupancy is sure to involve higher loads but also requires higher air change rates. Load changes and ventilation heat demand mean that the required heating output does not reduce with increasing room occupancy densities.

Variations of room occupancy densities
low   1 person + 1 PC + 100 W equipment, load 5 W/m², AC n= 0.5 h⁻¹
average 2 people + 2 PCs + 200 W equipment, load 10 W/m², AC n= 1.0 h⁻¹
high   4 people + 4 PCs + 400 W equipment, load 15 W/m², AC n= 2.0 h⁻¹

Fig. 3.1.18 **Natural light and shading**
If the provision of adequate natural light entry is not taken into account in the design of the shading, then this can lead to inadequate lighting levels even on sunny days.

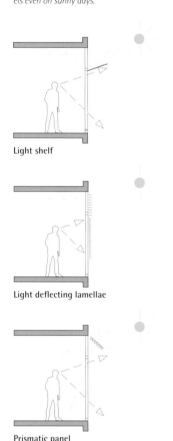

Light shelf

Light deflecting lamellae

Prismatic panel

Fig. 3.1.19 **Natural light deflection systems**
Deflection systems can direct light deep into the room and ensure better natural light provision.

Boundary conditions applicable to Figs. 3.1.20 and 3.1.21 unless varied as a parameter

Orientation	south
Facade area	13.5 m² (4.5 m x 3 m)
Glazing fraction	70%
Office area	22.5 m² (4.5 m x 5 m)
Reflectance of ceiling	80%
Reflectance of walls	40%
Reflectance of floor	20%
Transmittance	0.8

Use of natural light

The changes in the world of work, especially the increased use of computer monitors, bring with them new requirements for the use of natural light. More use must be made of natural light, but there must be no detrimental effects from glare. For this to be so, the amount of solar radiation admitted in summer should be kept as low as possible. Improved natural light provision has a great influence on the user's ability to perform at work and feeling of wellbeing, leading to an increase in productivity. The energy balance of the building can be considerably influenced by careful design of the lighting system. Looked at from the point of view of energy, the use of natural light is advantageous because of the electricity saved and because the heat input for identical light levels is up to ten times lower than for artificial light.

Fenestration and natural light In order to allow as much natural light to penetrate the room as possible, the skylight area should extend over the whole facade width. If the glazing fraction is kept small then two narrower windows are preferable to a single, centrally positioned window. The spandrel zone is of very little significance with respect to natural light levels at working height. It can even be opaque.

Use of light deflection systems Light deflection systems produce an even distribution in terms of daylight factors and improve lighting levels in the depth of the room. In its simplest form this can be sun shading with an upper part with differentially adjustable louvre angles. It can be installed in various positions in the facade. The natural light elements can be located outside in front of the facade, in the insulation glazing or inside the room. There are two types of natural light deflection systems: static and tracking systems. Moveable, guided tracking systems are controlled by the building management system. Light-deflecting venetian blinds are made to track the position of the sun to ensure the optimum light deflection. Moveable systems, e.g. retractable light-deflecting venetian blinds, can be retracted by a drive or manually when they are not needed. More efficient systems can be designed with light shelves, prismatic panels or holographic film.

bottom middle top

solar control glass [τ = 0.4] canopy no shading

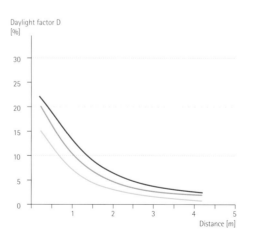

Fig. 3.1.20 **Daylight factor D in relation to the position of the window in the facade and the distance from the window**

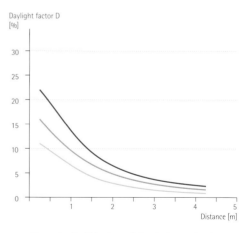

Fig. 3.1.21 **Daylight factor D in relation to the shading system and the distance from the window**

Use of energy

Facades are large surfaces, often exposed to the sun. Therefore they can also be used for energy gain. In addition to passive exploitation of solar energy by the glazing or by translucent insulation material (TIM), photovoltaic modules or solar heat collectors can be integrated into the facade. The energy systems should also perform facade functions so as to effect savings. The choice of systems is determined largely by the use of the building.

Translucent insulation material The integration of TIM elements in a solid single-skin facade can produce a delayed release of heat into the inside of the building. This is the equivalent of a load curve exhibited by administration buildings in which heating heat is normally only required during periods of little sunshine. One difficulty is shading in summer. TIM has particularly potential for use in buildings that have heating heat demand in the transition months, e.g. swimming pool buildings. If translucent insulation material without a storage wall is integrated into the facade, there is no time delay in the release of heat and the translucent material diffuses the light.

Air collectors integrated into facades Simple air collectors are advantageous for processes that require warm air, e.g. drying. They can also be used to condition rooms with low heat requirements. In the case of administration buildings, air collectors are mainly designed as double-skin facades, which can also act as noise insulation and weather protection whilst ensuring comfortable supply air temperatures in winter.

Water collectors integrated into facades For buildings with high hot water demand, the integration of water collectors into the facade is a viable solution. Direct integration into a facade can be by substitution for facade elements, which is a more economic solution than collectors positioned in front of the facade. Another positive effect is that the insulation required for the collector also contributes to the building insulation. Solar heating elements are not normally worthwhile in administration buildings, where there is hardly any demand for hot water. Heating heat demand is also extremely low and present only during periods of little sunshine. In this respect, heat obtained from solar heat elements is only usable from storage. In sunny summer months, the collectors would be unused and hence uneconomic.

Photovoltaic facades The integration of photovoltaic modules into a facade is accompanied by design and economic synergies when the modules form part of the exterior facade skin. The modules can be installed into mullion and transom facades or as a suspended skin on solid construction. Here they are replacing facade materials that would in any case be necessary. The fastenings also do not have to be specially provided. By the use of decentralised inverted rectifiers, the energy can be fed into the local electricity network. It should be borne in mind that the efficiency of photovoltaic cells decreases with increasing temperature. In this respect ventilated construction is advised. Depending on the arrangement and number of modules used, daylight penetration and the amount of shading may be influenced, which makes the use of photovoltaic facade modules with roof glazing of interest.

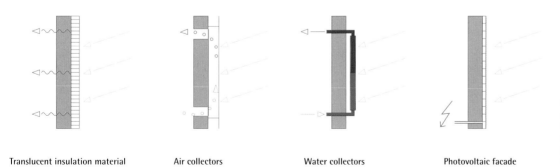

| Translucent insulation material | Air collectors | Water collectors | Photovoltaic facade |

Fig. 3.1.22 **Types of energy facade**
Active energy absorption at facades can be accomplished by various means. Depending on the system, the energy is released into the building by radiated heat, convection, warm water or electricity.

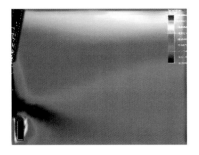

Fig. 3.1.23 **Fresh air supplied through a tilted window**
High airflow speeds and low air temperatures can be created at foot level when outside temperatures are low and fresh air enters directly through tilted windows. The radiator can no longer intercept the cold air drop.

Fig. 3.1.24 **Fresh air supplied through a facade optimised for ventilation**
An air mixing zone is created in which the cold outside air can be mixed with the warm room air. This avoids low temperatures at foot level.

Ventilation through the facade

No shafts, ducts or central ventilation equipment are required for ventilation through the facade. The air comes directly from the outside. Air quality cannot be adversely affected by dirty ducts or other system components and the user has full control over the air change rate. Heat recovery is only possible with an exhaust air heat pump in combination with a water-operated system. However, at locations with low air quality or high levels of dust and noise entry, the preferred method of supplying fresh air is through ducts or the building structure. In addition, direct ventilation through the facade with high outside air temperatures is linked to thermal discomfort, especially where a high air change rate is required.

Induction of supply air Supply air can be taken directly into the room without further measures at outside air temperatures of 5 to 24 °C. If the temperature is below this then by employing pulse ventilation thermal discomfort can be limited. Further possibilities include the mixing of supply air with warm room air in a mix zone or the introduction of air into the depth of the room. This requires appropriate construction measures in the room. Radiators near the facade can be used in conjunction with supply air preheating. Another possibility is supply air preheating in box windows or double-skin facades, which can provide ventilation with reduced entry of noise. However, in summer they have the disadvantage that the already warm outside air in the facade cavity is further heated by absorbed solar radiation. Comfortable ventilation is no longer possible. Air changes should be reduced to limit heat entry in summer when outside temperatures are above those inside. Another disadvantage of

ventilation through the facade in summer is the warmed facade boundary layer. In this boundary layer the air temperature is up to 10 K above the outside air temperature, depending on the wind conditions.

Ventilation elements Conventional tilt-and-turn fittings are generally not adequate to ensure natural ventilation the whole year round. Further elements are required depending on location and type of use. For noise loading and wind, bays with box windows or baffle panels are shown to be of benefit. They provide sound and wind protection as well as preheating the supply air in cold seasons. A smaller flap, opening directly to the outside, can allow facade ventilation in summer even in high wind speeds. This flap should have various opening angle settings to allow measured ventilation. The flap can provide pulse ventilation in summer in conjunction with a tilt-and-turn window. A controllable ventilation opening provides basic air changes, in some cases sensor controlled independent of the user.

Decentralised ventilation concepts Integrated facade ventilation units can be an effective addition to natural ventilation concepts. On days on which the window ventilation may cause thermal discomfort because the outside temperature is too hot or too cold, the integrated heating and cooling register tempers the supply air to a comfortable degree. The heating or cooling capacity is limited, however. Dehumidification is only possible in conjunction with condensate drainage pipework. There is one interesting alternative to central mechanical ventilation for ventilating individual rooms with increased air requirements, e.g. meeting or conference rooms.

	n [h⁻¹]
Windows and doors closed	0–0.5
Window tilted	0.3–1.5
Window half open	5–10
Window fully open	10–15
Windows and doors opposite open	> 40

Tab 3.1.1 **Number of air changes n for various types of window openings**

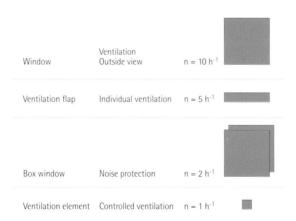

Fig. 3.1.25 **Form, function and typical air changes for various ventilation openings**

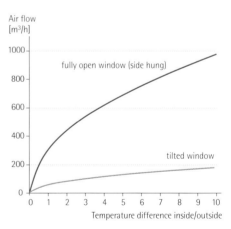

Fig. 3.1.26 **Airflow in relation to temperature difference and window setting** (after Pültz)

Sound insulation of facades

The increasing density of urban development makes building on sites exposed to noise unavoidable. In this situation sound insulation is becoming increasingly important. In the design of facades there are three aspects specific to sound insulation to be taken into account: the sound insulation effect of a closed facade, sound penetration when windows are open and the telephony effect whereby noise is transmitted by the intermediate cavity in a double-skin facade.

Sound insulation provided by the facade construction The objective of this sound insulation is to protect the user from unreasonable exposure to outside noise by adopting suitable facade design measures. The sound reduction index of a facade depends on the mass of the outside wall and the proportion and sound reduction index of the glazed areas. The frequency of the noise to be attenuated is also relevant. In theory, a doubling of the mass or frequency can be expected to produce an improvement of the sound reduction index of 6 dB. Curtain wall facades can provide an additional improvement of the sound reduction index of up to 15 dB in the area of the wall. Baffle panels or double-skin facades can also be used to improve sound insulation. Double-skin facades, if designed to optimise sound protection, can produce an improvement of up to 15 dB.

Noise penetration through open windows Noise penetration through open windows depends mainly on the size of the facade opening. A second facade plane such as a baffle panel or a double-skin facade can reduce the entry of noise even with the windows open. Sound blocking elements in the facade cavity can further improve this effect.

Noise protected openings can provide facade ventilation in single-skin facades even at noisy locations. The principle is based on multiple deflections in conjunction with sound damping elements. As a rule better sound insulation is provided by smaller ventilation openings. This can act against climatic requirements, e.g. if the openings in the outer skin are too small, it can result in overheating in the facade cavity.

Sound transmission from room to room Especially with unsegmented double-skin facades and office rooms with adjoining atria there is the danger of the telephony effect, in other words, the transmission of noise from room to room through the facade cavity or the atrium. This effect may be important for workplaces where confidential conversations take place. The participants in these conversations would find it particularly alarming if they could be heard elsewhere. This effect occurs even if the noise level in the room is very low.

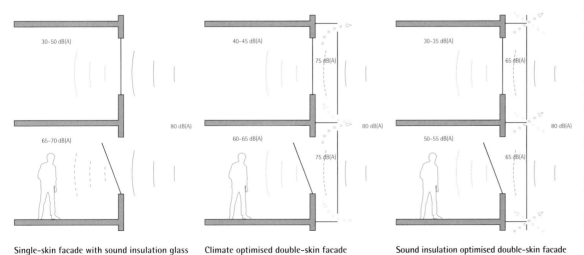

Single-skin facade with sound insulation glass   Climate optimised double-skin facade   Sound insulation optimised double-skin facade

Fig. 3.1.27 **Sound insulation for a single-skin facade with sound insulation glazing, and for double-skin facades optimised for climate and sound insulation respectively**
In the case of a single-skin facade, sound insulation glass can reduce noise by up to 50 dB. When the windows are open, the sound damping effect of the facade is extremely limited. In the case of a double-skin facade, the external skin has already reduced the sound loading to allow natural ventilation without serious detriment to comfort inside the room. The smaller the openings in the external skin, the better is the sound damping effect of the double-skin facade. This can also be achieved with sound blocking elements in the facade cavity. In the case of a double-skin facade optimised for sound insulation, the external skin can cut out up to 15 dB. If the openings are too small, this can result in overheating in the facade cavity, to the detriment of comfort.

Physical processes in facades

Fig. 3.1.28 Transmission heat loss

Transmission heat loss is the energy loss caused by heat conduction through the outer surface of the building. It is mainly determined by the thermal transmittance (U-value) of the individual exterior components and the temperature difference between the inside and outside. The U-value of the whole unit (e.g. the frame and glazing) is the relevant figure for transparent components.

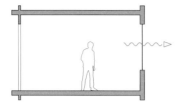

Transmission heat loss $Q_{Component}$

$$Q_{Component} = A_{Component} \cdot U_{Component} \cdot \Delta\Theta \cdot t \qquad [Wh]$$

$A_{Component}$ Area of componentl [m²]
$U_{Component}$ U-value of component [W/m²K]
$\Delta\Theta$ Temperature difference inside-outside [K]
t time [h]

	U [W/m²K]
2-pane heat insulation glass	1.4
3-pane heat insulation glass	0.6
New build to EnEV (wall)	< 0.35
Low energy house (wall)	< 0.25
Passive house (wall)	< 0.15

Fig. 3.1.29 Ventilation heat loss

Ventilation heat loss determines the energy loss caused by ventilation in winter. It depends mainly on the number of air changes and the temperature difference between inside and outside. At high rates of air change, ventilation heat loss is the largest contributor to the total heat loss.

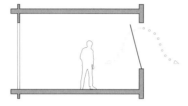

Ventilation heat losses Q_{Air}

$$Q_{Air} = V_{Room} \cdot n \cdot c_{Air} \cdot \Delta\Theta \cdot t \qquad [Wh]$$

V_{Room} Room volume [m³]
c_{Air} Heat capacity of air = 0.34 Wh/m³K
n Air changes [h⁻¹]
$\Delta\Theta$ Temperature difference inside-outside [K]
t Time [h]

	n [h⁻¹]
Window and door closed	0–0.5
Window tilted	0.3–1.5
Window half open	5–10
Window fully open	10–15
Windows and doors opposite open	> 40

Fig. 3.1.30 Total solar energy transmittance

The total solar energy transmittance for the facade is a function of the energy transmittance of the glazing, the glazing fraction and the reduction factor of the shading. The latter has to be specially calculated for internal systems as the energy transmittance is influenced by the reflectivity of the shading and glazing and the absorption properties of the glazing.

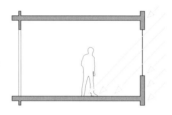

Total solar energy transmittance g_{tot}

$$g_{tot} = g \cdot F_c \cdot f \qquad [-]$$

g Energy transmittance of the glazing [-]
F_c Reduction factor of shading [-]
f Glazing fraction facade [-]

	g [-]
2-pane heat insulation glass	0.6
3-pane heat insulation glass	0.4
2-pane solar control glass	0.3

	F_c [-]
Shading lifted	1
External shading	0.1
Internal shading	0.5

Fig. 3.1.31 Daylight entry

The daylight factor is the ratio of the internal illuminance on a horizontal plane in the room and the illuminance on a horizontal plane outside under a fully overcast sky. The value of 1.5 times the window lintel height is used to calculate the depth of room that could be illuminated with natural light from a sidelight window.

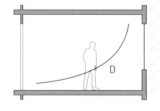

Daylight factor

$$D = E_p / E_a \cdot 100 \qquad [\%]$$

E_p Illuminance in the room [lx]
E_a Illuminance in the open [lx]

Illuminance depth in the room

$$\text{Illuminance depth} = 1.5 \cdot h_{Windowlintel} \qquad [m]$$

$h_{Windowlintel}$ Height from top of floor level to underside of lintel [m]

	D = 1%	D = 5%
Overcast sky (10,000 lx)	100 lx	500 lx
Clear sky (50,000 lx)	500 lx	2,500 lx

Fig. 3.1.32 Near-facade boundary layer

In summer the surface of a facade can heat up to temperatures of 40–80 °C depending on its reflective properties and colour. This heating up warms the air directly in front of the facade, which then moves upwards along the whole width of the facade. Depending on the wind, the boundary layer has temperatures between 5–10 °C above the outside air temperature and can be several metres thick.

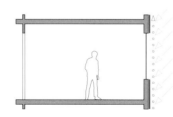

Boundary layer temperature close to facade $\Theta_{Boundarylayer}$

$$\Theta_{Boundarylayer} = \Theta_a + 10 \text{ °C} \qquad [°C]$$

Boundary layer temperature close to facade $\Theta_{Boundarylayer, wind}$

$$\Theta_{Boundarylayer, wind} = \Theta_a + 5 \text{ °C} \qquad [°C]$$

Θ_a Outside air temperature   [°C]

Internal surface temperature Θ_{si}

$$\Theta_{i0} = \Theta_i - \Delta\Theta \cdot U_{Wall} \cdot R_{si} \qquad [°C]$$

Θ_{i0} Internal surface temperature [°C]
Θ_i Room air temperature [°C]
$\Delta\Theta$ Temperature difference inside-outside [°C]
U_{Wall} U-value wall [W/m²K]
R_{si} Thermal resistance internal
     = 1.25 m²K/W

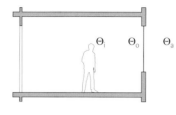

Fig. 3.1.33 **Internal surface temperature**
The surface temperature at the internal wall depends on the U-value and the difference between the inside and outside temperatures. Irradiance and the absorptance of the glazing also must be taken into account when considering internal surface temperatures. Irradiance plays a minor role near the walls.

	k [–]
Flat radiator	0.2
Radiator	0.4
Convector	0.8

Radiator output Q_{Rad} to counteract cold air drop *(after Nowak)*

$$Q_{HK} = \frac{A_U \cdot U \cdot \Delta\Theta}{k} \qquad [°C]$$

A_U Facade area [m²]
U U-value complete facade [W/m²K]
$\Delta\Theta$ Temperature difference inside-outside [K]
k Convective effect radiator [–]

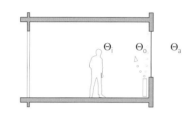

Fig. 3.1.34 **Cold air drop**
The room temperature near the window is noticeably cooled when the outside air and therefore the inside surface of the panels are cold. This gives rise to cold air drop at the window. This can be intercepted by a radiator near the window so that no circulating air current is formed, which would otherwise result in cold air and discomfort at floor level.

Boundary conditions

Window size	1.5 m x 1.25 m
Opening angle open window	90°
Opening angle tilted window	15°

Guidance values for air changes due to thermal currents

For fully open windows

$\Delta\Theta_{inside-outside}$ 20 K   approx.   1,500 m³/h
$\Delta\Theta_{inside-outside}$ 5 K   approx.   700 m³/h

For tilted windows

$\Delta\Theta_{inside-outside}$ 20 K   approx.   50 m³/h
$\Delta\Theta_{inside-outside}$ 5 K   approx.   25 m³/h

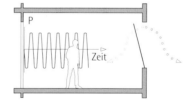

Fig. 3.1.35 **Air changes produced by thermal currents**
Air changes caused by thermal air currents through the open window establish themselves where there are temperature differences between inside and outside the room. The rate of air change depends on the window height and width, the opening angle, the airflow characteristics of the window opening and the temperature differ-

Boundary conditions

Wind velocity	1–4 m/s
$\Delta\Theta_{innen-außen}$	2–4 K

Calculation for air changes due to tilted window

50–100 m³/h

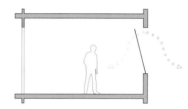

Fig. 3.1.36 **Air changes produced by the wind**
Wind-produced air changes take place in two ways. If air can flow through the building then air enters the room on the windward side, flows through the building by means of leakage and open doors, and exits on the leeward side. Pump effects, caused by pressure fluctuations from gusts of wind, can produce air changes through an opening.

	R'$_w$ [dB]
Aerated concrete 10 cm	41
Solid brick 24 cm	53
Heat insulation glass	30–35
Sound insulation glass	35–50

Sound pressure level L_i in the room directly at the facade

$$L_i = L_{ou} - R'_w \qquad [dB (A)]$$

L_a Sound pressure level external [dB (A)]
R'_w Sound reduction index facade total [dB]

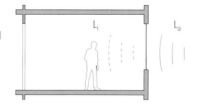

Fig. 3.1.37 **Sound reduction**
The sound reduction index of a facade determines how much sound is kept out by the closed facade. The weak points of a facade in terms of sound insulation are usually the windows. In the facade as a whole, the seals, window frames, the fittings and the details of the installation all have an effect on sound reduction.

Facade principles

The facade concept depends on the size and height of a building and its use and location. Influential factors include wind, noise, internal heat loads and type of ventilation. In addition, user comfort, architectural and town planning requirements are of crucial importance. The use of natural light, the possibility of natural ventilation and individual user control have become standard features.

Facade division Facades can be typically divided into three zones arranged vertically one above the other. On the top is the daylight zone, which provides natural lighting of the room. In the ideal situation light is deflected into the depth of the room so that the daylight factor does not drop as sharply further into the room. Light deflection into the depth of the room has the further advantage of reducing glare.

The middle zone provides the view and natural light when no direct sunlight strikes the facade. This area has shading so that during the summer months the amount of energy entering the room is reduced. In winter, when heat gain is desirable, internal shading improves visual comfort, especially at computer stations. The users can have individual control over this shading so that they can sit in the sun if they wish. This can be very pleasant, depending on the time of day and the type of activities being undertaken.

In the spandrel area, daylight plays a very minor role. This zone can provide outside views as required by the users. A glazed spandrel can give the user on the lower storeys a feeling of being continuously watched. For taller buildings, a transparent spandrel zone allows the user a view of the horizon and promotes a feeling of safety. However, there are people who are made to feel unwell by glazing that extends to the floor. As the spandrel zone contributes only slightly to natural lighting, reducing the entry of solar radiation in this area should be considered.

This can also be achieved whilst retaining a transparent appearance, for example, by using solar control glazing with a very low total solar energy transmittance, screen-printed glazing or metal grid structures in front of the glass. To a certain extent the outside view is retained. People cannot see in from outside and therefore the user may feel safer. In addition, ventilation elements can be installed in the spandrel area to allow natural ventilation without causing draughts.

Single-skin facades Single-skin building envelopes usually have very little distance between their functional elements. One example of this is the windowed facade, which, in its simplest form, consists of windows and solid wall surfaces but can also have number of functional elements. Ventilation, energy gain or light deflection elements are almost always positioned close to one another. This allows each element to be designed to best perform its function independently of the others. The glazing fraction is normally less and this has a positive effect on room climate. Single-skin facades can also be constructed as mullion and transom facades and the bays fitted with various functional elements. A single-skin facade offers no protection for shading and therefore any shading must be robust, for example fixed elements or wind resistant systems. A combination of a canopy and internal shading is an attractive alternative, which can, in some circumstances, provide the same result as external louvre systems in terms of heat gain.

Multiskin facades Double-skin facades have a second plane of glass positioned in front of the primary facade. The other functional elements are positioned in layers one behind the other, which means interaction of their functions cannot be avoided. The result is that the requirements of the individual functional layers are higher. One thing to keep in mind with regard to the provision of natural light is that light from outside has to

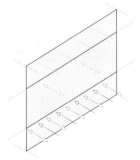

Fig. 3.1.38 **Facade division**
The facade is divided into three zones: the natural light zone, the view zone and the functional zone.

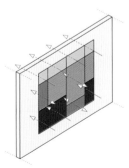

Fig. 3.1.39 **Single-skin facade**
In single-skin facades the individual functional elements are arranged close to one another.

pass through more than one layer and therefore suffers greater reduction. However, the lighting of the depth of the room ought to be just as good as for a single-skin facade. Therefore solar screening, which typically would be in the facade cavity, should be designed to permit adequate natural light to pass through into the room, whilst not having too detrimental an effect on the view. Another interaction is the supply air warming in the facade cavity. This is desirable in winter but can lead to comfort issues in summer. The overheating of the cavity in summer in certain building types can make mechanical ventilation essential. Depending on the design, the distance between the facade planes is somewhere between 0.2 m and 1.40 m. The cavity can be unsegmented, vertically (shaft facade) or horizontally (corridor facade). If divided horizontally and vertically the result is a box window facade. Double-skin facades are often chosen for aesthetic reasons. The homogenous exterior surface is hung off the main structure and gives a transparent light appearance to the building. In high-rise buildings, double-skin facades provide a solution to the problem of high wind pressures for windows with opening casements and solar protection exposed to the weather. The outer skin protects the facade openings, from which additional ventilation can be obtained when necessary. The second glazing plane also reduces wind pressure and the airflow through the building. In special cases, controllable flaps in the external skin determine the pressure conditions in the facade cavity, for example to achieve a specified airflow from outside to inside on all sides of the building.

Alternating facades The alternating facade is a combination of single- and double-skin facades and incorporates the principles of both types into an overall system. The disadvantages of the interaction of the individual layers of a multiskin system are avoided by the bays with single-skin facade elements. On the other hand, the advantages of the double-skin facade such as protection

from noise and wind, sheltered solar screening and the option of a comfortable supply of fresh air in winter are made available to the room.

Selection of concept The selection of the concept depends on the use, and functional and aesthetic aspects. If a building is exposed to high wind loadings this can give rise to two problems: solar protection is difficult to provide and natural ventilation requires special measures. The solution to these problems would be to construct the whole or part of the facade as double skinned. In a location with high noise loads, baffle panels or a partial double-skin facade would allow ventilation through the windows without admitting too much noise. It should be borne in mind for the double-skin alternatives that natural light has to pass through an extra plane of glass and will be correspondingly reduced. At low noise load locations or for building concepts with mechanical ventilation, a single-skin facade has many advantages. If necessary, the performance of the facade system can be improved by the integration of functional elements.

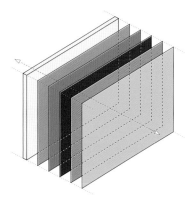

Fig. 3.1.40 **Multiskin facade**
In multiskin facades the individual functional elements are arranged one behind the other.

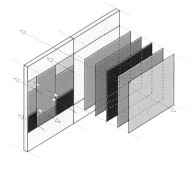

Fig. 3.1.41 **Alternating facade**
In alternating facades the functional elements are arranged both one behind the other and close to one another.

Light deflection
Shading
Energy gain
Ventilation
Internal and external visibility

Facade concepts

The choice of a facade type is made on the basis of location and use as well as the particular room climatisation requirements of the building. One important criterion is whether the sound load precludes natural ventilation through the windows. A decisive role is played by the desired glazing fraction and degree of transparency of the building. Overheating in the facade cavity is a particular characteristic to watch out for in double-skin facades. Other factors in the choice of facade concept include sound and odour transmission across the facade cavity, the space requirement, supply air requirements and the costs of maintenance and cleaning.

Windowed facade The windowed facade is the original form of facade. It consists of a solid, load-carrying wall with openings for light and ventilation. The solid parts provide thermal insulation and store a certain amount of heat. This cost-effective form of facade has good thermal properties and requires little maintenance. The amount of solar radiation admitted in summer is moderate. If the shading is provided on the exterior, it is exposed to the weather and cannot be used in strong winds. Ventilation through the facade only gives rise to discomfort when the outside temperatures are very low or very high. This type of facade is typical for residential and administration buildings in areas with no noise loading.

Element facade The element facade is a mullion and transom form of construction. In addition to transparent and opaque components, the facade can incorporate integrated functional elements for ventilation or providing natural light. It is a simple task to build in active energy systems. As the facade does not carry loads, the building can be erected quickly and a high degree of transparency can be achieved. The facade concept also allows a great deal of flexibility in design. The external shading is nevertheless open to the weather. The U-value of the facade depends greatly on the proportion of frame area. Opaque components lead to greater wall thicknesses, which can give rise to variations of internal wall profile. Heat stor-

age walls are unusual with these facades. This type of facade is typical for administration buildings in areas with no noise loading.

Baffle panel With a baffle panel, which can be additionally integrated into a windowed facade or a mullion and transom facade, the disadvantages of single-skin facades with regard to sound insulation and ventilation can be reduced. Noise level and wind pressure are reduced behind this attached and offset plate, thus allowing protected window ventilation. A baffle panel solution is simple to achieve and provides reliable weather and intruder protection for night cooling elements. Overheating of the facade cavity is less than for a double-skin facade. In winter the supply air is only minimally preheated. Baffle panels slightly limit the options for pulse ventilation and taking in air directly from outside. They are typically used in administration buildings at sites subject to medium levels of noise where night cooling is employed.

Alternating facade The alternating facade is a combination of single- and double-skin facades. It combines the advantages of both facade types in one concept. With an alternating facade every room has at least one double-skin and one single-skin facade element. Depending on the outside and inside climatic conditions, the user can ventilate the room through the single- or double-skin facade element. The alternating facade allows a high degree of user intervention and can offer comfortable conditions all year round. An alternating facade is expensive to construct and particular attention should be paid to shading in the single-skin facade bays. The small area involved means that this can be provided internally. Alternating facades are often found at noisy locations and when a high degree of user intervention is desired.

Box window facade A box window facade has the same effect as a double-skin facade that has horizontal and vertical divisions. It integrates equally well into a windowed facade or mullion and transom construction. The facade cavity can carry airflows vertically or horizontally through a continuous series of connections. Box window facades provide weather protection to shading, good sound insulation and comfortable supply air preheating in winter and the transition months. Overheating problems may arise in summer and direct supply air from outside is not possible. The box window facade can be used in residential and administration premises at noisy locations.

Corridor facade The corridor facade has horizontal bulkheads across the facade cavity dividing off each storey. Air changes are provided vertically at floor level or horizontally at the corners of the building. This reduces overheating of the air in the facade cavity. If air flows horizontally in the double-skin facade, it is often designed to control the air pressures in the facade cavity. The corridor facade requires more space and may lead to odour or sound being transmitted along the facade cavity. These facades are often used for administration buildings, in particular those with high wind loads.

Unsegmented double-skin facade Unsegmented double-skin facades have no horizontal or vertical divisions in the facade cavity. It can be designed with a cavity depth of less than 1 m or as a front glass wall at an offset of up to 5 m. Ventilation openings are typically positioned at the top and bottom. An unsegmented facade gives the building a uniform appearance and good sound insulation in normal circumstances. The height of the facade cavity can lead to severe overheating. The pressures in the facade cavity are not controlled, which can mean that odours and warm air can be transported through

it. Sound transmission from room to room can be more noticeable. These facades are often used with additional mechanical ventilation at very noisy locations.

Controllable double-skin facade A controllable double-skin facade is the most expensive type of facade to build. The whole external facade skin or individual flaps at ceiling and floor level on each storey can be opened. The controllable openings mean that the facade can be adjusted to suit the outside climatic conditions, thus avoiding overheating in summer. Sound insulation varies with the degree of opening. In summer there is a conflict between sound insulation and overheating. The facade is suitable for buildings in which natural systems are important in medium noise locations. Another typical area of use is in refurbished administration buildings.

Tab. 3.1.2 **Comparison of various facade concepts**

	Sound reduction effect with natural ventilation	Sound / odour transmission through facade cavity	Overheating of the facade cavity	Space requirement	Cleaning cost
Window facade	low	–	–	low	low
Element facade	low	–	–	very low	medium
Baffle panel	medium	–	low	low	medium
Alternating facade	high	–	– / high	medium	medium
Box window	high	–	high	medium	high
Unsegmented double-skin facade	very high	high	very high	high	very high
Corridor facade	high	medium	hoch	high	high
Controllable double-skin facade	variable	variable	low	high	very high

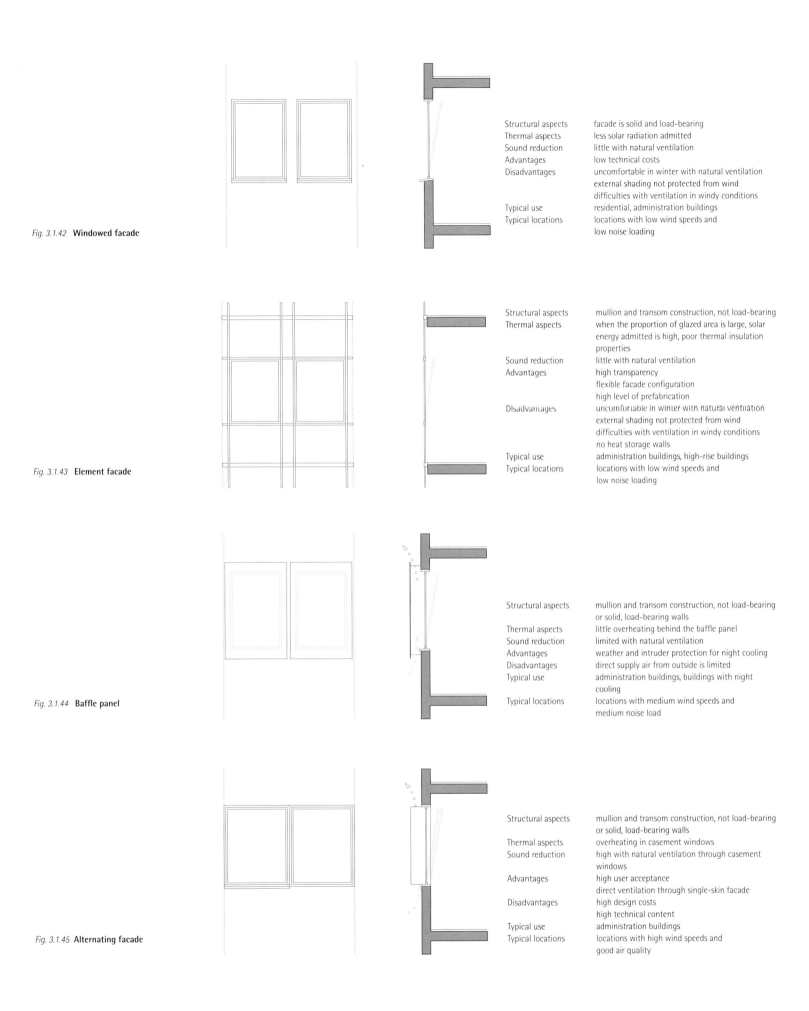

Fig. 3.1.42 **Windowed facade**

Structural aspects	facade is solid and load-bearing
Thermal aspects	less solar radiation admitted
Sound reduction	little with natural ventilation
Advantages	low technical costs
Disadvantages	uncomfortable in winter with natural ventilation
	external shading not protected from wind
	difficulties with ventilation in windy conditions
Typical use	residential, administration buildings
Typical locations	locations with low wind speeds and
	low noise loading

Fig. 3.1.43 **Element facade**

Structural aspects	mullion and transom construction, not load-bearing
Thermal aspects	when the proportion of glazed area is large, solar
	energy admitted is high, poor thermal insulation
	properties
Sound reduction	little with natural ventilation
Advantages	high transparency
	flexible facade configuration
	high level of prefabrication
Disadvantages	uncomfortable in winter with natural ventilation
	external shading not protected from wind
	difficulties with ventilation in windy conditions
	no heat storage walls
Typical use	administration buildings, high-rise buildings
Typical locations	locations with low wind speeds and
	low noise loading

Fig. 3.1.44 **Baffle panel**

Structural aspects	mullion and transom construction, not load-bearing
	or solid, load-bearing walls
Thermal aspects	little overheating behind the baffle panel
Sound reduction	limited with natural ventilation
Advantages	weather and intruder protection for night cooling
Disadvantages	direct supply air from outside is limited
Typical use	administration buildings, buildings with night
	cooling
Typical locations	locations with medium wind speeds and
	medium noise load

Fig. 3.1.45 **Alternating facade**

Structural aspects	mullion and transom construction, not load-bearing
	or solid, load-bearing walls
Thermal aspects	overheating in casement windows
Sound reduction	high with natural ventilation through casement
	windows
Advantages	high user acceptance
	direct ventilation through single-skin facade
Disadvantages	high design costs
	high technical content
Typical use	administration buildings
Typical locations	locations with high wind speeds and
	good air quality

Structural aspects	mullion and transom construction, not load-bearing or solid, load-bearing walls
Thermal aspects	overheating in the facade cavity
Sound reduction	high with natural ventilation
Advantages	protected shading
Disadvantages	high technical content
Typical use	administration buildings, residential buildings, high-rise buildings
Typical locations	locations with high wind speeds and high noise load

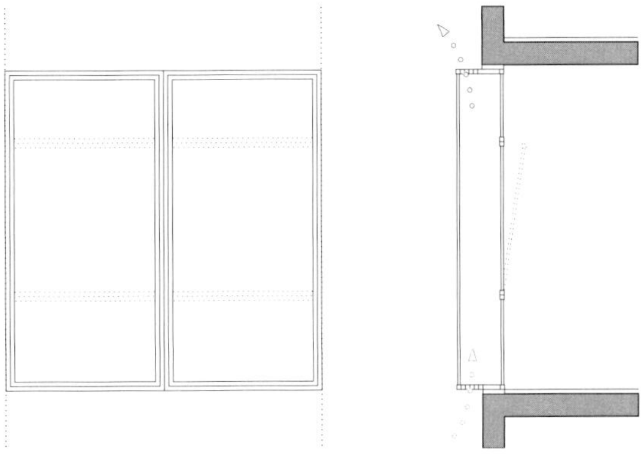

Fig. 3.1.46 **Box window facade**

Structural aspects	generally the facade is not load-bearing
Thermal aspects	overheating in the corridor
Sound reduction	high with natural ventilation
Advantages	air pressures in the facade cavity can be controlled the corridor can be used as a gathering or meeting place
Disadvantages	high technical content
Typical use	administration buildings, high-rise buildings
Typical locations	locations with high wind speeds and high noise load

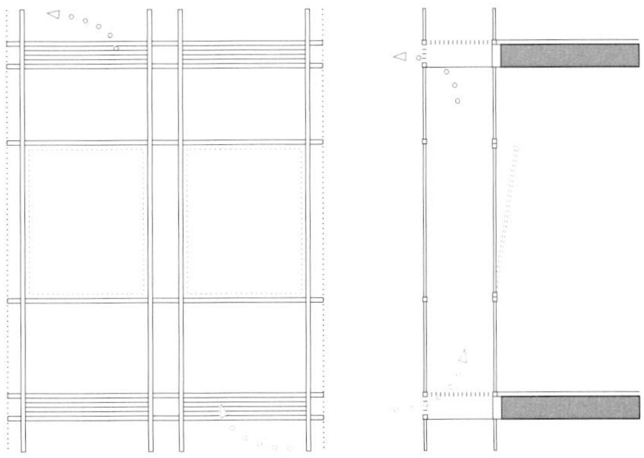

Fig. 3.1.47 **Corridor facade**

Structural aspects	generally the facade is not load-bearing
Thermal aspects	severe overheating in the facade cavity
Sound reduction	very high with natural ventilation
Advantages	high transparency uniform appearance
Disadvantages	additional mechanical ventilation necessary high sound and odour transmission from room to room air pressures in the facade cavity are not controlled
Typical use	administration buildings
Typical locations	locations with high wind speeds and very high noise load

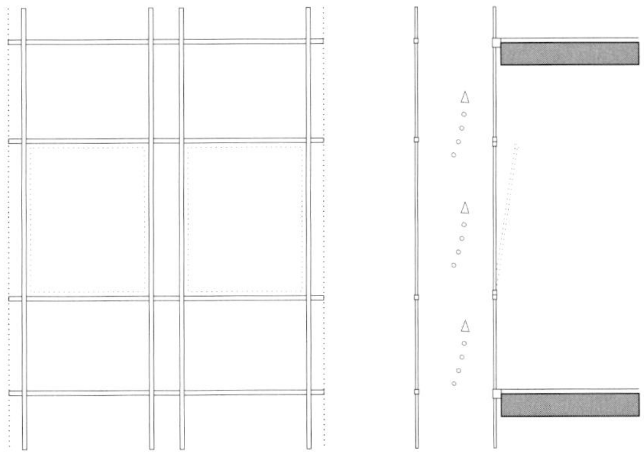

Fig. 3.1.48 **Unsegmented double-skin facade**

Structural aspects	generally the facade is not load-bearing
Thermal aspects	no overheating in the facade cavity
Sound reduction	little to high with natural ventilation depending on control
Advantages	adjustable to outside conditions by means of control systems high transparency
Disadvantages	very high technical content
Typical use	administration buildings, as facing panel in refurbishment projects
Typical locations	locations with high wind speeds and medium noise load

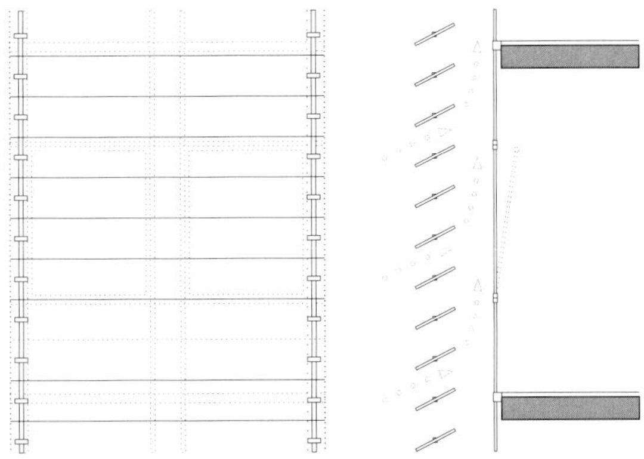

Fig. 3.1.49 **Controllable double-skin facade**

Required sound reduction effect
with open windows

Typical glazing fraction

low
<15 dB

medium
15–25 dB

high
>25 dB

low
<30%

medium
30–70%

high
>70%

Window facade

Box window facade

Element facade

Corridor facade

Baffle panel

Unsegmented double-skin facade

Alternating facade

Controllable double-skin facade

Fig. 3.1.50 **Decision chart for practical facade concepts**
The important criteria in the selection of a facade system are the sound reduction effectiveness of the facade with open windows and the transparency of the building, which depends on the glazing fraction. Suitable systems result from the combination of the selected initial criteria. The different specific characteristics of each system are shown by colour coding. The coloured squares represent three grades of performance: good (filled), medium (half-filled) and poor (empty).

Thus the combination of requirements of medium sound reduction with a high glazing fraction results in the recommendation of a controllable double-skin facade. This ensures good ventilation in windy conditions (yellow) and has a high space requirement due to the second facade plane (orange). The controllability avoids overheating in the facade cavity (red). With the flaps closed, however, sound and odour can be transmitted from room to room through the facade (green). The cost of cleaning is high due to the large glass area and technical equipment (blue).

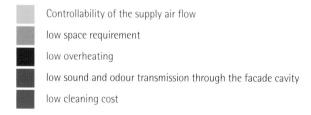

Controllability of the supply air flow

low space requirement

low overheating

low sound and odour transmission through the facade cavity

low cleaning cost

Deflected light

The Zusatzversorgungskasse des Baugewerbes building (an occupational health insurance office) in Wiesbaden was designed with a combined system of external shading and light deflection vanes. In the open condition under a cloudy sky, diffuse natural light is deflected into the room. When the sun is shining the elements are guided automatically by the building management system to suit the position of the sun. The light deflection plates are moved in the direction of the building to provide maximum shading. Direct, glare-free light is deflected on to the floor by aluminium profiles in the middle part. The lower element provides shading. There is always visibility through the lower part of the facade even with full shading deployed. The office rooms have additional internal glare protection, which can be adjusted by the user.

Controlled air

The building was designed so that the offices are totally naturally ventilated through the facade. The wooden facade consists of two alternating elements: a fixed glazed window made from triple heat protection insulation glazing and a thermally insulated panel, which extends as an opening casement over the full height of the facade. Supply air flows through the opaque facade elements into the room. Controllable vents are positioned at the top of the facade. They provide user-dependent natural ventilation of the room. Convectors in the sill-mounted boxes with an output of 210 W each ensure comfortable supply air temperatures even when the outside air is cold. The air flowing through the vents is optimally distributed between the top and bottom opening slots so as to achieve adequate air changes even in no-wind conditions. If the office is not in use, the system goes to stand-by mode. On someone entering the room, movement sensors switch the ventilation, heating and artificial lighting system into full operation mode. First all four vents are opened and the room is thoroughly ventilated. Night heating convectors also come into operation when outside temperatures are low. The ventilation flaps are controlled in response to the outside temperature. The ventilation flaps and convectors can be set manually so that the user has individual control over room climate. The opaque facade flaps can be opened like French windows, providing the user with a direct outside view. In winter the convectors switch off when the openings are open. To prevent the convectors from freezing in winter, they have their own glycol circuit. The transmission heat loss of the building is intercepted by a component heating system, which can also be used for cooling in summer.

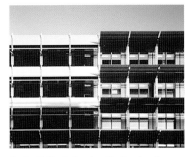

Fig. 3.1.51 South facade with closed and open light deflection vanes
When the sun shines, the greater part of the direct solar radiation is blocked. Highly reflective aluminium sheets guide part of the solar radiation to an aluminium light reflector. From there the light is deflected without glare into the room. When the sky is cloudy and the shading element is open, the aluminium sheets direct diffuse light into the room.

Construction: 2002
Use: offices
Client: Zusatzversorgungskasse des Baugewerbes
Architect: Herzog + Partner, Munich
Energy planning, building services: Ingenieur-
    büro Hausladen, Kirchheim, Munich
Facade: wooden construction with triple heat
    protection insulation glazing and thermally
    insulated panels, ventilation flaps
Energy concept: combined energy system with
    power-heat coupling, two gas-fired com-
    bined heat and power plants for electrical
    power and heat generation, absorption
    chillier, heating and cooling by thermo-
    active ceilings, window ventilation

Fig. 3.1.53 Section of facade
Light deflection using vanes. Top in solar radiation, bottom in diffuse light.

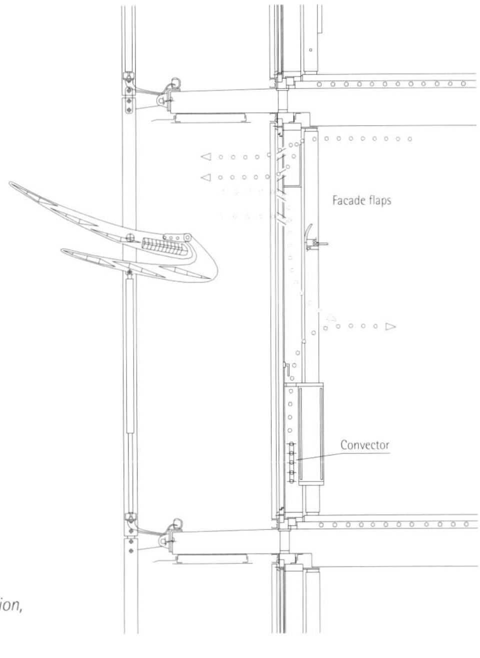

Facade flaps

Convector

Fig. 3.1.54 Facade section
Airflow through facade flaps and convector.

Fig. 3.1.52 Detailed view of the ventilation elements
The glass plate optimises the air changes through the flaps.

Displacement ventilation system
Displacement diffusers QL-I, Trox

Mixed flow ventilation system
Swirl diffusers RFD 160, Trox

Displacement ventilation system
Floor diffusers FB 200, Trox

Ventilation systems

The ventilation of a building is a core component of building technology. Air changes provide people with fresh air to breath, take away pollutants, contribute to the thermal behaviour of the building and are an important parameter in the feeling of wellbeing. Along with building ventilation stand quantifiable parameters such as capital investment, maintenance and operating costs, construction costs and level of energy savings balanced against softer factors like comfort and quality of use.

Building geometry plays a significant role in the ventilation concept. An optimised plan arrangement increases the proportion of floor area that can be naturally ventilated by avoiding large room depths or by keeping them to a minimum. The noise load can be minimised by facing the office space away from the street. The building structure (e.g. stairwell, atrium) can be included in the airflow concept. Natural driving forces such as wind and thermal currents can then be exploited.

Good air quality is a prerequisite to the user's feeling of wellbeing. Air changes must not be so low that the emissions of equipment and materials are not conducted away. By selecting materials with lower odour emission and dispensing with textiles and carpets, the required basic number of air changes can be reduced and energy saved. Improved air quality means that ducts in mechanical ventilation systems require less cleaning. Recirculatory air operation is not recommended on grounds of hygiene.

Natural ventilation requires neither technical installations nor energy to drive the system. The user has individual control over the ventilation and enjoys extensive outside views. Current trends are moving in the direction of controlled natural ventilation. This involves air changes produced by pulse ventilation through ventilation flaps.

Heat recovery, adiabatic cooling systems, supply air collectors and underground ducts can be used in conjunction with mechanical ventilation, thus allowing the expenditure on ventilation heating and cooling refrigeration to be reduced. With appropriate building design, this technology is replacing conventional systems.

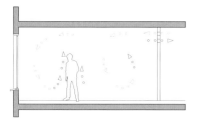

Fig. 3.2.1 **Mixed flow ventilation with tangential introduction of supply air**
Tangential supply air introduction has the air inlet and outlet on the same side, which reduces the installation costs.

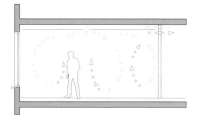

Fig. 3.2.2 **Mixed flow ventilation with radial introduction of supply air**
Radial supply air introduction leads to a vigorous mixing with the room air. This allows lower introduced air temperatures to be used but also results in higher rates of air change.

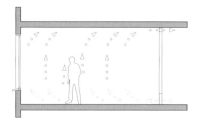

Fig. 3.2.3 **Displacement ventilation**
With displacement ventilation the air is 2 K lower than room air temperature and introduced low speed at the floor into the room. It gives very good air quality at low rates of air change.

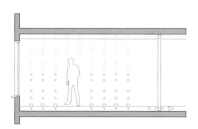

Fig. 3.2.4 **Laminar flow ventilation**
With laminar flow ventilation, air flows from one room surface to the opposite surface, ensuring that the air is very clean.

Air conduction in rooms

Air conduction in rooms can be performed in various ways. In principle there are three types of ventilation: mixed flow, displacement and (low turbulence) laminar flow ventilation. The determining factors are the required air quality and room conditioning by air.

Mixed flow ventilation With mixed flow ventilation, supply air is introduced into the room at high speed. Depending on the design of the diffusers, the air is either blown far into the room or quickly mixed with the room air by swirl diffusers or the induction effect. High air speeds and temperature differences quickly subside, although overall, a high rate of air change is required. Ventilation relies on the dilution principle, whereby the air quality at all points in the room is roughly the same. This mixing of air allows supply air at a different temperature to that of the room air to be used for cooling or heating. Supply air temperatures of between 10 and 40 °C are possible.

The advantage of mixed flow ventilation is that the air can be introduced into the room through small supply air openings at all points of the room. This usually simplifies installation. Little energy is used, as the temperature of the supply air is independent of the room temperature and therefore does not have to be increased or decreased.

Mixed flow ventilation is often used if the requirements for air quality are not very high or a greatly increased rate of air change is already required for thermal reasons. It can also contribute to air conditioning, e.g. by extending the performance of thermally activated components or improving the options for individual regulation of a room. In most cases mixed flow ventilation is found in residential premises. Low occupancy densities in these buildings mean that air quality is not a crucial problem. A window can be opened at any time. In residential buildings, the need to remove moisture determines the required air change rate. Another area of use for mixed flow ventilation is in rooms with very high rates of air change as a result of the type of use, such as exhibition centres, concert halls and pubs.

Displacement ventilation With displacement ventilation, fresh air is introduced through large area diffusers at a low air speed (less than 0.2 m/s) and at supply air temperature of approximately 2 K less than the room temperature. A pool of fresh air forms in the room. The warmed fresh air moves upwards at sources of heat such as people and equipment and is extracted at ceiling level. To ensure the formation of the fresh air pool and avoid loss of thermal comfort, the supply air temperature must be within a narrow range. Therefore the cooling performance of displacement ventilation is low, achieving values in the order of only 10 W/m². As the supply air temperature must be less than the room temperature,

room heating from ventilation is not an option. Therefore additional water operated heating systems are necessary. With respect to the energy use, displacement ventilation can have the disadvantage that the air must be preheated almost to room temperature in spite of the need for cooling.

For large rooms there is the advantage that displacement diffusers can ventilate a surrounding area of up to 15 m radius. Therefore the number of ventilation diffusers required is low. If the horizontal distribution takes place in the suspended ceiling, the near-floor introduction of supply air results in high installation costs as vertical ducts to the floor are required. Displacement ventilation ensures that people are always breathing good quality air.

Displacement ventilation is particularly suitable for office buildings as it provides good air quality with relatively low volumes of air. It has become the preferred means of ventilation.

Laminar flow ventilation With laminar flow ventilation the air is introduced over a large area of one room-defining surface, e.g. at the ceiling, and extracted by suction at the opposite surface. All points in the room experience defined, low turbulence air changes. This may be required where there are requirements for micro-organisms and dust particles to be removed, such as in clean rooms, laboratories or operating theatres. The introduction of air over large areas involves high installation costs.

Air conduction in the building

Optimised air conduction in the building provides energy savings and ensures a high degree of comfort. The various types of air conduction are differentiated by the way the air is introduced into the room, the opportunities for pre- and post-conditioning and the form of heat recovery. To save driving, heating and cooling energy, the airways and temperature levels of the air zones are matched to one another and extensive use is made of thermal currents and wind conditions. Other criteria include the air quality and the required air changes. Rooms in continuous occupation by the user should have the best air quality. From there the air can overflow into areas in less complete occupation such as connection zones or exhaust air rooms such as sanitary zones.

Introduction of air The air can be conducted through the facade or by a central ventilation system into the room. From the point of view of air quality and user acceptance, it is preferable to bring in air through the facade. A central supply air conditioning system is required at heavily loaded locations, where high rates of air change are necessary or there are special requirements. This can incorporate heat recovery by means of heat exchangers. In addition, possible comfort issues due to excessively hot or cold supply air are avoided.

Air conduction Supply and exhaust air flows can be conducted through air ducts from the central plant to the rooms. Alternatively, just the exhaust or supply air ducts can be ducted, whilst the second airway is routed through the facade or internal shafts, stairwells, atria, or other special access zones. If both airways are ducted,

then pressures can be defined and controlled. The detrimental effects of odour and noise are avoided. If an airway runs through a component within the building structure, then the costs of air conduction are reduced and the exhaust air can be used for tempering the building component. This can be accompanied by undesirable transmission of odour, noise and heat. When a whole section of a building is used as a second airway, it is also difficult to balance air flows and to avoid uncontrolled air changes, in particular those caused by thermal currents or wind. A further problem is the provision of the required overflow openings. They must have a slight resistance to flow and, at the same time, satisfy fire protection requirements. Sound transmission from the circulation zones into the occupied rooms should be avoided.

Heat recovery If both airflows are ducted then any type of heat recovery can be used. If exhaust air exits through an atrium, heat recovery can be either by a central ventilation plant or a system that is connected into a circuit. No heat recovery can take place with the exhaust air conducted through a facade into the open air. If the supply air is introduced through the facade, then heat recovery is only possible using an exhaust air heat pump which delivers its heat to the heating system, as there is no central supply air flow.

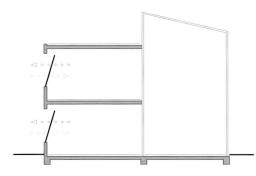 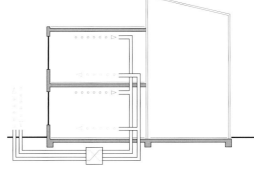 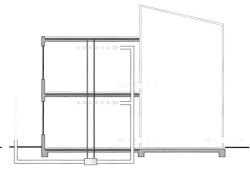

Fig. 3.2.5 **Supply air conducted through the facade**
If supply air is introduced through the facade, the result is high air quality and high user acceptance. Precautions must be taken at the facade in connection with air conditioning so that no noise can enter or thermal discomfort occur. Direct heat recovery is not possible.

Fig. 3.2.6 **Ducted supply and exhaust air**
Conducting the air flows in ducts allows defined ventilation and control of the rate of air change, supply air temperature and air moisture content. Ventilation depends on the pressure relationships within the building as a whole. Heat recovery is certainly possible. It creates no undesirable odour transmission. Rooms with large depths can be ventilated.

Fig. 3.2.7 **Supply or exhaust air through an atrium**
Atria, circulation zones or internal shafts can be used for conducting supply or exhaust air. The other airway is routed through the facade or ducts. Thermal currents and wind can provide some of the driving energy. There is the danger of uncontrolled air flows which may transport undesirable odour or heat. Sound transmission within the building should be avoided. Heat recovery is only possible to a limited extent. Exhaust air can be used for tempering the atrium. Supply air can be preheated in the atrium.

Ventilation concepts

The design of ventilation concepts is closely linked with the use of the building, the functional requirements of the facade and the plan layout. Therefore the ventilation concept and the building structure should be developed in parallel. Ventilation concepts are differentiated by the type of drive, the way the air is conducted through the building and the air flow in the room. This can have consequences for the energy required to drive the system, the feasibility of heat recovery, technical costs, and thermal and acoustic comfort.

Window ventilation Window ventilation is a very simple ventilation strategy with little technical content and high user acceptance. Supply and exhaust air are conducted through the facade. The ventilation of a room is independent of the rest of the building. This form of ventilation is suitable for unpolluted locations with moderate rates of air changes and low thermal loads.

Supply air introduced through the facade, overflow into an atrium This simple system uses thermal forces and has high user acceptance. Supply air is introduced into the room through windows or special supply air openings in the facade. Particular attention should be paid to thermal discomfort. The exhaust air overflows into the atrium, where it provides a little heat. The air flows directly into the open air driven by thermal currents through openings in the upper part of the atrium. This concept is suitable for unpolluted locations with moderate thermal loads in conjunction with unheated atria.

Supply air introduced through the facade, ducted mechanical exhaust air This form of ventilation is the simplest mechanical concept and has a high user acceptance and defined rates of air change. Supply air is introduced into the room directly from the outside through special ventilation openings in the facade. This must be done in a way that avoids creating draughts and low room air temperatures. Exhaust air is extracted mechanically through a duct and can be fed through an exhaust air heat pump. As there is no single supply airflow, the heat recovered must be transferred into a water-operated system. This type of ventilation is suitable for locations with good air quality and offers a means of removing pollutants and moisture from a room.

Secondary flow from an atrium, ducted mechanical exhaust air With this concept the atrium can be used to temper the supply air, thus avoiding noise load or air pollutants. The outside air flows unrestricted through opening flaps into the atrium, is warmed there and then overflows into the offices. The exhaust air is extracted from the offices through ducts. Heat recovery using a waste air heat pump is an option. This concept provides an alternative in cases where the introduction of supply air through the facade is not possible due to the location or use of the building.

Ducted mechanical supply air, exhaust airflow through the facade This concept allows defined supply air conditioning and avoids unintentional heat transmission through the facade. The supply air is conditioned in a central ventilation plant and conducted to the room through ducts. There it flows into the room as displacement air, which the user finds pleasant. The exhaust air flows out freely through openings in the facade and can also take away solar heat loads. This concept is suitable for polluted locations, especially in conjunction with a double-skin facade with variations in ventilation strategies to suit the season.

Ducted mechanical supply air, overflow into an atrium This concept allows defined supply air conditioning in conjunction with partial heat recovery. Supply air is prepared in a central plant and ducted to the rooms, where it enters as displacement air. Exhaust air enters the atrium through overflow openings where it has a tempering effect. From there it flows through openings directly into the open air. Heat recovery is possible using an exhaust air heat pump or a system that is connected into a circuit. This form of ventilation is suitable if defined supply air conditions or high rates of air changes are required.

Mechanical supply air through an atrium, ducted mechanical exhaust air This system allows the atrium to be used for preheating the supply air. Supply air is blown mechanically into the atrium. A certain amount of preheating takes place in the atrium due to solar and internal heat gains. The air enters the rooms through overflow openings. Mechanical exhaust air extraction through ducts ensures defined rates of air change. This concept is suitable for small building units in which there is no intensive use of the atrium or special requirements for air quality.

Ducted mechanical supply air, mechanical exhaust air through an atrium This concept allows defined supply air conditions and high rates of air change. Supply air is prepared in a central system and ducted to the rooms, where it enters as displacement air. The openings for supply air can be set in any position. The exhaust air flows through overflow openings into the atrium from where it is mechanically extracted and conducted to the ventilation equipment. This can allow an efficient form of heat recovery. This concept is suitable where there are special requirements for ventilation, in particular with high rates of air change.

Ducted mechanical supply and exhaust air This system is the most expensive ventilation system but it offers the option of efficient heat recovery and defined supply air conditions. Supply air is prepared in a central ventilation system and ducted to the rooms, where it enters as displacement air. The exhaust air is extracted from the room through ducts and conducted to the ventilation equipment. This can incorporate heat recovery by means of heat exchangers. This concept is suitable for polluted

locations and types of use where there are high requirements for supply air conditions and for high rates of air change.

Supply air by local ventilation unit, exhaust air by local ventilation unit This system offers a high degree of flexibility with a low space requirement but leads to high maintenance costs. Supply air is introduced into the room directly from the outside through local ventilation equipment in the facade. The same equipment conducts the exhaust air to the outside. The local ventilation equipment can provide heat recovery. Supply air can be heated and cooled to a certain extent. This concept is suitable for buildings that are mainly naturally ventilated and conditioned and with individual rooms in which special requirements for ventilation apply.

Tab. 3.2.1 **Comparison of various ventilation concepts**
Various types of heat recovery system:
Exhaust air heat pump (EAHP), in-circuit system (ICS), heat exchanger (HE).

	Capital cost	Drive energy	Maintenance	Space requirement	Heat recovery
Window ventilation	–	–	–	–	not possible
Supply air introduced through the facade, overflowing into an atrium	very low	–	low	–	EAHP
Supply air introduced through the facade, ducted mechanical exhaust air	low	low	medium	medium	EAHP
Secondary flow from an atrium, ducted mechanical exhaust air	low	low	medium	medium	EAHP
Ducted mechanical supply air, exhaust air flow through the facade	low	low	medium	medium	not possible
Ducted mechanical supply air, overflow into an atrium	low	medium	medium	medium	EAHP, ICS
Mechanical supply air through an atrium, ducted mechanical exhaust air	medium	medium	medium	high	EAHP, ICS, HE
Ducted mechanical supply air, mechanical exhaust air through an atrium	medium	medium	medium	high	EAHP, ICS, HE
Ducted mechanical supply and exhaust air	high	high	medium	very high	EAHP, ICS, HE
Mechanical supply and exhaust air by local ventilation units	high	high	very high	low	HE

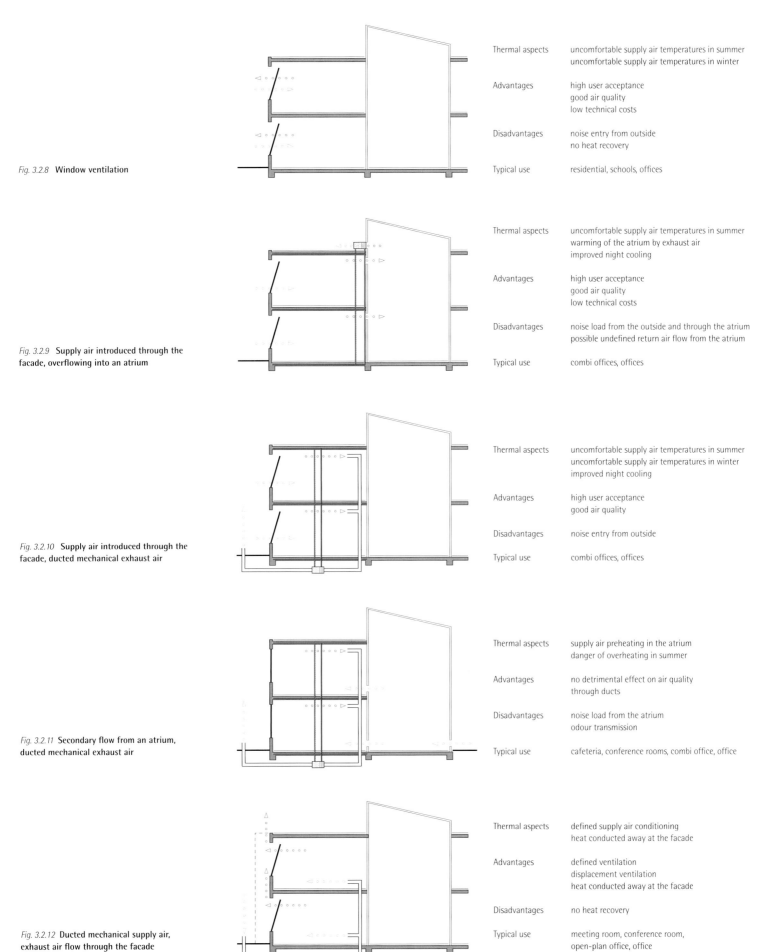

Fig. 3.2.8 **Window ventilation**

Thermal aspects — uncomfortable supply air temperatures in summer
uncomfortable supply air temperatures in winter

Advantages — high user acceptance
good air quality
low technical costs

Disadvantages — noise entry from outside
no heat recovery

Typical use — residential, schools, offices

Fig. 3.2.9 **Supply air introduced through the facade, overflowing into an atrium**

Thermal aspects — uncomfortable supply air temperatures in summer
warming of the atrium by exhaust air
improved night cooling

Advantages — high user acceptance
good air quality
low technical costs

Disadvantages — noise load from the outside and through the atrium
possible undefined return air flow from the atrium

Typical use — combi offices, offices

Fig. 3.2.10 **Supply air introduced through the facade, ducted mechanical exhaust air**

Thermal aspects — uncomfortable supply air temperatures in summer
uncomfortable supply air temperatures in winter
improved night cooling

Advantages — high user acceptance
good air quality

Disadvantages — noise entry from outside

Typical use — combi offices, offices

Fig. 3.2.11 **Secondary flow from an atrium, ducted mechanical exhaust air**

Thermal aspects — supply air preheating in the atrium
danger of overheating in summer

Advantages — no detrimental effect on air quality
through ducts

Disadvantages — noise load from the atrium
odour transmission

Typical use — cafeteria, conference rooms, combi office, office

---

Fig. 3.2.12 **Ducted mechanical supply air, exhaust air flow through the facade**

Thermal aspects — defined supply air conditioning
heat conducted away at the facade

Advantages — defined ventilation
displacement ventilation
heat conducted away at the facade

Disadvantages — no heat recovery

Typical use — meeting room, conference room,
open-plan office, office

Thermal aspects	defined supply air conditioning warming of the atrium by exhaust air
Advantages	defined ventilation displacement ventilation
Disadvantages	noise load from the atrium
Typical use	meeting room, conference room, open plan office, combi office, office

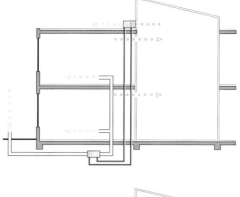

Fig. 3.2.13 Ducted mechanical supply air, overflow into an atrium

Thermal aspects	supply air conditioning danger of overheating in summer
Advantages	heat recovery with heat exchanger
Disadvantages	noise load from the atrium odour transmission
Typical use	cafeteria, conference rooms, combi office, office

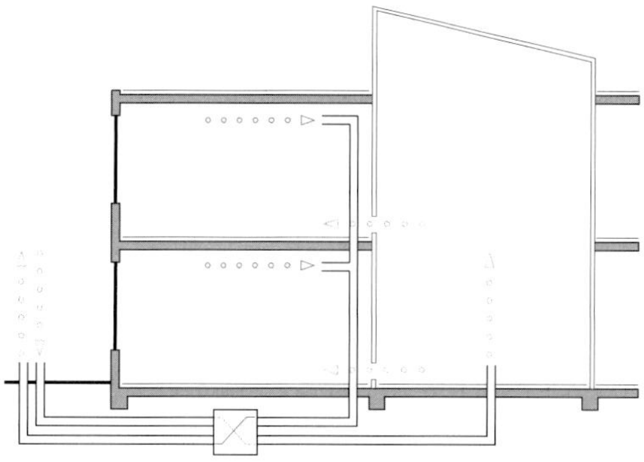

Fig. 3.2.14 Mechanical supply air through an atrium, ducted mechanical exhaust air

Thermal aspects	defined supply air conditioning
Advantages	defined ventilation displacement ventilation heat recovery with heat exchanger
Disadvantages	noise load from the atrium
Typical use	meeting room, conference room, open plan office, combi office, office

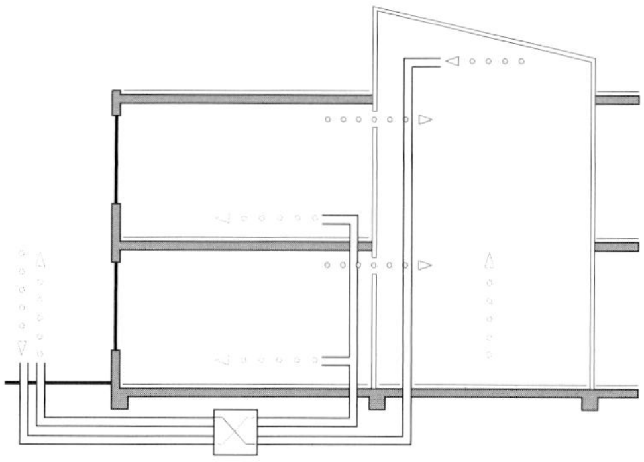

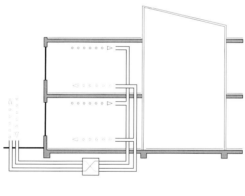

Fig. 3.2.15 Ducted mechanical supply air, mechanical exhaust air through an atrium

Thermal aspects	defined supply air conditioning
Advantages	defined pressure conditions defined ventilation displacement ventilation heat recovery with heat exchanger no noise load
Disadvantages	high technical content
Typical use	meeting room, conference room, cafeteria open plan office, combi office, office, residential

Fig. 3.2.16 Ducted mechanical supply air, ducted mechanical exhaust air

Thermal aspects	defined supply air tempering
Advantages	low space requirement can be retrofitted flexibility no noise load
Disadvantages	high maintenance cost high energy cost
Typical use	conference room, office

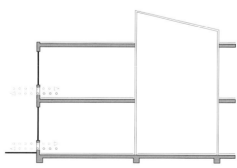

Fig. 3.2.17 Supply air by local ventilation unit, exhaust air by local ventilation unit

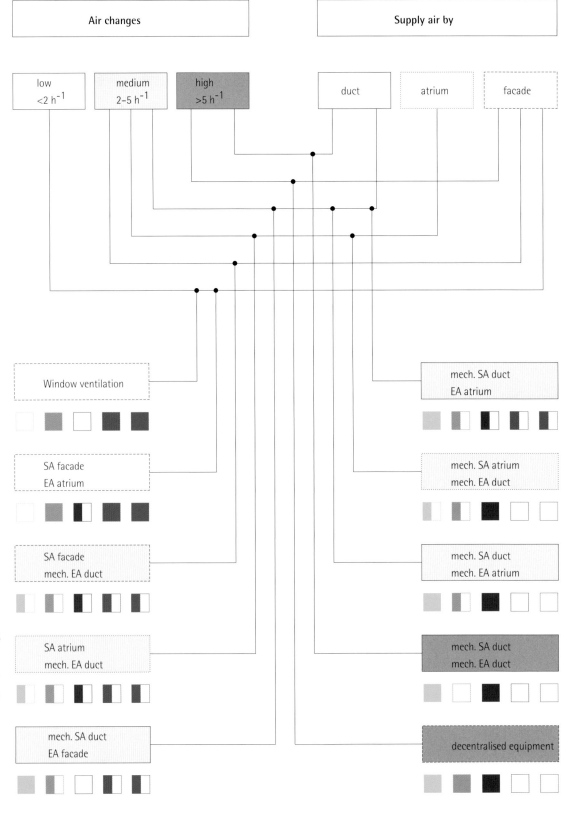

| Air changes | | | Supply air by | | |

low
<2 h⁻¹

medium
2–5 h⁻¹

high
>5 h⁻¹

duct

atrium

facade

Window ventilation

mech. SA duct
EA atrium

SA facade
EA atrium

mech. SA atrium
mech. EA duct

SA facade
mech. EA duct

mech. SA duct
mech. EA atrium

SA atrium
mech. EA duct

mech. SA duct
mech. EA duct

mech. SA duct
EA facade

decentralised equipment

Fig. 3.2.18 **Decision chart for ventilation concepts**
The important criteria in the choice of ventilation systems are the required rates of air changes and the conduction of the supply air. Suitable systems result from the combination of the selected initial criteria. The different characteristics of each system are shown by colour coding. The coloured squares represent three grades of performance good (filled), medium (half-filled) and poor (empty). Therefore the example of a combination of high rates of air change with supply air through the facade results in ventilation from local equipment. This would allow defined ventilation (yellow) with low space requirement (orange) and heat recovery (red). However, local equipment has a high drive energy demand (green) and has a high technical content (blue).

defined ventilation

low space requirement

heat recovery

low drive energy requirement

low technical costs

Climate spiral, engineering competition

An important component of an air conditioning concept for the proposed BioParc in Dresden was the possibility of reversing the direction of airflow by mechanical means depending on the season. In winter, when the high temperatures in the facade cavity can preheat the supply air, the airflow moves through the double-skin facade into the offices and from there into the atrium. The exhaust air leaves through the atrium roof. If the temperatures in the facade cavity are too high due to outside air temperatures or solar radiation, then the direction of airflow is reversed. Supply air is then precooled by passing through an underground duct and blown into the atrium and flows from there into the offices. Exhaust air flows through the facade to the open air so that the high facade cavity temperatures do not have an effect on the rooms. Flaps in the outer facade skin control of the positive and negative pressure ring.

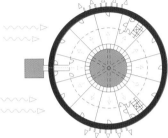

Fig. 3.2.19 Diagram showing the principle of the facade as a positive and negative pressure ring

Fig. 3.2.20 View of BioParc, Dresden
(Figs. Bernhardt and Partner, Darmstadt)

Construction: competition
Use: offices
Client: Klaus Tschira Stiftung, Saxony
Architect: Bernhardt & Partner, Darmstadt
Energy planning, building services: Ingenieurbüro Hausladen, Kirchheim, Munich
Facade: transparent double-skin facade as a climate skin and aerodynamic element
Energy concept: seasonal ventilation concept, earth pipe, foundation slab cooling, heating and cooling by thermoactive components, recooling at night, heat recovery by heat pump in the atrium roof

Night ventilation

All workstations in the office building for the Krankenversorgung der Bundesbahnbeamten building (a health insurance office) in Kassel are naturally lit and ventilated. The optimum combination of thermal storage mass and free night ventilation makes mechanical cooling equipment unnecessary. The offices have no suspended ceilings or impact sound insulation. All reinforced concrete structural components are open to view in the room. Opening windows are used to cool the offices. Protection against rain, wind and intruders is provided by glass panels fixed 10 cm in front of the window units (baffle panels). Fire protection requirements mean that the hallways extend in every direction up to the facade. At these points, room-high ventilation flaps at the facade serve to cool the core zone. Cold outside air flows through these flaps to cool the ceilings, floors and solid wall panels and flows through a smoke and heat vent roof flap in the stairwell.

Fig. 3.2.22 Offices of the Krankenversorgung der Bundesbahnbeamten (KVB), Kassel (Photo: Bieling & Bieling Architekten, Kassel)

Construction: 2000
Use: administration building
Client: Deutsche Bahn Immobilien GmbH
Architect: Bieling & Bieling Architekten, Kassel
Energy planning, building services: Ingenieurbüro Hausladen, Kirchheim, Munich
Facade: fully glazed facade with single panels fixed in front of facade, internal shading
Energy concept: good A/V ratio, thermoactive ceiling, night cooling, natural ventilation and lighting

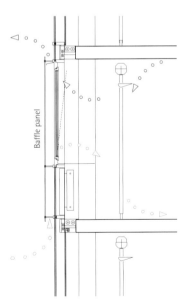

Baffle panel

Fig. 3.2.21 Detailed section of the facade showing the ventilation concept with baffle panel

"If Nature had been comfortable, mankind would never have invented architecture."

Oscar Wilde 1854–1900

Ribbed radiator
Thermostatic valve
Sprinkle head

Downlight
Solar protection control
Chilled ceiling

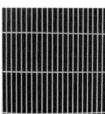

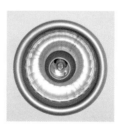

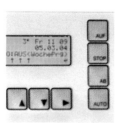

Convector grille
Recirculation cooler
Exhaust air unit

Room conditioning systems

Technical systems are needed to be certain of achieving the desired room temperature and the necessary room ventilation conditions. Knowing the requirements of both user and client is important to the selection of the right concept. The more accurately the requirements are determined, the better will be the suitability of the room conditioning concept. If they cannot be specified, such as in the case of investor projects for which the use will not be clear until later, then a flexible approach to concept selection and adequate options for retrofitting should be adopted.

Changed working structures and rapid developments in communications technology require flexibility from buildings with respect to room division, type of use and the ability to retrofit. Where high flexibility is wanted the room climatisation concept has to be designed to provide it, so, for example, adopting concrete core activation in the ceilings would exclude double floors and suspended ceilings. The use of chilled ceilings means that changing the room division is only possible at great expense. With respect to possible later changes of use, it is often wise to provide heating and cooling water pipework from the start.

Advances in electronics have led to many more types of programmable controls and regulators being available. Often no provision is made for simple and intuitive user interfaces. In some cases the user is left having no control over the system. User control is important to avoid the feeling of powerlessness. In many cases, ordinary rotary switches are a worthwhile alternative to central, programmable regulation concepts.

The use of regenerative heating and cooling energy sources is advisable from an ecological point of view. They have only small useable temperature differences and are limited in output. The choice of an appropriate heating and cooling transfer system must take this into account.

Buildings of the 1960s and 70s were conditioned by air conditioning systems. High cooling loads demanded correspondingly high quantities of air, which consumed considerable energy, had a high technical content and took up a lot of space in the building. Often discomfort occurred because of convective energy release, high air speeds and reduced air quality. Therefore there was a move to separate room conditioning from ventilation.

Room conditioning concepts

The various heating, ventilation and cooling technologies can be combined to give rise to different room conditioning concepts. They are distinguished from one another by their different output capabilities, system temperatures, controllability, user acceptance and costs. The concept for room climatisation is a decisive parameter in the later functioning of a building.

Window ventilation with radiators This concept represents the simplest technical form of room conditioning. Heating is provided by radiators positioned under the windows. Ventilation is through the window or special ventilation elements. Ventilation heat losses are higher as heat recovery is not possible. Window ventilation has a high user acceptance, but can also lead to discomfort in winter when outside temperatures are low. Removal of heat from the room is done only by ventilation. Depending on the outside temperature, a certain amount of the heat load can be conducted away by window ventilation. Control of room temperature is by thermostatic valves; the rate of air change can be set individually by the user. This concept is a good solution at locations without pollution, wind and noise loads and with low heat loads in the rooms.

Window ventilation with thermally activated components and booster heaters This concept offers good levels of comfort with little technical content and a low energy demand. Background heating of the building is provided by thermoactive ceilings. Additional booster heaters are required to adjust room temperature and preheat the supply air entering through the windows. Two heating control systems are required because of the different and high system temperatures. Thermally activated components can be driven with low system temperatures and effectively operated with a heat pump. Window ventilation is associated with low technical content but does not allow heat recovery. Thermally activated components can provide comfortable room cooling with low temperature differences between the coolant and the room with the result that regenerative cooling energy sources can be efficiently exploited. The time phase shift caused by the inertia of the mass allows night cooling. In conjunction with window ventilation, thermally activated components offer great cooling potential due to the large heat transfer surfaces involved. The inertia of the mass prevents any form of quick response control. On the other hand, load peaks are smoothed so that the outputs of the heating and cooling systems can be designed with lower reserve capacities. Individual room control is possible to a very limited extent and separate floor-by-floor billing cannot

be provided. This concept can be expected to provide extensive comfort at low cost with low energy demand at locations where there is no noise load and regenerative cooling energy is available.

Natural ventilation with chilled ceilings and radiators This system has a quick response to controls but has a high energy demand. Radiators under windows provide heating by warming the incoming supply air to a certain extent. Heat recovery is not possible. Chilled ceilings provide flexible cooling. The generally high output is limited on hot humid days because of the danger of condensation when windows are opened. Chilled ceilings can offer improved room acoustics through the design of the suspended ceiling and space for technical installations below it. The cost of technical control equipment is very high because of the necessary reduction of the cooling output at high air humidities. Alterations to the room geometry involve a lot of work to the technical installations. The choice of cooling generation equipment is limited due to the low system temperature. Nevertheless, this concept will be very effective on almost any day of the year at unpolluted locations in buildings with high internal heat loads.

Local ventilation equipment In buildings that are almost entirely naturally ventilated, local ventilation equipment should be considered for rooms with increased air requirements. With the adoption of a well-insulated building envelope, the equipment could also be used for heating. The air changes necessary for good hygiene must also be provided. Preheating the supply air avoids comfort problems in winter. Ventilation heat losses can be reduced if the equipment allows heat recovery. Cooling loads may be covered to some extent in summer. If no condensate drainage pipework is planned for the building then cooling performance is very limited because of the condensate accumulation. Local ventilation equipment can be controlled very effectively to ensure temperatures remain in the lower range. The concept offers flexible cooling. However, the maintenance costs of the equipment are very high and it must be cleaned regularly.

Local ventilation equipment with thermally activated components Both systems are enhanced when local ventilation equipment is combined with thermoactive ceilings. Background heating is provided by the thermoactive ceiling. Low system temperatures and the inertia of the mass have a positive effect. Additional heating can be installed along with local ventilation equipment to avoid discomfort caused by ventilation and to provide individual room control. Local ventilation equipment ensures adequate air changes take place without loss of comfort. Cooling the supply air in summer can reduce further contributions to the heat load. When combined with the cooling potential of thermally activated components, a medium level of total cooling output can be achieved. The local equipment can overcome some of the disadvantages of the poor control capability of thermoactive ceilings. Local equipment can be retrofitted following a change of mind by the user or a change of use. This concept is very suitable for polluted locations, for buildings which have to be highly flexible and have medium climate loads.

Mechanical ventilation with thermally activated components The combination of thermally activated components and mechanical ventilation extends the scope of use of thermoactive ceilings. Thermally activated components at low system temperatures provide the heating. Ventilation can be used for heating when a sudden need for heat arises but then there will no longer be any displacement ventilation in the room. Heat recovery reduces the ventilation heat loss, preconditioning the air prevents comfort problems associated with the introduction of supply air. If the mechanical supply air is dehumidified then this can mitigate the problem of condensation to a certain extent and therefore increase the effectiveness of thermally activated components. When combined with cooling of the supply air, total output is in the medium range. The control options are limited from the overall point of view; however, when load changes occur ventilation can be adjusted quite rapidly. This system can deal with average cooling loads at polluted locations and the use of regenerative energy sources is perfectly possible.

Mechanical ventilation with heated or chilled ceilings This system is a widely adopted solution in conventional types of building. Additional radiators can provide heat or, if the facade is sufficiently insulative, the chilled ceilings may be adequate when used as heating surfaces. Mechanical ventilation allows supply air to be introduced without detriment to comfort or heat recovery. Chilled ceilings have a high potential output, in particular where mechanical supply air deals with any condensation problem. In addition, mechanical ventilation does not add any further heat load to the room. The system can be effectively controlled as the storage mass is thermally decoupled. Energy transfer through large surfaces allows small system temperature differences to be used, which means that the energy is used more efficiently. Suspended ceilings conceal versatile space for services. Chilled ceilings can also improve room acoustics. This concept is suitable for polluted locations with high internal heat loads and high requirements for room acoustics. There is useful installation space above suspended chilled ceilings.

Air conditioning systems An air conditioning system provides heating, cooling and ventilation from a central plant. The introduced air can also be used to control humidity. The ventilation units can filter pollutants, dust and pollen from the air. These systems can have very high cooling outputs but the energy and capital costs are also very high. As the system is very cost intensive, the plant and control technology must be carefully designed to match the actual requirements of the user. User intervention is limited and therefore the system does not always receive user acceptance, most of all when it is not operated correctly. The multiple pipes and equipment rooms take up a lot of space.

Tab. 3.3.1 **Comparison of various room conditioning concepts**

	Capital costs	Energy requirement	Maintenance	Space requirement
Window ventilation, radiators	very low	low	very low	low
Window ventilation thermoactive ceiling, radiators	low	medium	very low	very low
Window ventilation chilled ceiling, radiator	high	high	high	medium
Local ventilation equipment	medium	medium	very high	very low
Local ventilation equipment with thermoactive ceiling	high	medium	very high	very low
Mechanical ventilation, thermoactive ceiling	high	very low	medium	medium
Mechanical ventilation, heated / chilled ceiling	high	medium	very high	high
Air conditioning system	very high	very high	very high	very high

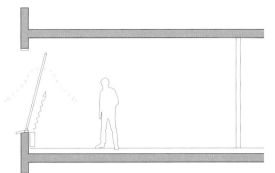

Heating output	40–100 W/m²
Cooling output air	depends on outside air temperature
Cooling output water	none
System temperature heating	35–80 °C
Controllability	good
Advantages	comprehensible
	direct user intervention
Disadvantages	uncomfortable ventilation in winter
	entry of noise and dust
	no cooling in summer
	no heat recovery
Typical uses	offices, residential

Fig. 3.3.1 **Window ventilation with radiators**

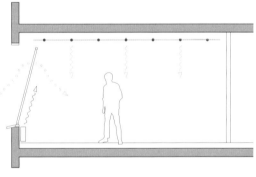

Heating output	50 W/m²
Cooling output air	depends on outside air temperature
Cooling output water	40 W/m²
System temperature heating	25 °C / 35 °C (thermoactive ceiling/radiator)
System temperature cooling	18 °C
Controllability	limited
Advantages	radiated heat output
	time phase shift
	smoothing of peak loads
	regenerative heat and cooling energy sources
Disadvantages	impact sound transmission
	poor room acoustics
	no suspended ceilings
	uncomfortable ventilation in winter
	entry of noise and dust
Typical uses	offices, residential

Fig. 3.3.2 **Window ventilation with thermally activated components and booster heaters**

Heating output	40–100 W/m²
Cooling output air	depends on outside air temperature
Cooling output water	30–100 W/m²
System temperature heating	35–80 °C
System temperature cooling	16 °C
Controllability	very good
Advantages	high level of comfort
	wide range of installation options
Disadvantages	output limited on hot, humid days
	room alterations are expensive
	uncomfortable ventilation in winter
	entry of noise and dust
	no heat recovery
Typical uses	meeting room, conference room, cafeteria

Fig. 3.3.3 **Natural ventilation with chilled ceilings and radiators**

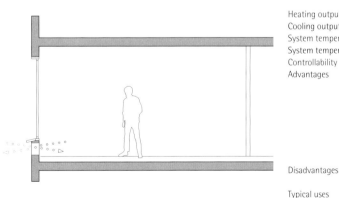

Heating output	40 W/m²
Cooling output air	30 W/m²
System temperature heating	30–40 °C
System temperature cooling	16 °C
Controllability	good
Advantages	short supply air path
	comfortable supply air introduction
	high flexibility
	can be retrofitted
	minimum installation in room
	comprehensible
	direct user intervention
	can incorporate heat recovery
Disadvantages	high maintenance cost
	risk of contamination
Typical uses	meeting room, office, residential

Fig. 3.3.4 **Local ventilation equipment**

Heating output	60–80 W/m²
Cooling output air	30 W/m²
Cooling output water	40 W/m²
System temperature heating	25 °C / 30 °C (thermoactive ceiling/local ventilation equipment)
System temperature cooling	18 °C / 16 °C (thermoactive ceiling/local ventilation equipment)
Controllability	good
Advantages	short supply air path, comfortable supply air introduction room alterations are inexpensive time phase shift, smoothing of peak loads regenerative heat and cooling energy sources heat recovery, individual room control
Disadvantages	high maintenance cost, risk of contamination no individual room billing impact sound transmission, poor room acoustics

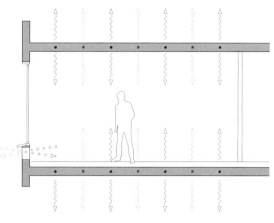

Fig. 3.3.5 **Local ventilation equipment with thermally activated components**

Heating output	40 W/m²
Cooling output air	8 W/m²
Cooling output water	45 W/m²
System temperature heating	25 °C / 30 °C (thermoactive ceiling/mechanical ventilation)
System temperature cooling	18 °C
Controllability	very limited
Advantages	heat recovery comfortable ventilation in winter low heat entry in summer can incorporate air dehumidification
Disadvantages	no individual room control no individual room billing impact sound transmission poor room acoustics no suspended ceilings
Typical uses	office, meeting room

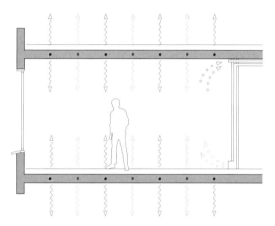

Fig. 3.3.6 **Mechanical ventilation with thermally activated components**

Heating output	50 W/m²
Cooling output air	8 W/m²
Cooling output water	80 – 100 W/m²
System temperature heating	30 °C
System temperature cooling	16 °C
Controllability	very good
Advantages	no problems with falling below dew point high level of comfort wide range of installation options user intervention
Disadvantages	room alterations are expensive limited heating output
Typical uses	meeting room, conference room, cafeteria

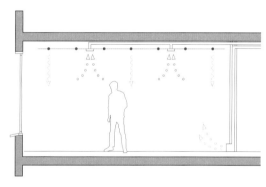

Fig. 3.3.7 **Mechanical ventilation with heated or chilled ceilings**

Heating output	70 W/m²
Cooling output	80 W/m²
System temperature heating	40 °C
System temperature cooling	6 °C
Controllability	good
Advantages	humidification and dehumidification suitable for extreme climate zones
Disadvantages	high maintenance cost no direct user intervention detrimental to air quality high energy cost high capital cost
Typical uses	laboratories, offices with high occupancy densities, meeting room, conference room,

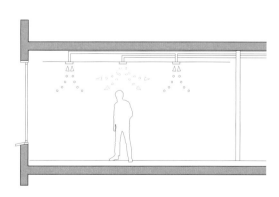

Fig. 3.3.8 **Air conditioning system**

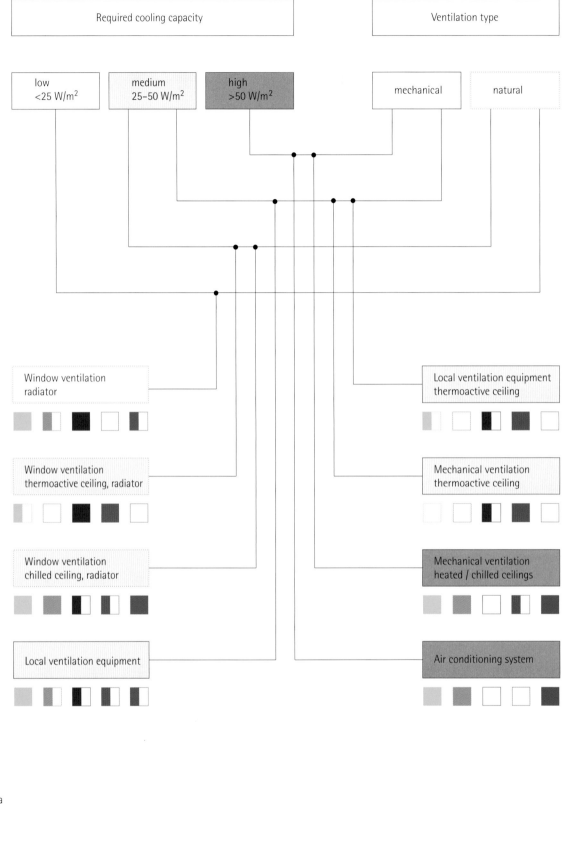

Required cooling capacity

| low <25 W/m² | medium 25–50 W/m² | high >50 W/m² |

Ventilation type

| mechanical | natural |

Window ventilation
radiator

Window ventilation
thermoactive ceiling, radiator

Window ventilation
chilled ceiling, radiator

Local ventilation equipment

Local ventilation equipment
thermoactive ceiling

Mechanical ventilation
thermoactive ceiling

Mechanical ventilation
heated / chilled ceilings

Air conditioning system

Fig. 3.3.9 **Decision chart for room conditioning**
The important criteria in the selection of room conditioning systems are the expected cooling load requirement and the type of ventilation. Suitable systems result from the combination of the selected initial criteria. The different specific characteristics of each system are shown by colour coding. The coloured squares represent three grades of performance good (filled), medium (half-filled) and poor (empty).

Thus, for example, a combination of low loads with natural ventilation results in window ventilation with radiators. This has good controllability (yellow) and possibility of space for installations in ceiling area (orange). The ceilings can remain free for use as activated thermal storage masses. The energy requirement is low (red). Regenerative energy gain for heating is not possible due to high feed flow temperatures (green). The system allows good room acoustics and protects against impact sound transmission (blue).

Controllability

Space for installations in ceiling area

Low energy requirement

Regenerative energy gain

Room acoustics

Plug-In, competition contribution

The technical and room conditioning concept for the proposed Event and Delivery Centre for the BMW plant in Munich had to interplay in an exciting way with the dynamism of the architecture. The main task in the design consisted of creating many different indoor climates and the consequent development of a building envelope in which the greatest possible number of technical functions could be integrated. This "climate skin" was to be formed as a perforated structure with a shape similar to a curved perforated plate. Prefabricated round units for the various functions could then be inserted into the holes in the structure. This approach allows the envelope to be adapted to satisfy all the different requirements. Like motor vehicle manufacture, this modular approach with prefabricated elements provides maximum flexibility in use.

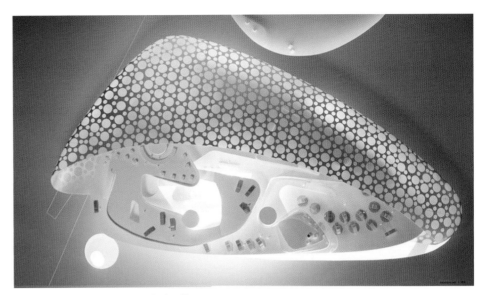

Fig. 3.3.10 **Building layout with organisational inner zone**
(Fig. Auer+Weber+Architekten, Munich)

Exhaust air element | Heat recovery | Energy spot | Light diffuser | Light deflection | Photovoltaic | Through flow element

Fig. 3.3.11 **Possible uses of plug-ins**

Construction: competition
Use: event and delivery centre
Client: BMW AG, Munich
Architect: Auer + Weber + Architekten, Munich
Building services: Ingenieurbüro Hausladen, Kirchheim, Munich

Facade: climate skin as an active skin with prefabricated functional elements
Energy concept: climate islands, heated or chilled panel sails, thermally activated components, mechanical ventilation with heat recovery, decentralised post-conditioning of the supply air, light deflection modules, direct energy control and absorption

Fig. 3.3.12 **View inside the large hall with defined climatised inner zones and variable climate islands**
(Fig. Auer+Weber+Architekten, Munich)

Fig. 3.3.13 **Climate skin with the option of inserting modular elements**
(Fig. Auer+Weber+Architekten, Munich)

Typologies

Imagine you are building a bank. You want it to be an attractive and prestigious building. You want your staff to enjoy working in it and to identify themselves with your bank. And since building in an environmentally friendly way is not only important for you personally, but also enhances your image, you want a zero-energy bank. Energy-efficiency is good for prestigious buildings, too. Inside your bank, you need a generous entrance area, plenty of space for your clients and, above all, lots of offices for your highly qualified staff. Since there is a lot of money involved in banking, working places should be as comfortable as possible to ensure that your employees can concentrate properly. So much for their requirements.

You have already purchased a piece of land for your building – close to the city centre and convenient for transport. This, of course, means that both your staff and approximately 10,000 other commuters will be driving past your premises every day. The noise environment they produce will be approximately equal to that generated by a medium-sized pneumatic hammer. Your piece of land lacks the necessary distance and buffer zones. This makes you think of home, where your study, which also faces west, is usually much too warm in summer, so that you frequently use this fact as an excuse to go and play golf. Briefly, you try to work out in your head how much it would cost you if all your staff were to go to the golf course in summer because of overheated offices.

"The best office is the back seat of an automobile."

Jean Paul Getty 1892–1976
American oil industrialist

Administration buildings

**BMW "Four Cylinder" Building, Munich, 1972,
Architect: Prof. Karl Schwanzer**
*All 18 storeys including the facade were pre-
fabricated on site and raised hydraulically on a
concrete spine, which now contains stairwells and
lifts. The building is fully air conditioned; the windows do not open.*

**Stadttor ("City Gate"), Düsseldorf, 1997,
Architects: Petzinka Pink & Partner**
*Two 16-storey columns support the penthouse
floor and enclose a 56 m high glass hall. The
whole building has a double-skin facade which
serves as a climate buffer and offers the user the
option of window ventilation. The facade cavity is
accessible from the rooms.*

**Dobler Headquarters, Klaus in Vorarlberg, 2001,
Architect: Hermann Kaufmann**
*The office building is a solid, load-bearing frame
constructed from concrete slabs on steel columns
with prefabricated timber facade elements with
copperplate cladding; these elements offer high-
thermal insulation. The buildings are heated with
a central wood-chip combustion plant. The office
building also has a background ventilation system.*

Fig. 4.1.1 **Typical types of administration building**

The categories include block and comb, internal courtyard and atrium, narrow-plan and point-block high-rise. The form of a building has consequences as much for technical and constructional aspects of the building as for its energy and room climatisation requirements. Comfort is a particularly important factor to be borne in mind for administration buildings.

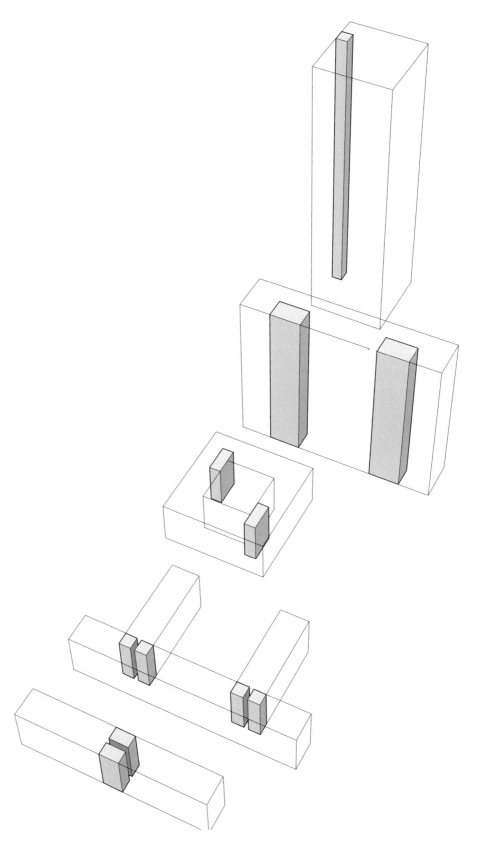

Building forms

The external form of an administration building has many consequences for its technology, economy, energy and room climatisation. It determines the ratio of main to the secondary functional areas and the surface to volume ratio, and has a decisive influence on shaft cross section and the length of cables, ducts, pipes etc. In addition, the possibility of natural ventilation, use of natural light and the aerodynamic pressure distribution on the building envelope depend on the building form. The requirements of fire protection, in particular for adequate escape and rescue routes, must likewise be taken into account. The overwhelming majority of completed buildings fall into the categories of block and comb, courtyard and atrium, narrow plan and slender point-block high-rise.

Block The block is a long, narrow building that is considerably longer than it is high. Blocks can be arranged singly or aligned with others. Vertical access routes are located centrally or at the ends. Depending on its depth, all typical office concepts can be accommodated in a block. A north–south orientation of the main facade is beneficial to room climatisation in summer. The large facade area usually provides enough natural light and good lighting of the depth of the room. Natural ventilation is also perfectly possible.

Comb The comb structure consists of several parallel blocks connected by a transverse block at one end. The parallel blocks can be aligned singly or in pairs. The vertical access routes and services shafts are generally found at the intersection points with the transverse block. The cross block often has special uses. The comb structure allows good use of natural light and ventilation. The bottom storeys are in partial shade from the building opposite, which means that they are not heated up as much in summer. Protected internal courtyards, possibly closed off at the ends with glazing, can be formed between the teeth of the comb so that the comb structure can be adopted even at locations near to heavily used roads.

Internal courtyard and atrium The internal courtyard consists of buildings grouped around a courtyard. This permits the buildings to have longer sides, as the rooms on the inside can be lit and ventilated from the internal courtyard. The rooms facing towards the courtyard are sometimes in shade. They do not heat up as much in summer, but the lower storeys receive reduced natural light. The rooms facing the internal courtyard are relatively sheltered from the wind.

The atrium is a courtyard covered with a glass roof, which reduces the area of heat-dissipating surfaces. In winter this creates an intermediate climate zone, which can also allow natural ventilation even on cold days. If through-ventilation is inadequate, air temperature in the atrium can rise to a very high value in summer, which can adversely affect natural ventilation. Natural light is reduced in quality because the roof permits less daylight to enter. In rooms facing the atrium this can lead to user acceptance problems.

Narrow-plan high-rise The narrow-plan high-rise is a block with many more storeys. The narrow-plan form may lead to two different types of facade being used, one for the two narrow sides and one for the two main facades. In general, the two main facades can be different designs, as it is possible to deal with each compass orientation in different ways with special facade concepts. A north-south orientation reduces the risk of overheating in summer. The ratio of the main to the secondary functional areas reduces with increasing height, but not as unfavourably as with point-block high-rises. Access routes can be located internally or in the outside faces of the building. If the longer side is transverse to the prevalent wind direction, considerable differences in pressure may arise between the windward and leeward sides. As narrow-plan high-rises generally have a large room depth, individual offices cannot be adopted everywhere in the building without some difficulty. Normally a mix of combi or open-plan offices is used.

Point-block high-rise Point-block high-rises are high buildings with a square or circular shape in plan. The ratio of the main to the secondary functional areas reduces with increasing height. The extensive vertical services and access routes require long lengths of cables, ducts, pipes etc. and very large areas occupied by services shafts and lifts. Point-block high-rises normally have a homogeneous building envelope, which means that orientation does not significantly influence architectural form. Wind pressure increases with height, which means exterior solar protection cannot be used and special measures must be adopted if windows are to be capable of being opened. If point-block high-rises are circular in cross section, then large pressure differences can arise between the positive and negative pressure zones when wind speeds are high. The relatively large outside surface area has a favourable effect on the availability of natural light. The building is usually exposed and therefore virtually unaffected by the shadows of neighbouring buildings.

Individual office

Occupants	1
Room size	10.8 to 16.5 m²
Occupancy density	10.8 to 16.5 m²/person
Lighting	5 W/m²
Av. int. loads	25 to 36 W/m²
Air requirement	1 x 25 m³/h = 25 m³/h
Air changes	0.5 to 0.8 h⁻¹
Light	natural light
Heating	radiator
	thermoactive ceiling
Ventilation	window ventilation
Cooling	–

Double office

Occupants	2
Room size	18 to 30 m²
Occupancy density	9 to 15 m²/person
Lighting	5 W/m²
Av. int. loads	27 to 42 W/m²
Air requirement	2 x 20 m³/h = 40 m³/h
Air changes	0.6 to 0.9 h⁻¹
Light	natural light
Heating	radiator
	thermoactive ceiling
Ventilation	window ventilation
Cooling	possible

Combi office
Combi zone

Occupants	variable (assume 4)
Room size	27 m²
Occupancy density	6.75 m²/person
Lighting	8 W/m²
Av. int. loads	22 W/m²
Air requirement	4 x 25 m³/h = 100 m³/h
Air changes	1.2 h⁻¹
Light	natural light through offices
	additional lighting required
Heating	thermoactive ceiling
	VAC
Ventilation	exhaust air
	overflow openings
	supply and exhaust air
Cooling	thermoactive ceiling
	HVAC

Individual cells

Occupants	1
Room size	9.5 m²
Occupancy density	9.5 m²/person
Lighting	5 W/m²
Av. int. loads	35 W/m²
Air requirement	1 x 25 m³/h = 25 m³/h
Air changes	0.9 h⁻¹
Light	natural light
Heating	radiator
	thermoactive ceiling
Ventilation	window ventilation

Open-plan office

Occupants	50
Room size	400 m²
Occupancy density	8 m²/person
Lighting	8 W/m²
Av. int. loads	46 W/m²
Air requirement	50 x 30 m³/h = 1500 m³/h
Air changes	1.1 h⁻¹
Light	natural light in facade area
	additional lighting required
Heating	HVAC
Ventilation	mechanical ventilation
Cooling	chilled ceiling, HVAC

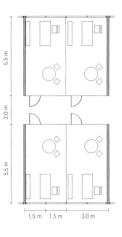

Fig. 4.1.2 **Individual office**
Facade grid 1.35 and 1.5 m

Fig. 4.1.3 **Double office**
Facade grid 1.5 and 1.35 m

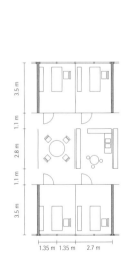

Fig. 4.1.4 **Combi office**
Facade grid 1.35 m

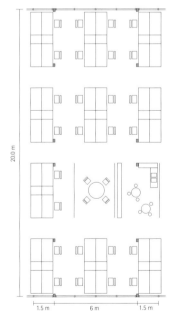

Fig. 4.1.5 **Open-plan office**
Facade grid 1.5 m

Types of office

In earlier times individual and double offices were the most common types, but since then changes in the world of work have produced a host of new office concepts. The first change was the introduction of open-plan offices, which have been more recently followed by combi offices and business clubs. Each type of office has its own characteristic heat load (Table 4.1.1 and Fig. 4.1.9). In addition, there are consequential effects for lighting and ventilation, for room climate and the associated technical installations.

Individual offices Individual offices with typical dimensions 2.7 x 4.0 m or large individual offices with dimensions 3.0 x 5.5 m have areas of 10.8 and 16.5 m² respectively. Individual offices with their shallow room depth are easy to light naturally and can be ventilated through the facade. The internal loads are between 25 to 36 W/m². As individual offices are occupied by one person only it makes sense to allow this person to set the room climate and ventilation. Radiators are a suitable means of heating. Ventilation can be through the windows. This gives the user the opportunity of individual intervention. With moderate proportions of window area and exterior solar protection, individual offices have small heat loads and therefore can be designed without cooling.

Double offices Double offices have typical dimensions of 4.5 x 4.0 m or 5.4 x 5.5 m, which result in office areas of 18 to 29.7 m². The occupancy density is between 9.0 to 15 m²/person. The room depth still offers plenty of potential for natural lighting and ventilation. The internal loads are higher with double offices than with individual offices. They are between 27 and 42 W/m². The users in double offices should also be able to control their room climate, as two people can normally agree on this. The required air changes can also be provided through windows. If the double offices frequently contain more people, for example for discussions or meetings, then ventilation through the facade becomes difficult. The thermal loads can be so high that mechanical cooling is necessary. It may be necessary to take measures to improve room acoustics. This can be accomplished with furniture and wall cladding.

Combi offices Combi offices have office cells at the facades and an assigned common zone to the inside. This combi zone serves as a circulation area and offers space for setting things down and meetings. Staff tea kitchens and photocopying machines are often sited there. Permanently assigned desks can only be made to operate in the combi zone with some difficulty. The internal loads are fairly low at 22 W/m². The possibility of providing light and ventilation to the combi zone through the facade is often limited, which means additional lighting and mechanical ventilation are necessary. At 9.5 m², the size of the individual work space is relatively small. The internal heat loads are around 35 W/m². The climate in the office cells in the combi offices should be able to be set individually. Ventilation can be through the windows. The combi zone is illuminated through the individual offices and for this the internal walls must be relatively transparent. The combi zone must be mechanically ventilated; if necessary the supply air can be provided to the combi zone by overflow from the individual offices. However, a minimum rate of air change is necessary through the facade.

Open-plan offices Open-plan offices have large room depths of 20 to 30 m. The offices may have an area as large as 1,000 m². The partition walls are low and serve principally to provide privacy. Occupancy density is very high at 8.0 m²/person. Up to 50 employees can work in an average-sized office with an area of 400 m², a facade length of 40 m and a room depth of 20 m. This produces a high internal load of approximately 46 W/m². Room acoustics are relatively poor because of the many sources of noise. Therefore measures to improve the acoustics are normally unavoidable. The high density of technical installations usually requires double floors, which stops them from acting as thermal storage masses. Continuous additional lighting is required because of the great room depth. The high heat loads mean that cooling must be part of the design. Open-plan offices must be able to offer a pleasant room climate for numerous different users. Therefore individual intervention in climate control is not an option. The high quantity of air required means mechanical ventilation is necessary, normally along with mechanical humidification and dehumidification. Natural ventilation usually plays a subsidiary role.

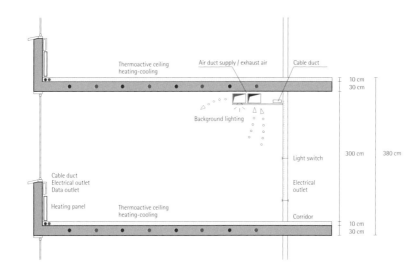

Fig. 4.1.6 Installation concept with exposed ceilings

Advantages
Exposed thermal storage mass
Low storey height

Disadvantages
Little flexibility
Difficult room acoustics
Less space for technical installations
Displacement ventilation expensive to
provide

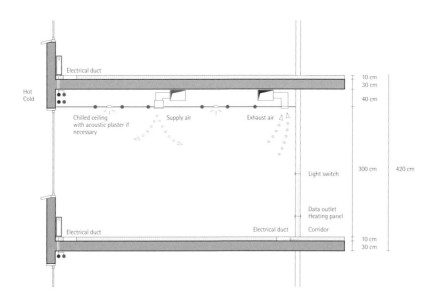

Fig. 4.1.7 Space for installations in the suspended ceiling

Advantages
Good room acoustics
Simple integration of lighting
High cooling output
Extensive installation space
Luminaire ventilation extraction possible

Disadvantages
High storey heights in building
No active thermal storage masses
Little flexibility for electrical and
data distribution

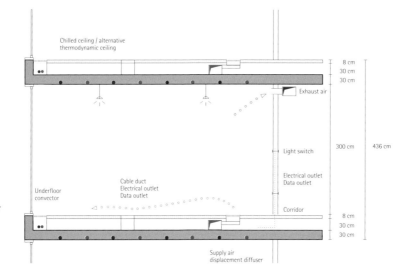

Fig. 4.1.8 Installation space in double floor

Advantages
High flexibility for data and
electrical services
Displacement ventilation easily provided
No visible heating elements on the facade

Disadvantages
Possible room acoustics problems
No unobstructed heat transfer through the floor
Larger storey height required

Integrated technology

With the increasing demands on room climate and the requirements of mechanical ventilation, extensive technical systems have to be integrated into the building. This integration is achieved within vertical shafts, horizontal distribution ducts, and installation zones in the rooms.

Rooms and their uses are frequently changed nowadays and it is therefore necessary for the installation concept to incorporate a high degree of flexibility. When drawing up layouts, it is important to ensure that the vertical shafts can be integrated into the building without staggering their routes. Ventilation ducts occupy the most space. When dimensioning shafts, you should ensure that there is enough space for the duct itself, its installation and the future maintenance of the fire dampers. The pipes for heating, cooling, water, waste water, and conduits for electricity and data installed in the vertical shafts must be easily accessible at the connection points on each storey.

Horizontal distribution in the building is mainly along cable channels, which run in the basement and lead to the shafts. On each floor the cables, ducts and pipes are taken to the individual rooms. In large projects, the rooms in the basement must be of appropriate height to allow adequately dimensioned channels. Depending on the building services concept, a higher storey height may also be required in the above-ground storeys, for example when ventilation ducts have to be accommodated in the corridors. The required installation space for the horizontal distribution infrastructure increases with the number of rooms to be supplied. To keep storey heights to an economic minimum, it might be worthwhile installing additional shafts.

The installation of the cables on each floor or to the individual rooms can be in a double floor, above a suspended ceiling or exposed in the room. Other possibilities include installation zones in the windowsill areas or ducts in floor screeds. The trend towards thermally activated components and night cooling requires thermal storage masses that can be activated and exposed floors and ceilings. This could mean that installation concepts such as double floors or suspended ceilings cannot be considered in the solution. In addition to the lack of installation space, it is difficult to integrate luminaires and take measures to improve room acoustics.

Installation concepts with exposed ceilings The installation space can be lost if ceilings and floors are left unclad so that they can be used for concrete core activation. Alternatively, data and electrical cables can be routed next to the facade and along the internal walls. Air conduction is under the ceiling in the area of the internal walls. Elements for background lighting, improving room acoustics and chilled ceilings can also be fitted into this suspended zone. Likewise it is also used for further hori-

zontal distribution of electrical cables, in particular for connecting switches and socket outlets on the internal walls. A heater at the facade can be an additional means of individual control of room conditions.

Installation space in the suspended ceiling If the room has a full-surface suspended ceiling it can be used as a chilled ceiling and as a means of improving room acoustics. Lighting and ventilation fitments can also be installed there. The installation space can be used for heating and cooling system pipework and ventilation ducts. Holes have to be provided in the concrete slab to connect up the radiators. The electrical and data cables are laid in ducts in the floor screed.

Installation in double floors The area under the double floors is used for electrical and data cables, ventilation ducts and heating pipework. Displacement diffusers can be installed close to the ducts and the underfloor convectors integrated into the double floors. Cooling can be by thermoactive ceiling or flush-fitted chilled ceiling. Luminaires can be attached directly to the structural slab.

Device	Output [W] in operation	Output [W] Standby / off
Computer + monitor	150	15 / 5
Laser printer	190	2 / 1
Inkjet printer	20	2 / 1
Copier	1,100	27 / 1
Fax	20	2 / 0
Desk light	11	0
Gen. lighting/m²	5	0
People	120	80

Tab 4.1.1 **Typical heat outputs in offices**

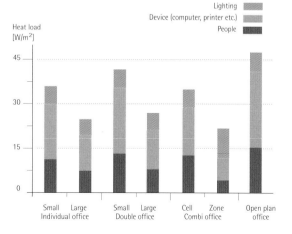

Fig. 4.1.9 **Internal heat loads for various types of office**

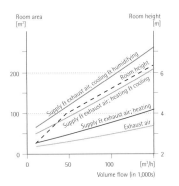

Fig. 4.1.10 **Space requirement of HVAC systems**
Irrespective of the HVAC system, the required room height depends on the airflows.

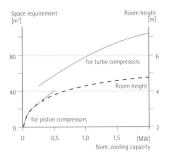

Fig. 4.1.11 **Space requirement of refrigeration plants**

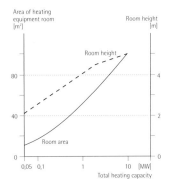

Fig. 4.1.12 **Space requirement of heating plants**

Fig. 4.1.13 **Schematic section showing the location of ventilation equipment rooms**
An important factor in deciding the location of the equipment rooms is the requirement for heat recovery using a heat exchanger. Another criterion is the location of the outside air intake point. If outside air can be taken in from near ground level or an earth pipe is planned, the equipment room should be located in the basement, otherwise a roof location is often the best solution. Equipment rooms in the middle of the building reduce the required shaft area. The significance of the location of the equipment rooms increases with the number of storeys in the building.

Equipment rooms

In administration buildings there are heating, sanitary, and electrical equipment rooms and, depending on use, ventilation and refrigeration plants. The great amount of space and installation work required make ventilation equipment rooms the most difficult to integrate. Electrical and heating equipment rooms are typically located in the basement because of the energy supply connections. Location in other parts of a building is also possible. The choice of location of refrigeration plants should take into account the need for sound insulation.

Ventilation equipment rooms The number and cross sectional area of shafts can be minimised by optimally positioning ventilation equipment rooms. Supply and exhaust air plants require the most space, especially when heat recovery involving rotary or plate heat exchangers is used, a solution which needs the supply and exhaust air to be conducted to one point in the building. If the outside air is taken in at ground level or if preconditioning in an underground duct is planned then locating the ventilation plant in the basement makes good sense. The top storey is the best location in heavily polluted locations. This also applies to exhaust air only plants, to systems without heat recovery or with heat recovery by means of a system connected into a circuit or by an exhaust air heat pump. Separate supply and exhaust air equipment rooms allow savings on shaft area but heat recovery is less efficient. With tall buildings, a ventilation plant in the middle storeys of the building requires the least shaft cross sectional area as it can serve the floors above and below it. These plants are also used to divide tall buildings in services storeys, which can often be recognised from the outside (Fig. 4.1.13).

Refrigeration plants The generation of cooling energy is often associated with vibration and noise. Therefore if it is located elsewhere than in the basement very good sound insulation will be required. As refrigeration machines need some form of recooling, the location should take into account the adjacent space required by recooling plants or heat exchangers. Siting the recooling plant inside the building should be avoided as it must be supplied with a considerable volume of air. Normally the roof offers the best solution.

Electrical and ITC equipment rooms Depending on the ITC concept, buildings can sometimes require large server rooms. Due to their high heat loads, these rooms must have adequate ventilation and often extensive cooling. Normally server rooms are cooled using recirculation air cooling.

Meter rooms The position and size of the meter room needs to be clarified at an early stage as the utility services providers often have their own requirements. The meter room should always be positioned at an external wall near the public utilities services as a short connection to the public supply keeps construction costs down. Moreover, the responsibility of the supplier usually ends at the meter and unnecessary deviations are often not accepted.

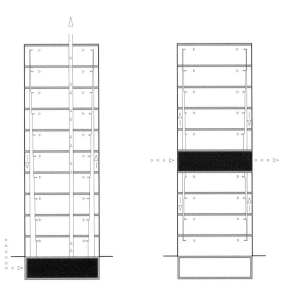

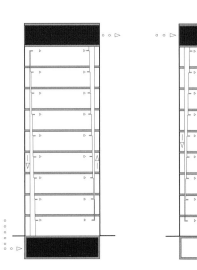

Energy Info Box

The new building for the Centre for Sustainable Building in Kassel is a research facility that seeks to provide maximum user comfort for minimum energy consumption. The use of a mechanical ventilation system with heat recovery was stipulated at an early planning stage. In addition, the climatisation concept had to include tempered zones on different floors and heating circuits for specific rooms. The interactions between ventilation, heat transfer system, room climate and user behaviour within the building are measured and analysed. Pipework is installed in the concrete ceilings and in the floor screeds of the rooms on the second, first and ground floors. The rooms are tempered by heated/chilled ceilings or underfloor heating or cooling. Every office has a separately controllable circuit in the ceiling and the floor screed. In the normal mode of operation, the screed provides heating and the ceiling provides cooling. The building components with water flowing through them are used in summer for cooling, when cold water is circulated in the solid ceiling slabs and/or floor screed. More pipework in the building foundations recools the water warmed by this process. The heating feed flow temperature is set in relation to the outside air temperature. Screed and ceiling temperatures are regulated as a single system by suitable controls. This creates a thermoactive ceiling that gives up its energy evenly above and below. For this reason the thickness of impact sound transmission insulation is limited to 2 cm.

Fig. 4.1.14 **Centre for Sustainable Building in Kassel**
View from southeast

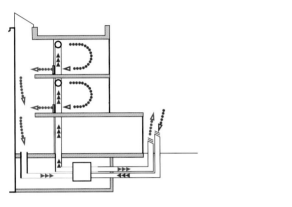

Fig. 4.1.15 **Ventilation schematic supply air**
Supply air is conducted into the offices and flows from there through overflow openings into the atrium.

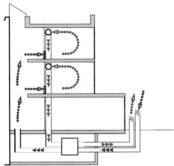

Fig. 4.1.16 **Ventilation schematic exhaust air**
The supply air flows through the heat recovery system into the atrium and flows from there through overflow openings into the offices and laboratories.

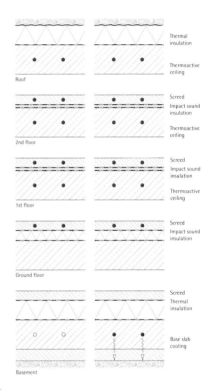

Fig. 4.1.17 **Position of the pipework in ceiling slabs on different storeys and the type of tempering in summer and winter**

Construction: 2001
Use: demonstration and research facility
Client: Centre for Sustainable Building, Prof. G. Hausladen, Prof. G. Hauser, Prof. G. Minke, Kassel
Architect: Jourdan & Müller PAS, Frankfurt a. Main, Prof. J. Jourdan, Seddig Architekten, Kassel; I. Seddig, R. Fehrmann
Building services: Ingenieurbüro Hausladen, Kirchheim, Munich, J. Bauer, Ingenieurbüro Springl, Ingolstadt, P. Springl
Facade: triple insulation glazing in highly thermally insulated frames
Energy concept: low energy house, component heating and cooling system, foundation slab, ventilation system with heat recovery

Fig. 4.1.18 *The view of the building at night shows up the printed balustrade zones designed to reduce the amount of solar energy admitted.*

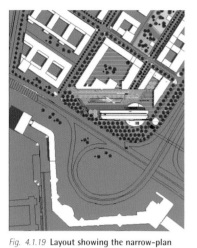

Fig. 4.1.19 **Layout showing the narrow-plan high-rise**
(Fig.: Auer+Weber+Architekten, Munich)

Light-tech, two competition contributions

A **light-tech high-rise** was designed in a two-stage competition for a concept involving a narrow-plan high-rise and a point-block high-rise on a noisy site at the intersection of the middle ring road and motorway.

Achieving comfort and user friendliness with the minimum of building services technology is a most important consideration in the development of the facade and building services technology concepts. To create a high-quality user environment, the building should be naturally ventilated and provided with extensive daylighting. Users should also be able to exercise individual control over their room climates and understand how the system interacts with their surroundings. Reducing the technical content should result in a lower energy demand and reduced capital and maintenance costs. The aim of

the facade concept was to produce a solution that would combine formal and functional aspects.

Alternative narrow-plan high-rise As a departure from the requirements of the town plan, the longitudinal axis of the building was turned through almost 90° to result in a north-south orientation of the main facades. This enabled the heat load of the building to be considerably reduced. The building is also aligned along the main wind direction to reduce the pressure difference between the two facades. This avoids unintentional airflows through the building and high opening forces on windows and doors.

The double-skin facade permits air to flow horizontally and vertically through it so that no overheating of the facade cavity occurs. Inside the double-skin facade cavity the shading and light deflection systems can be protected against the weather.

Fig. 4.1.22 **Alternative narrow-plan high-rise**
(Fig.: Auer+Weber+Architekten, Munich)

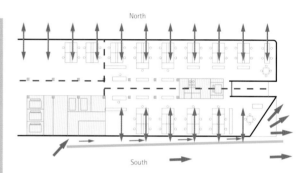

Fig. 4.1.20 **Natural ventilation through the facade**
(Fig.: Auer+Weber+Architekten, Munich)

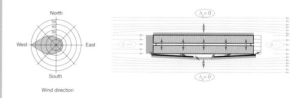

Fig. 4.1.21 **Aerodynamic alignment of the building**
(Fig.: Auer+Weber+Architekten, Munich)

Construction: competition
Use: administration building
Client: Langenscheidt KG, Munich
Architect: Auer + Weber + Architekten, Munich
Building services, energy technology: Ingenieurbüro Hausladen, Kirchheim, Munich
Facade: narrow-plan high-rise option: transverse through flow double-skin facade, point-block high-rise option: alternating facade
Energy concept: window ventilation and thermoactive ceilings

Alternative point-block high-rises The facade concepts were united in a single concept that was based on the formal theme of the grid in order to exploit the advantages of single- and double-skin facades. The facade consists of internal shading and direct opening windows for summer ventilation and a box window with a baffle panel and intermediate shading. Each element fills a complete bay in facade grid. The internal shading reduces the glazing fraction, considerably cutting down the amount of solar energy admitted. The elements are positioned alternately vertically and horizontally. In this way each office has at least one double-skin and one single-skin facade element.

The openings in both facade types have three different settings: they may be tightly closed, have a small open gap or be completely open, to allow both background ventilation and pulse ventilation. The user is able to use the options in the opening elements of each facade type in response to his own needs and the outside climatic conditions. The system is simple to comprehend and offers many different ways of influencing internal climate conditions.

The shading elements are divided into two spatially separated groups to avoid it being necessary to switch on artificial lighting to compensate for low light levels inside the rooms when the shading elements are closed during sunny weather. The top part of the lamella curtain has a light deflection zone, which can be adjusted to suit the user. The flatter lamella angle deflects the sunlight into the depth of the room.

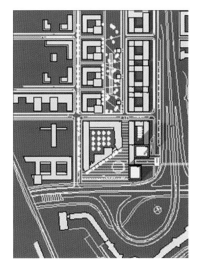

Fig. 4.1.23 **Layout showing the point-block high-rises**
(Fig.: Auer+Weber+Architekten, Munich)

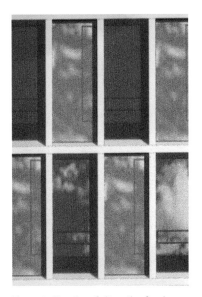

Fig. 4.1.24 **Elevation of alternating facade**
(Fig.: Auer+Weber+Architekten, Munich)

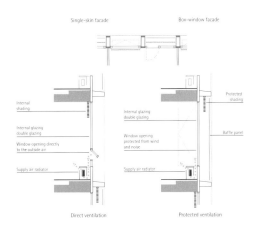

Fig. 4.1.25 **Alternating facade**
An alternating facade has alternating box window and single-skin facade elements. Each room has both facade types.

Fig. 4.1.26 **Alternative point-block high-rise**
(Fig.: Auer+Weber+Architekten, Munich)

Fig. 4.1.27 **Hypothekenbank Munich**

Construction: 2002
Use: offices
Client: Hypothekenbank Munich
Architect: Lanz Architekten + Generalplaner
    GmbH, Munich
Energy planning, building services: Ingenieurbüro
    Hausladen, Kirchheim, Munich
Facade: combined facade
Energy concept: natural ventilation, thermoac-
    tive ceilings in combi offices, chilled ceilings
    on the directorate floor, compression chillers,
    cooling tower

Hypothekenbank Munich

The local conditions at the site for the new building for the Münchener Hypothekenbank required a special approach to its planning and design right from the start. The plot was close to the city centre on the heavily trafficked Karl-Scharnagl-Ring. The main facade faces west. The impressive corporate image entrance hall gives access to conference rooms and eating facilities on the same floor. Offices are located on the first to fourth floor. The directorate rooms are in the penthouse on the top storey. Offices in the standard storeys are laid out in opposing pairs with internal combi zones. In the planning of the building it was particularly important to ensure that the users would be able to control individual room climates by means of window ventilation, heating controls and variable lighting.

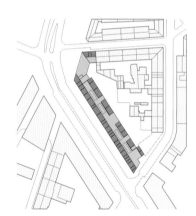

Fig. 4.1.28 **Urban planning situation**
Circulation zones and the location of office rooms in the standard floor

Facade With a sound load of between 75 and 80 dB(A) at times of peak traffic on the Karl-Scharnagl-Ring, the noisy location and the west-facing main facade required a special facade design. The west facade has a relatively low glazing fraction of about 50% and is made up of an alternating combination of single-skin and box-window facade elements (Fig. 4.1.29). A box window with an opened internal window admits much less noise than an open window in a single-skin facade. This allows all offices to have natural ventilation through their windows. This facade concept offers the user the individual extensive outside views through the single-skin facade as well as comfortable ventilation without noise. Exterior solar protection is positioned in front of the single-skin facade elements. Solar protection glass in the casement windows reduces solar input. Internal glare protection can be lowered when required.

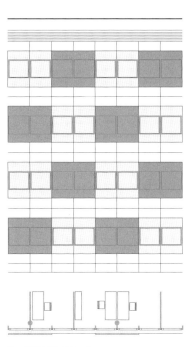

Fig. 4.1.29 **West facade**
Single-skin facade and box-window elements - alternating pattern

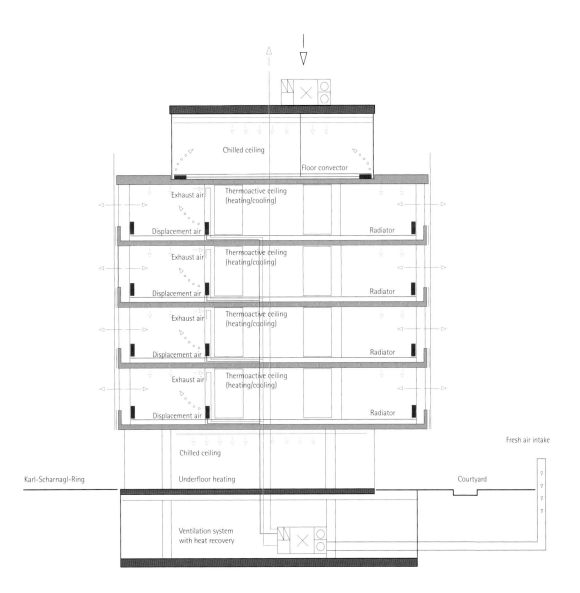

Fig. 4.1.30 **Heating, ventilation and cooling concept for the Münchener Hypothekenbank – typical cross section**

Radiator

Cooling stack
with free cooling (hybrid cooler)
Thermoactive ceiling for tempering
the core of the chilled ceiling
in special rooms

Ventilation concept
Window ventilation on the courtyard side
Window ventilation and displacement
air on the road side
Ventilation system in special rooms

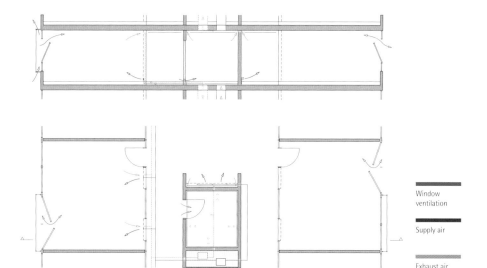

Window
ventilation

Supply air

Exhaust air

Fig. 4.1.31 **Ventilation on standard floors**
Section (above) and plan (below)

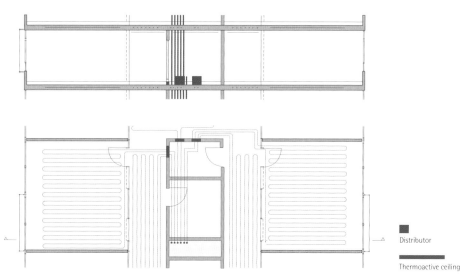

Feed

Return

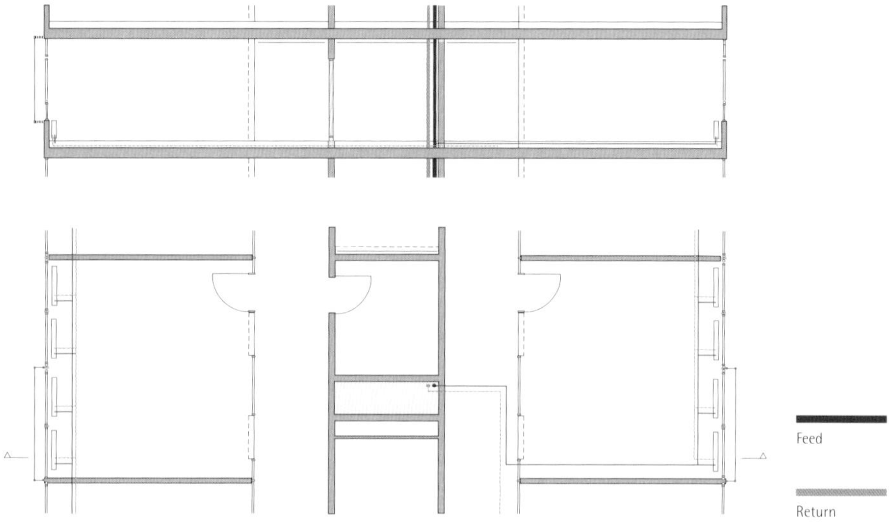

Fig. 4.1.32 **Heat distribution on standard floors**
Section (above) and plan (below)

Distributor

Thermoactive ceiling

Fig. 4.1.33 **Thermoactive ceiling on standard floors**
Section (above) and plan (below)

Ventilation concept The office rooms on the east side of the building facing into the internal courtyard are ventilated exclusively through windows. The entrance hall is ventilated through opening flaps. The background ventilation to the offices on the road side is provided by mechanical ventilation. Natural ventilation is always available through the box windows (Fig.4.1.31). Pulse ventilation from the single-skin facade can be used to prevent heated air in the facade cavity from entering the office.

The combi zones in the standard storeys and special rooms on the ground floor such as canteen, kitchen and conference rooms are mechanically ventilated. The outside air is extracted from the internal courtyard and delivered through an earth pipe to the ventilation plant. From there it is distributed into the rooms and exhausted through exhaust air fans in the roof, after heat recovery. On the directorate floor, two independent air conditioning units on the roof provide mechanical ventilation.

Heating and cooling concept A district heating connection occupies little space in the heating equipment room and has an available heat energy capacity of 1,000 kW for peak periods. Heat transfer in the office rooms is by panel heaters (Fig. 4.1.32); on the directorate floor and in other corridor areas it is through underfloor convectors. The entrance hall is tempered through floor heating, underfloor convectors and facade heating.

Two compression refrigeration machines provide cooling energy and can be used by free night cooling when outside temperatures are low. Thermoactive ceilings limit the room temperature on the standard floors to 28 °C (Fig. 4.1.33). Rooms on the directorate floor and the conference rooms on the ground floor have a higher degree of comfort with maximum temperatures of 26 °C due to the use of chilled ceilings.

Integration of technical systems The equipment rooms for heating, cooling, electricity supply, sprinklers and ITC are concentrated in the first basement and in parts of the second basement (Fig. 4.1.34–Fig. 4.1.36). Five main shafts in the central zone are used for vertical distribution. Horizontal distribution in each storey is by double floors. Installations are not located under the ceiling in order not to reduce the effectiveness of the thermoactive ceilings. Therefore artificial lighting for the offices is provided by floor lamps. The building management and services systems can be controlled from a control centre in the basement.

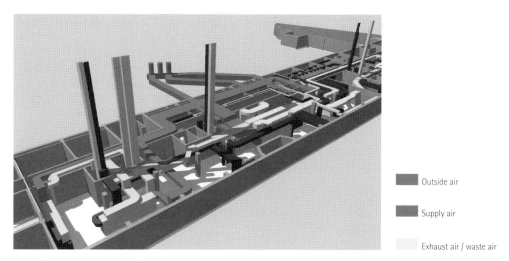

Outside air

Supply air

Exhaust air / waste air

Fig. 4.1.34 **Perspective of ventilation equipment room in first basement**

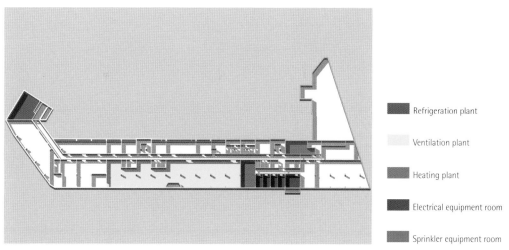

Refrigeration plant

Ventilation plant

Heating plant

Electrical equipment room

Sprinkler equipment room

Fig. 4.1.35 **Building services equipment rooms in first basement, plan**

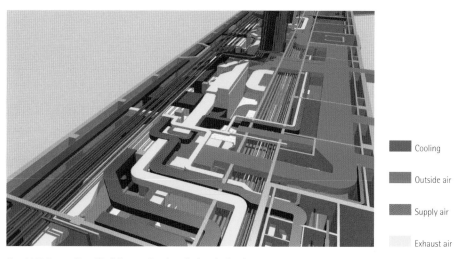

Cooling

Outside air

Supply air

Exhaust air

Fig. 4.1.36 **Perspective of building services installations in first basement**

Typologies | Administration buildings

Fig. 4.1.37 **View of trade exhibition tower**
Construction: 1999
Client: Deutsche Messe AG, Hanover
Architect: Herzog+Partner, Munich
Building services: Ingenieurbüro Hausladen,
Kirchheim, Munich

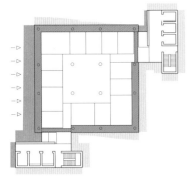

Fig. 4.1.38 **Plan of standard floor**
with wind pressure distribution on the facade

Administration building
Deutsche Messe AG, Hanover

A new building was added to the Deutsche Messe AG administration building in Hanover in 1999.

The new building is 85 m high and has 20 storeys. The 14 storeys above the three-storey entrance hall are used solely for offices. The upper floors accommodate the directorate and conference and meeting areas. The plan layout is square with a side length of 24 m. The floor space on each level can be split between open plan, combi or individual offices. This building is special because of the way the various systems in the building are integrated into an overall concept that ensures higher comfort, lower energy consumption, and the exploitation of sun and wind for tempering and ventilation.

Two attached towers form the accesses to the building and contain the stairs, lifts, sanitary provisions and all the vertically running installations. The building services floors are housed on the roof of the northeast tower (Fig. 4.1.37). A ventilation tower projects above the northern access tower by about 30 m. Thermal buoyancy is used as the main engine for naturally ventilating the whole building. The building is a reinforced concrete frame, stiffened by the two access towers. The cladding to the towers consists of a ventilated, ceramic curtain wall facade. The floor slabs are in situ concrete and function as exposed thermal storage masses in the completed building.

Facade A significant component of the architectural concept is the form of the facade. The external skin is designed as a double-skin facade with horizontal separation (corridor facade) at each storey. The external and the internal facade skin consists of insulating glazing (U = 1.1 W/m²K). The insulation glazing of the external skin made thermal separation of the projecting ceiling unnecessary. The separation of each storey simplified fire protection. The columns are located in the facade cavity so as not to take up usable space. Shading elements are also in the facade cavity and are therefore protected from the weather and can be operated independently of the wind. The inner facade is constructed of timber and glass.

Ventilation concept The ventilation concept of the building is largely based on natural ventilation through the windows. The facade cavity acts as a buffer zone for wind and heat. Ventilation louvres are incorporated into the outer skin and allow the flow through and pressures in the facade cavity to be controlled. Whatever the prevailing wind conditions, the building can be naturally ventilated throughout the year.

The outer facade skin has eight strips with ventilation louvres that control the flow of air into and out of the facade cavity. The ventilation louvres can be set in six different positions. Temperatures are measured at various points and used to determine the required settings for the facade openings. Different ventilation strategies are called upon to suit the season, time of day, insolation, wind speed and direction. The flow of air always moves from the outside to inside (Fig. 4.1.38). Hence window ventilation is possible even in high winds.

The flaps are mainly kept closed during cold times of the year and air changes are restricted to a minimum. In summer they are wide open so that heat stored in the facade cavity is conducted away by a high rate of air change. Window ventilation is augmented by mechanical ventilation systems with heat recovery. The facade plinth houses the supply air duct for the mechanical ventilation system. The ventilation system provides a 1.5 rate of air change. The supply air duct can be controlled and easily cleaned by wide opening flaps. Windows and supply air openings are linked to one another (Fig. 4.1.39). When the window is opened in a room, the supply air outlet is closed by a mechanical link. The exhaust air system continues to operate. Thus the user can decide whether to retain the preconditioned air from the supply air duct or ventilate the room from the facade cavity.

Heating and cooling In order to avoid the use of mechanical refrigeration machines, room conditioning is provided by thermoactive ceilings, which are recooled during the night. The recooling plant (hybrid cooler) on the roof of the building achieves coolant water temperatures of 18 °C during summer nights. Heating of the building is provided by thermoactive ceilings. There are no additional night heating radiators.

Fig. 4.1.39 Internal view of the office looking onto the ventilation element

*"I dreamt that I dwelt in marble halls
With vassals and serfs at my side."*

*Alfred "Poet" Bunn 1796–1860,
The Bohemian Girl (1843)*

Atria

Prisma, Frankfurt/Main, 2002,
Architects: Auer + Weber + Architekten
The internal atrium is integrated into the room cli-
matisation and ventilation concept. The supply air
is taken in either through the double-skin facade
or from the atrium, allowing the required supply
air conditions to be selected to suit the climatisa-
tion situation.

Continuing Education Academy Mont Cenis,
Herne, 1999, Architects: Jourda Architects,
Hegger Hegger Schleiff Architekten
The atrium forms a space protected from the
weather in which the usage units are arranged
like houses. It forms an intermediate climatic zone
with Mediterranean temperatures. The hall is not
climatised.

Hong Kong and Shanghai Bank, Hong Kong
1985, Architects: Foster and Partners
The internal atrium of the Hong Kong and Shang-
hai Bank is used as circulation zones and offices.
Computer-controlled light shelves deflect natural
light into the building. The atrium is fully air con-
ditioned.

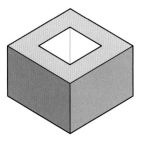

Internal
Lighting: difficult in the lower storeys
Ventilation: difficult conduction of supply air
In summer: danger of overheating in the upper storeys
Particular characteristics: access zone

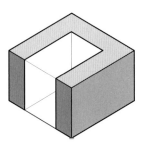

Open to one side
Lighting: good
Ventilation: good
In summer: effective shading required
Particular characteristics: sound insulation

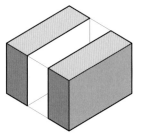

Open to two sides
Lighting: difficult in the lower storeys of the middle zone
Ventilation: through-ventilation possible
In summer: thermally less critical
Particular characteristics: passageway

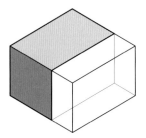

Open to three sides
Lighting: good
Ventilation: good
In summer: thermally critical, efficient shading required
Particular characteristics: winter garden

Fig. 4.2.1 **Atrium construction forms**

Building forms

More and more atria are being designed as integral parts of administration buildings. They are used as access zones, passageways and light wells. They can also be incorporated into the room climatisation and ventilation concept. Atria can improve the area/volume ratio and the ratio of the main to the secondary functional areas and therefore the requirements for internal walls. In comparison with the enclosed internal courtyard of ancient times, today's solution offers many more options for layouts, which in turn create quite different kinds of relationships between internal and external space.

Internal atrium The enclosed atrium is the original form of light well. No horizontal outlook is possible; light enters the room from above only, creating an introverted, non-directional impression of the space. Ventilation comes either from ventilation openings in the ground floor area or through ventilation ducts. Internal atria are often used as access areas. Overshadowing or shading is necessary to prevent overheating of the upper parts of an atrium.

Atrium, open to one side A facade glazed to the outside world creates an impressive visual relationship with the environment. The atrium faces a particular direction. Natural light also penetrates the lower parts of the atrium through the vertical glass face. Fewer problems occur for lighting offices in the lower storeys as they can be faced towards the atrium. Ventilation openings can be installed at the bottom of the vertical face to allow a good

through-flow of fresh air in the summer. Efficient shading is necessary to limit the amount of solar radiation admitted. There is the danger of cold air drop in winter due to the large area of glass.

Atrium, open to two sides The two sides of the atrium are contained by long blocks. The two opposing glazed surfaces on the narrow sides create the characteristics of a passageway, which may have an introverting effect, depending on the length of the atrium and the design of the glazed facades. Light entering at the sides means that the areas near the vertical glazed surfaces have ample natural light. In the middle zone the intensity of illumination drops off considerably in the lower storeys, depending on the length of the atrium. Ventilation flaps can be incorporated into the vertical faces to allow vertical and horizontal flows of fresh air. The vertical surfaces exposed to sunlight require efficient shading. Cold air drop and draughts in certain wind conditions should be kept in mind.

Atrium, open to three sides The position of the building on one side makes the atrium like a winter garden, creating a very highly transparent intermediate zone, which is protected from the weather. The exposed situation results in a high amount of admitted solar radiation. The building can be very deep as it is illuminated from both sides. The large glazed surface can lead to thermal problems in summer so that very good through-ventilation and efficient shading are particular aspects to consider. This type of solution is often built at heavily trafficked locations to provide sound insulation.

Uses

Atria have three main types of use: the atrium as a passageway, as an access zone, as a provider of light and air (Fig. 4.2.3). The important difference is in the type of interaction with the associated usable rooms. Depending on the design, rooms may face outwards into the atrium only or have other external facades.

The atrium as a passageway The simplest function of an atrium is one of a circulation area that is sheltered from the effects of the weather. It forms an independent space. Interaction with the associated rooms does not take place or is very restricted, with the effect that these areas must have other lighting and ventilation facilities available. The atrium adopts a character more like an enclosed external space than an internal space and becomes a passageway, an arcade or a thoroughfare.

Atrium as a circulation zone The atrium in this case provides horizontal and vertical access to the building, which allows the user to create a lively and interesting space. The rising arrangement of offices takes up more area. Light from two sides of the rooms permits greater depth. If the atrium is used for access, higher temperatures must be ensured in winter. Mechanical supply air or exhaust air is often integrated into this type of atrium.

Atrium for lighting and ventilation If the atrium is used to provide light and ventilation to rooms oriented towards the atrium, then care should be taken to ensure adequate natural light in the lower storeys as well as good air quality and consistent thermal conditions. A width to height ratio of 1:1 is the ideal value to ensure good lighting. Good ventilation is required in the summer. Pair of linked useable rooms can allow large building depths. Ventilation of these rooms in winter is comfortable as the supply air is prewarmed in the atrium, but in summer there is the risk of overheating. Depending on use, the atrium may give rise to problems with noise and odour transmission.

22 °C	Prolonged stay
	Meeting
	Office zone
	Restaurant
18–20 °C	Temporary stay
	Cafeteria
	Staff tea kitchen
10–14 °C	Exhibition area
	Circulation space
	Corporate image area

Fig. 4.2.2 **Temperature in the atrium in relation to use and duration of occupation**
The shorter the duration of occupation, the lower are the requirements for comfort. Fluctuations can be tolerated. The degree of interaction of the functions of the adjoining rooms with the atrium generally determines the requirements in relation to the atrium.

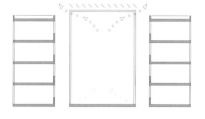

Fig. 4.2.3 **Uses of atria**
Schematic cross section

Atrium as a passageway
No ventilation to the atrium
No sound or odour transmission

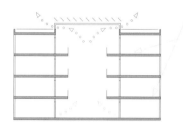

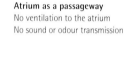

Atrium as a circulation zone
Mechanical ventilation through the atrium
Reduced sound and odour transmission

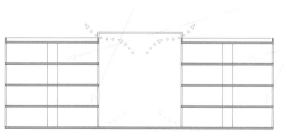

Atrium for lighting and ventilation
Window ventilation to the atrium, if necessary
Mechanical ventilation of the atrium space
Pronounced sound and odour transmission

Ventilation

Atria can be integrated into a building's ventilation concept, either natural or mechanical. There are three ways of doing this: natural ventilation through the atrium, the supply air atrium and the exhaust air atrium. The choice of ventilation type is tightly linked to the thermal conditions in the atrium, the outside conditions and the requirements for air quality in the offices.

Natural ventilation through the atrium With natural ventilation through the atrium, ventilation is provided through windows opening into the atrium. In winter the air in the atrium is prewarmed and used for ventilating the offices, thus avoiding any comfort problems. If ventilation is provided only from the atrium, then in summer there can be a serious risk of overheating in the adjoining rooms. Adequate shading is an important consideration. To ensure adequate air quality and to avoid disturbing odours it is necessary for the atrium to receive a generous through-flow of air. This can be provided either by having adequately sized openings or mechanical supply air ventilation.

If mechanical through-ventilation is employed for the atrium, the supply air can be preconditioned. This is particularly attractive in the summer when preconditioning can be by underground duct or ground water. Particular attention should be paid to the possibility of disturbance caused by noise from the atrium or by the transmission of sound from room to room. The concept is suitable for locations at which no direct window ventilation is possible because of external noise.

Supply air atrium In summer the supply air can be cooled, for example in an earth pipe, so that the temperature in the atrium is below the outside air temperature. Air flows from the atrium through overflow openings into the rooms and conducted out through the facade. In this way the heat input from the facade is very small. No solar loads should be allowed to warm the supply air in the atrium. A supply air atrium can be the solution if there are no odours in the atrium and in summer the amount of solar radiation admitted can be efficiently limited. In winter, passive solar gain warms the supply air so that the ventilation heat requirement is reduced and the supply air can be introduced in a comfortable manner into the room.

Exhaust air atrium Supply air flows directly into rooms through the facade or from a mechanical ventilation system. This allows air of a higher quality to be conducted directly into zones where people are present over prolonged periods. Exhaust air flows through overflow openings into the atrium (Fig. 4.2.4) and from there through the roof directly to the open air or taken back through a duct to a central ventilation system (Fig. 4.2.5).

The warm exhaust air contributes to the tempering of the atrium. For this reason the concept is particularly suitable for circulation zone atria. In winter the mechanically conducted supply air must be tempered to the required temperature. Supply air conducted through the facade must be introduced in a way that is not detrimental to comfort. Heat recovery is simple to incorporate in the main exhaust flow. Supply air can be preconditioned in a central plant so that the thermal conditions are improved in summer.

Fig. 4.2.4 **Overflow openings to the atrium**
Regional Office for Statistics and Information, Schweinfurt

Fig. 4.2.5 **Exhaust air ducts at the passenger lift**
Regional Office for Statistics and Information, Schweinfurt

Conditioning

If possible, atria should not be actively heated or cooled. However, additional local measures are necessary in order to improve thermal comfort. The large volume of an atrium means that the room conditioning system should be designed to provide comfortable conditions in the places where people are frequently present for long periods (Fig. 4.2.6). Cold air drop presents a particular problem, as does overheating in the upper storeys.

Cold air drop Underfloor convectors in front of the facade can prevent cold air drop at tall glass surfaces. Additional means of heating may be required for various facade levels with atrium heights of more than 10 m. They can be in the form of finned tubes or heated facade profiles. Areas near the facade should not be designated as places where people are present for prolonged periods. Local means of heating, such as radiators or suspended heating panels, are useful for improving comfort in these defined informal meeting areas. Underfloor heating may be used to provide background tempering of the atrium if required. If appropriate the gallery areas can be heated by wet heating systems. If the atrium is mechanically ventilated, the supply air may be preconditioned using regenerative energy sources such as earth pipes or ground water.

Cooling atria The large areas of glass predispose atria to overheating in summer. Good through-ventilation is required in addition to efficient shading. A higher atrium roof is an efficient way of improving the thermal conditions in the upper storeys. Thermally driven through-ventilation requires adequately sized ventilation flaps in the base and roof areas of the atrium. The flaps should be automatically controlled. If underfloor heating is installed, it can also be used for cooling. The supply air should be precooled with mechanical ventilation. Regenerative sources of cooling energy such as ground water or earth pipes are promising solutions for cooling atria.

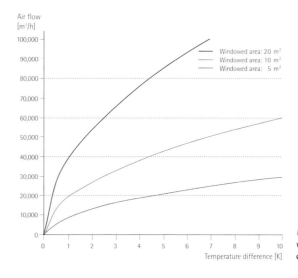

Fig. 4.2.6 **Intensity of ventilation for various window sizes in a glazed hall using thermal air currents** *(after Pültz)*

Natural light

The difficult aspect in the design of atria is to allow as much natural light as possible to enter the useable rooms but avoid overheating in summer. In winter a high amount of admitted solar radiation is desirable to exploit passive solar gain, but on the other hand care must be taken to avoid the nuisance of glare from direct sunlight. To satisfy these conflicting requirements the shading in the roof and vertical surfaces should be designed in detail. In addition to the entry of radiation through the transparent surfaces, the supply of natural light has a crucial influence on the atrium geometry (Fig. 4.2.7).

In the lower storeys, the supply of natural light decreases with increasing atrium height and decreasing atrium width. Circulation zones and galleries reduce the supply of natural light to the associated rooms. Light-coloured wall and floor surfaces have a positive effect on room brightness. If necessary, light deflection systems can also be used.

The large area of glazing makes atria susceptible to overheating in summer, making efficient shading essential. The ideal solution is an external shading system. If shading systems are located internally to escape the weather then adequate rear ventilation of the shading must be provided. Another option is the integration of shading grillages in the plane of the glass. Direct views from the room can no longer be guaranteed in that case.

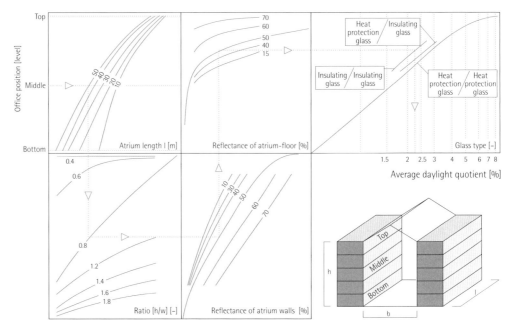

Fig. 4.2.7 **Calculation of daylight quotients in linear atria**
The calculation of daylight quotients in offices based on the level of the office room, atrium length, height-to-width ratio, wall reflectance, floor reflectance and the glazing characteristics is carried out in five stages:

1. *Level of the room (top, middle, bottom of building)*
2. *Intercept on the atrium length curve (10–50 m)*
3. *Read off the height to width ratio (0.4–1.8)*
4. *Intercept on the wall reflectance curve (10 to 70 %)*
5. *Intercept on the floor reflectance curve (15 to 70 %)*
6. *Intercept on glazing characteristics curve*
7. *Read off the daylight quotient*

Dynamic ventilation,
competition contribution

A natural ventilation concept was developed for the Adidas factory outlet in Herzogenaurach. The high rate of through-ventilation of the sales hall by means of ventilation openings in the roof fits the context of sportiness, dynamism and freshness.

The flow of air through the hall is caused by the wind creating a negative pressure zone over the roof. The aerodynamic effect is enhanced by the projecting canopy, which is designed to behave like an aircraft wing flap. The overhang also provides optimum shading. In winter and summer the supply air is brought preheated or cooled into the building through an earth pipe. The direct conduction of exhaust air through the roof is an effective means of removal of the heat given off by the lamps. The additional tempering of the ceiling creates a comfortable radiation ambiance at all times of the year.

Fig. 4.2.8 **View into the sales room**
(Fig.: Auer+Weber+Architekten, Munich)

Fig. 4.2.9 **Breathing skin**
(Fig.: Auer+Weber+Architekten, Munich)

Construction: competition
Use: retail building
Architect: Auer + Weber + Architekten, Munich
Building services, energy technology: Ingenieur-
büro Hausladen, Kirchheim, Munich
Facade: fully glazed facade with ventilation openings in the roof
Energy concept: natural ventilation with wind assistance

Fig. 4.2.10 **Aerodynamic canopy**
(Fig.: Auer+Weber+Architekten, Munich)

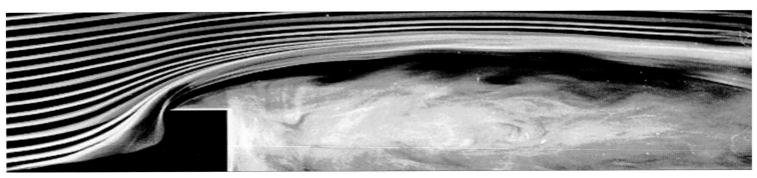

Fig. 4.2.11 **Exploitation of wind forces**
(Fig.: Auer+Weber+Architekten, Munich)

Fig. 4.2.12 E.ON Bayern Customer Centre, Weiden

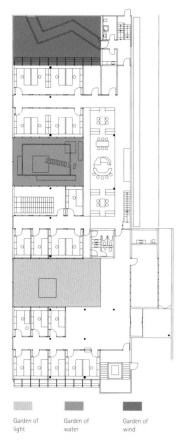

Garden of light | Garden of water | Garden of wind

Fig. 4.2.13 **Plan of the first floor**

Construction: 2003
Use: customer centre
Client: E.ON Bayern AG
Architect: SHL-Architekten, BDA Weiden, Dipl.-Ing.
    Dr. Emil Lehner, Dipl.-Ing. Stefan Kunnert
Building services, energy technology: Ingenieurbüro
    Hausladen, Kirchheim, Munich
Facade: functional facade with daylight deflection
    and shading system
Energy concept: earth pipe, thermoactive ceilings,
    ventilation system with heat recovery

E.ON Bayern Customer Centre, Weiden

The three-storey building runs east-west and is a compact rectangular solitary structure with side lengths of 19 x 55 m. The building is divided into three office zones, two internal atria, the light garden and the water garden, and a communal zone with multifunctional working and communication areas to the south (Fig. 4.2.13). The working zones generally look out to the east and west of the building. Transparent corridor walls and fully glazed internal facades with sliding elements create an open and communicative working environment. The atria open the building to the north and determine the visual relationships, the ventilation and the lighting concepts. They serve as reception halls for customers as well as display areas, informal meeting places and conference areas for employees. To prevent overheating from solar radiation, the atrium roofs have a very effective tracking external shading system with metal louvre light deflectors.

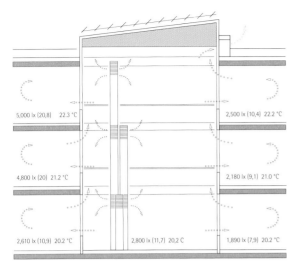

Fig. 4.2.14 **Section through the atrium showing temperatures and illuminance on a winter's day**
In winter and in excessively strong winds the atrium is ventilated mechanically.

5,000 lx (20,8) 22.3 °C   2,500 lx (10,4) 22.2 °C

4,800 lx (20) 21.2 °C   2,180 lx (9,1) 21.0 °C

2,610 lx (10,9) 20.2 °C   2,800 lx (11,7) 20,2 C   1,890 lx (7,9) 20.2 °C

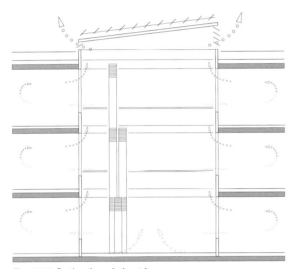

Fig. 4.2.15 **Section through the atrium**
Mechanical ventilation is switched off in the transition months.

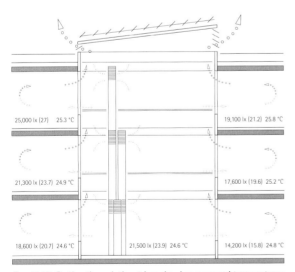

Fig. 4.2.16 **Section through the atrium showing measured temperatures and illuminance on a summer's day**
The atrium is mechanically ventilated

25,000 lx (27) 25.3 °C   19,100 lx (21.2) 25.8 °C

21,300 lx (23.7) 24.9 °C   17,600 lx (19.6) 25.2 °C

18,600 lx (20.7) 24.6 °C   21,500 lx (23.9) 24.6 °C   14,200 lx (15.8) 24.8 °C

Energy concept A media duct running under the building brings fresh air and all services supply cables and pipes to the vertical riser shafts. The building has thermoactive ceilings, which provide background heating in winter and cooling in summer. Additional heating energy is produced from a heat pump connected to a series of boreholes. Cooling is obtained directly from the boreholes. If this cooling energy is inadequate, the heat pump can be used for cooling. The glazed equipment room is an eye-catching feature.

Ventilation concept The office rooms on the east and west sides are supplied with fresh air from their windows, which also provide direct views to the outside. In the other rooms, large sliding window elements facing into the atria provide ventilation. The atria have a number of ventilation strategies to suit the season. The atria are mechanically ventilated in winter and in unfavourable wind conditions. In summer, the supply air is precooled in an earth pipe. Large ventilation flaps ensure adequate air changes in the transition months.

During winter the system provides airflows of 3,000 m³/h to the large atrium and 2,000 m³/h to the smaller atrium. Fresh air is taken in from the outside in the "Wind Garden", prewarmed in an earth pipe and reheated in the central ventilation system. Heat recovery from the exhaust air and the heat pump provides the required heating energy. Supply air at a temperature of approximately 21 °C is blown through vertical pipes into the atria (Fig. 4.2.14). As an aid to improved mixing, the air is fed into the space at different heights. Air is expelled mechanically through a ventilation unit on the roof, which extracts the air from extra-high points in the atria. Heat recovery operates using a system connected into a circuit.

If the outside temperatures are high enough, the mechanical ventilation system switches off and window louvres open. The atria are then ventilated naturally (Fig. 4.2.15). Air flows through horizontal glass louvres in the lower part of the northern facade with an open area of approximately 10 m² per atrium. Air flows out naturally at the eastern and western high points of both atria through opened louvres with an open area of up to 18 m², depending on the air velocity and atrium temperature.

If the atria are overheating or the outside temperatures exceed 28 °C, precooled air at approximately 18 °C from boreholes is blown in through ventilation pipes (Fig. 4.2.16). This doubles the rate of air changes from that of the winter. Exhaust air is conducted out through flaps at high points in the atria.

Fig. 4.2.17 **Glass supply air pipes in the atria**

"... the environment itself is more of an occasion than a cause: it simply provides the necessary means for spiritual growth..."

Maria Montessori 1870–1952
Italian doctor and educationalist

Educational buildings

Primary school, refurbishment 2004,
Architect: Gerhard Müntinga
Small schools are generally individually designed
and there is little differentiation between the room
requirements. Primary schools place a great deal
of emphasis on comprehensibility and identifica-
tion. Small schools normally have window ventila-
tion and a conventional heating system.

Staufer High School, Pfullendorf, 1997,
Architect: Prof. Christine Remensperger
A trend from the 1970s is the grouping of different types of schools into educational centres. In
addition to general purpose classrooms these large
schools have a large number of technical and specialist subjects with different uses. Climatic conditions in summer and ventilation are two points to
be given special attention.

University of Applied Sciences Ulm, 1963,
Architect: Günter Behnisch
The size and fitting out of technical colleges and
universities depend on the faculties present. In
addition to administration areas, these buildings
have large teaching and seminar rooms. Rooms
and laboratories are subject to frequent changes
of use, which demands great flexibility in the technical installations.

Fig. 4.3.1 **Small classrooms**
Nursery and primary schools
Divided for different uses
15 to 25 people

Occupants	20
Room size	40 m²
Lighting	5 W/m²
Av. int. loads	45 W/m²
Air requirement	20 x 20 m³/h = 400 m³/h
Air changes	400 m³/h / (5 x 8 x 2.5) m³ = 4 h⁻¹
Heating	radiators
	underfloor heating
Ventilation	natural

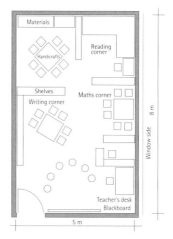

Fig. 4.3.2 **Seminar rooms**
Standard classroom for all school types
Religious and specialised instruction, small number of specialist rooms
25 to 35 people

Occupants	30
Room size	70 m²
Lighting	5 W/m²
Av. int. loads	55 W/m²
Air requirement	30 x 25 m³/h = 750 m³/h
Air changes	750 m³/h / (7.5 x 9.5 x 3) m³ = 3.5 h⁻¹
Heating	radiators
	underfloor heating
Ventilation	natural
	mechanical

Fig. 4.3.3 **Lecture theatres**
Large room for secondary schools and high schools
Lectures and specialised instruction
50 to 500 people

Occupants	100
Room size	115 m²
Lighting	5 W/m²
Av. int. loads	110 W/m²
Air requirement	100 x 25 m³/h = 2,500 m³/h
Air changes	2,500 m³/h / (9.5 x 12 x 4) m³ = 5.5 h⁻¹
Heating	radiators
	VAC
Ventilation	mechanical
Cooling	VAC
	chilled ceiling
	underfloor heating

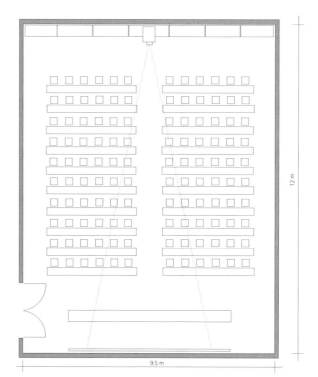

Typology

The time that students spend in all kinds of educational buildings is continuing to grow. Clients and architects are paying increasing attention to designing teaching rooms to be as healthy and comfortable for their occupants as possible. The era of full air conditioning in schools with sealed facades is past, as it is in administration buildings. However, the requirements relating to room air quality are particularly high in seminar rooms. Sustained periods in poor air leads to reduced concentration, tiredness and headaches. Room sizes vary depending on type of use and age group. Classrooms generally have an area of about 2 m² per person. The figure may go up to 3 m² for rooms with working and utility areas that accommodate different uses. The room plans are rectangular or square. Clearance to the ceiling is between 2.5 and 3.4 m.

Small classrooms This type of room is mainly found in nursery and primary schools. Characteristically these rooms are divided internally, occupied by small classes and in continuous use throughout the school day. The rooms may be ventilated by windows if the location is not noisy or polluted. The difficulty lies in continuously ventilating the rooms. Ventilation by tilt-turn windows creates draughts for the places near the windows when outside temperatures are low. In addition they cannot be adjusted in reaction to changes in wind and temperature conditions. With small classes and an open form of teaching, this problem can be countered by regular pulse ventilation. In this case, the teacher is responsible for adequate air quality. This method does not achieve an even, high air quality. Facades with different sizes and arrangements of ventilation flaps in which small ventilation openings can be permanently left open without causing draughts are one alternative (Fig. 4.3.4). Small classrooms can be heated with radiators or underfloor heating.

Seminar rooms Seminar rooms are used by normal-sized classes, which as a rule frequently change classrooms. Seminar rooms are seldom other than standard in layout and equipment as they are mainly used for specialist lectures or instruction. In most cases these rooms are ventilated through windows. Seminar rooms fitted with tilt-turn windows are usually only ventilated during breaks because of possible draughts. This leads to a continuous reduction in air quality. In addition to various ventilation openings in the facade, an exhaust air system with secondary flow through the facade represents a cost-efficient option for continuous ventilation. A mechanical supply and exhaust air system is often only installed in schools in special rooms such as chemistry laboratories, kitchens, assembly halls or gymnasiums. At very noisy or polluted sites, natural ventilation and secondary flow through the facade can be ruled out as a ventilation concept. Something approaching natural ventilation in the classroom can be obtained from an atrium into which clean outside air is supplied with precautions against noise. This is primarily a solution for small school buildings in which the atrium is not a permanent place for informal meetings or breaks from work. If this is not the case the disadvantages of internal sound transmission become too great. Radiators and underfloor heating are suitable for heating. With large exposed thermal storage masses particular care must taken with the acoustics.

Lecture theatres The possible high occupancy density of lecture theatres leads to a large air requirement. The use of a mechanical supply and exhaust air system is normally the rule for these rooms. CO_2-based control is a worthwhile option for matching the airflow to the actual demand. As the CO_2 content of the room air is directly proportional to the number of people present, it can be used as a means of limiting the air changes to the rate required. Additional free window ventilation is also worthwhile. At low occupancy densities, window ventilation can be used to provide rapid change of air during breaks. The high internal loads in lecture theatres usually give rise to a requirement for cooling. Radiators, chilled ceilings or an HVAC system are suitable for room conditioning.

Orientation and facade design The character of a room is heavily influenced by its orientation and solar penetration. Visible solar radiation makes a significant contribution to the physical and psychological feeling of wellbeing. Classrooms should therefore be oriented so that the room receives direct sunlight at least for part of the teaching day.

Classrooms facing south on the other hand receive direct solar radiation even in winter. Shade can be relatively easy to provide in summer by roof projections or permanent external shading features. As an alternative to a fully southern orientation, educational buildings may deviate to the east from this direction. An east, west or a fully northerly orientation should be avoided if possible. Glazed east and west facades can very easily lead to overheating of the rooms and are relatively difficult to shade without completely obstructing the view. Glare protection should be arranged so that in the fanlight area as large an area of window remains free to provide natural light.

Natural light Children experience their environment mainly with their eyes. They learn through seeing and observing. A good lighting concept promotes successful learning. Natural light plays a major role in teaching. Experiments in the 1970s with windowless classrooms that were intended to keep all outside distractions away from the children were quickly seen as a poor idea. Today each seat in a classroom is entitled to receive the best possible quality of natural light and have an outside view.

The quality of natural light is determined by several factors. The student's field of view should not contain any areas of excessive luminance contrast as this can lead to glare. This should be particularly borne in mind with a flexible arrangement of tables, as the students will all be sitting at different directions with respect to the window. Disturbing shadows created by bright spotlights should be avoided in working areas. All workplaces, including

inside a classroom, must achieve a daylight quotient of at least 2%.

Good illumination in the depth of the room is created by windows extending up to the underside of the ceiling. Glazing the windowsill area brings no advantages in this respect. Ideally a band of windows should run across the whole width of the room so that dark corners are avoided. Lighting classrooms from two sides improves the evenness of illumination of the room. Skylights in an extensively glazed access corridor or an atrium improve the lighting conditions in the classroom. If the classroom has two opposing external walls, the second band of windows should not be much smaller than the main band, as a higher luminance contrast between window and wall will result in increased glare. With indirect lighting through a corridor or an atrium, luminance contrast plays a subordinate role as the amount of natural light admitted is substantially reduced and no direct sunlight falls on the second band of windows. The windows can be reduced in size to prevent possible disturbance from people passing the room.

Artificial light Teaching rooms normally have a nominal illuminance of approximately 500 lx. Lighting does not have to be shadow-free with a perfect light incidence but deep shadow should be avoided. Fluorescent lamps are suitable for providing basic lighting. Halogen lamps can set the tone. Artificial light should try to reproduce as closely as possible the distribution and colour of natural lighting; a warm white to neutral white colour of light is most suitable. The arrangement of the lights must avoid creating glare between the students or teacher and the blackboard. The blackboard should be free of reflections of light sources. The correct choice of light sources allows differently used areas of a room to receive the appropriate lighting. This is important for classes where different forms of teaching are carried out. Withdrawal areas can

Fig. 4.3.4 **Ventilation openings in the facade**
Various sizes and arrangements of ventilation openings in the facade can provide natural ventilation. The fanlight zone provides a good level of natural light in the room depth.

Fig. 4.3.5 **Lecture theatre**
Good room acoustics are achieved from acoustic elements in the ceiling and the seat coverings.

be provided with less intensive lighting, display items and notice boards can be highlighted with targeted lighting. The colour and texture of the surface and the appropriate direction of lighting can produce individual, interesting and varied interior space that motivates the occupants and fosters concentration.

Sound insulation In addition to the load due to outside noise imposed on a room, the acoustic behaviour inside the room plays a major role. Concentration levels of teachers as well as children quickly declines if speech can be understood only with difficulty because of the high level of noise. Heavily trafficked roads should be avoided in the selection of the site, or the classrooms should be made to face away from the road. If not, the facade should be designed to ensure sound protection, which would normally require mechanical ventilation.

Favourable reverberation times and an even sound field are necessary if people are to understand what is being said. With even, short sound wave paths and good distribution all seats enjoy the same quality of acoustics. Good intelligibility of speech is associated with reverberation times of 0.8 to 1.0 seconds. Reverberation times in unoccupied classrooms are frequently above these values due to the acoustically hard surfaces used. A long reverberation time means that teacher and students use relatively little energy to achieve a specific volume but speech intelligibility drops off markedly. Rooms with components that resonate easily, e.g. wood or wood-based materials, do not normally require further acoustic measures. If a classroom requires large thermal storage masses for temperature reasons or uses the floor or ceiling for room conditioning, then other measures must be taken to improve room acoustics. This may involve sound-absorbing elements on the walls or by the appropriate selection of furniture (Fig. 4.3.5).

Energy generation The selection of the method of energy generation for educational establishments is based on the size and position of the building, the heating, hot water and cooling energy requirements. Energy generation is an important part of our everyday life. To help to impart this importance to children and young people, energy generation systems should be installed in accessible positions. The technical plant and fittings become visual objects that become part of the teaching environment.

Schools are supplied with energy from oil or gas-fired boilers or from district heating systems. Normally the hot water heating requirement is low and so hot water can be provided locally. Providing there are no specified restrictions on energy generation, schools can be heated by coal or wood. Pellet heating systems are very suitable for school central heating as they can be effectively regul-

ated and hardly ever breakdown. If a suitable source of heat such as ground water or moist earth is available, the heat requirement in connection with radiant panel heating can also be covered by a heat pump.

As well as conventional heat energy generators, small combined heat and power plants (CHP) may also be suitable for covering the basic heating load for larger school buildings. This is an attractive option for sports hall annexes, which have a high hot water heat requirement even in summer and can provide a long annual operating period for the CHP. Alternatively a solar installation can be used to provide hot water.

There can be a requirement for cooling energy as well as heat in very large school buildings and universities. Depending on the required output, the demand can be supplied from district heating, CHPs or compression or absoption refrigeration machines. Often a local heating or cooling network can satisfy the demand. The requirements depend on the uses of the buildings.

All teaching buildings have large roof areas, which can be used to generate electricity from solar energy. The photovoltaics can become part of the teaching environment of the school and help to create the building's identity.

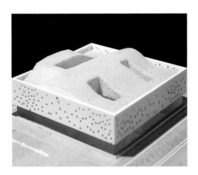

Fig. 4.3.6 model with internal atrium and wave-shaped roof reminiscent of dunes
(Fig.: HENN ARCHITEKTEN, Munich)

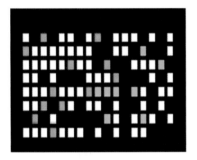

Fig. 4.3.7 RGB pixels
(Fig.: HENN ARCHITEKTEN, Munich)

Pixel, competition contribution

The design for the Media Production City in Riyadh layers ancient Arabic Moorish typology with a medial architecture of light. A strict, massive wall arranged in a square encloses the sculptural building form. The fully glazed transparent ground floor offers views into the shimmering and colourful television world.

The structural grid of 8.10 x 8.10 m facilitates a straightforward addition of further floors. The interior of the building is penetrated by three right-angled light-flooded atria, which can be screened from the sun during the day. The air volumes form a linking space between the floors. The organic form of the roof landscape is reminiscent of wind-formed sand dunes.

The ground floor is extensively glazed on all sides. The building appears inviting and transparent to the visitor. The facade offers space for information, projections and for light installations. The upper floor and the roof landscape are surrounded by a stone facade which protects the building from heat. This is perforated by small irregularly placed openings. These are an abstract symbol representing digitalised pictures. The transfer medium of pictures and television is the pixel. The facade translates this medium architecturally. Each of the little openings is fitted with RGB – lights, red, green, blue. With these, colours and pictures can be generated which can continually change, fade and overlap.

High cooling effect is realised through adiabatic cooling with fountain and plants in the atrium. Thermally activated ceiling through embedded water pipes as a primary cooling system for the upper floors achieves high thermal comfort through radiation cooling.

Split systems for peak cooling. High utilization of daylight through rooms with light exposure from the atrium as well as light exposure from slots in the exterior facade to capture the zenith light. Elements for channelling light to achieve high illumination of large room.

Fig. 4.3.8 Media Production City – Night view of pixel facade
(Fig.: HENN ARCHITEKTEN, Munich)

Construction: competition
Use: administration building
Architect: HENN ARCHITEKTEN, Munich
Energy concept: Ingenieurbüro Hausladen, Kirchheim, Munich,
    J. Bauer
Facade: front solid wall with openings
Energy concept: thermally activated components for basic cooling,
    evaporation cooling by wells and planting in the atria, great use
    of natural light

Faculty of Educational Sciences, University of Brixen

The new building for the Faculty of Educational Sciences at the University of Brixen was handed over to the university in March 2004. The very compact square building has outside dimensions of 75 x 75 m and consists of a three-storey outer ring raised off the ground and a core area of four large buildings. The new building has space for about 1,700 students and a gross floor area of 23,000 m² including the underground car park.

The corridor on the inside of the ring forms a climate buffer for the adjoining rooms (Fig. 4.3.10). The stairwells are located at the corners of the ring. In the core area the escape stairwells have been placed at the ends of the four buildings. The circulation zones are not heated; they are only tempered from the adjoining rooms. This creates a buffer zone to protect against high heat losses.

Fig. 4.3.9 **Faculty of Educational Sciences, University of Brixen**

Construction: 2004
Use: educational building
Client: Autonomous Province of Bozen
Architects: Kohlmayer Oberst Architekten, Stuttgart
Building services, energy technology: Ingenieurbüro Hausladen, Kirchheim, Munich
Facade: element facade with opaque ventilation elements, alternating external translucent and internal translucent storey-high glass panels
Energy concept: district heating, thermoactive ceilings, natural ventilation, mechanical ventilation with heat recovery and cooling registers in the core areas, ground water cooling, night ventilation

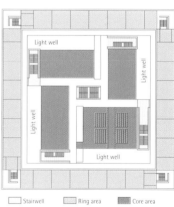

Fig. 4.3.10 **Schematic plan first floor**

Facades The ring area contains the rooms with high daylight requirements such as seminar and administration rooms and professors' offices. The external facade of the ring is a combined facade with projecting and indented elements in which recessed, transparent, storey-high glass panels alternate with similar translucent panels in the plane of the facade. The rooms receive indirect natural light from the corridor and translucent internal walls. The external facade consists of solar protection glass with a high natural light transmittance. Additional mobile shading in the form of stainless steel louvred blinds is positioned alternately in front of and behind the glass elements (Fig. 4.3.11). The shading is moved automatically by the building management system. The controlling parameter is the measured solar radiation. The user has the opportunity to switch off the automatic control and operate the shading manually.

The four-storey core area with lightwells contains rooms with lower natural light requirements and shorter periods of use, such as laboratories, library, main lecture theatre, dining hall and informal meeting rooms. Natural light comes from the lightwells. The core area and the corridor side ring facade have transparent, storey-high windows without shading. The core area receives adequate shading from the outside ring and has internal shading. High temperatures in the corridors in summer are to be expected.

Ventilation concept All rooms are naturally ventilated through motor-operated window flaps. The opaque ventilation elements are located in the side recesses. The window flaps are capable of fine adjustment so that air can flow into the rooms in all weathers without causing drafts. In summer the ventilation flaps provide night cooling of the rooms. The raised ring and the chimney effect of the core in summer produce good through-ventilation and removal of heat. In almost all parts of the building, exposed concrete floor slabs act as a thermal storage mass to make a considerable contribution to the stabilisation of room climate in summer.

Rooms in the core area are naturally ventilated through motor-operated skylights. The window flaps are controlled in response to the time of day and weather. Direct wind pressure is kept off the facade of the core area by the outside ring and therefore fresh air can enter the room in controlled amounts even when outside temperatures are low.

The room depth and the high occupancy density required additional mechanical ventilation with heat recovery. Heat recovery is by cross-flow heat exchangers with an effectiveness of approximately 60%. Four air changes per hour are provided for rooms with high occupancy, one air change for the rest. Air changes are controlled to meet actual need except for the toilets and library. Supply air in summer as in winter has a temperature of 20 °C.

The Aula Magna, the University's main auditorium, has an air conditioning system with heat recovery for use when occupancy densities are high during official functions (Figs. 4.3.12 and 4.3.13). Air changes are designed as 25 m³/hperson. Temperature regulation is performed by the air conditioning system, which can handle any large fluctuations in load. A CO_2 sensor controls air quality.

An earth-air heat exchanger is used to precondition the outside air in summer and winter. The earth pipe

Fig. 4.3.11 **Shading**
In the offices and seminar rooms, the shading elements are positioned alternately inside and outside the room.

lies partially in ground water and therefore is capable of high output. The concrete pipe was placed in an extended excavation parallel to the external wall to minimise construction costs. The pipe diameter is between 1.2 and 2 m and is therefore accessible and easy to clean. The earth pipe is 200 m long and serves three ventilation equipment rooms. Outside air is taken in from the northern planted area of the site so that pollutant content is kept to a minimum.

Heating and cooling concept Heating and cooling of rooms is by individual room-controlled underfloor heating in conjunction with unregulated building component activation (thermoactive ceilings). The building is divided into 20 control zones.

The unregulated thermoactive ceilings work from an outside temperature (average previous day) of below –5 °C as heating. Control works using outside air temperature with a maximum feed temperature of 27 °C. The thermoactive ceilings switch off if the temperature difference between the feed and return is less than 3 K. At an outside air temperature greater than 18 °C, the thermoactive ceilings work as coolers with a constant feed temperature of 16 °C. Cooling mode switches off if the return temperature is below 20 °C.

Offices and seminar rooms can be individually regulated by means of the underfloor heating. The target temperature is determined centrally by the building management system. User intervention in this is not intended. Heating is set in operation at an average outside temperature of under 16 °C. Underfloor cooling is set in operation at an average outside temperature of 20 °C and at

a room temperature of over 24 °C. The estimated output for heating the university is 80 W/m², and for cooling, 58 W/m².

Generation of heating and cooling energy The required heating output of 930 kW to heat the whole building complex is made available from the newly constructed district heating network for the Brixen area. Heat is supplied from a gas-fired combined heat and power plant. The local authority at Brixen has set itself the objective of constructing a biogas-fired combined heat and power plant to supply CO_2-neutral heat energy in the future.

The extensive ground water pipework system under the university allows regenerative provision of cooling energy from the ground water. Ground water is extracted from a well (max. 20 l/s) and introduced into the building's cold water system after passing through a heat exchanger. The building is cooled by thermoactive ceilings, underfloor cooling, air cooling in the ventilation system and by recirculatory air coolers.

The equipment rooms and shafts are integrated into the building in such a way that capital and maintenance costs can be reduced to a minimum. Ventilation equipment rooms are located in different parts of the complex. Most of the equipment rooms are on the end walls of the buildings where vertical riser shafts are installed with fire protection bulkheads. One or two shafts serve a floor, which allows fire dampers to be installed centrally in the basement. This allows an overall fire protection concept to be adopted and low maintenance costs.

Fig. 4.3.12 **Internal view of the Aula Magna**

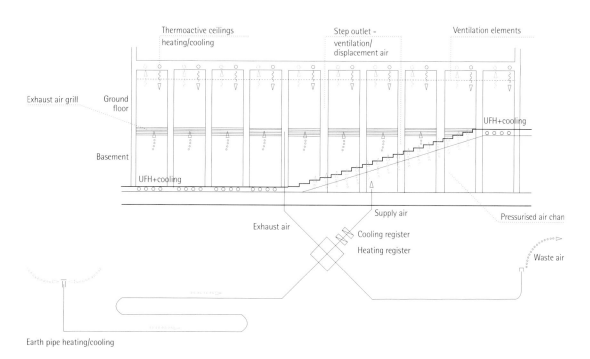

Fig. 4.3.13 **Air conditioning concept for the Aula Magna**
An air conditioning system provides conditioning to the Aula Magna when occupancy density is high. In other conditions, the auditorium can also be naturally ventilated through skylight flaps.

"Private faces in public places
Are wiser and nicer
Than public faces in private places."

W.H. Auden 1907–1973
Orators (1932), dedication

Assembly rooms

Herz-Jesu Church, Munich, 1998,
Architects: Allmann, Sattler, Wappner
Smaller public assembly rooms have various uses, ranging from club meetings to concerts or theatrical performances. Comfort requirements are high.

Divisible sports hall at Rossäcker, Weinsberg, 2002,
Architects: Büro für Architektur
At any one time sports halls are in use by only a few people. It is only when competitive events are held that occupancy density is high. For most of the time, sports halls are like small halls in terms of their low comfort requirements.

Trade Exhibition Hall 26 Hanover Messe, 1996,
Architects: Herzog + Partner
These large halls host trade fairs, concerts and sporting competitions. Seated public events such as congresses and classical music concerts are also held to maximise use. The climate concept must therefore incorporate a lot of flexibility to be able to adapt to suit the various uses. Frequent modifications require a very high degree of flexibility.

Fig. 4.4.1 **Small halls**
Community centres, exhibition rooms

Uses   celebrations, exhibitions,
            seated concerts

Heating   radiators
            underfloor heating
            air heating

Ventilation window ventilation
            mechanical ventilation

Cooling   night cooling
            underfloor heating
            air cooling

Fig. 4.4.2 **Sports halls**
School and sports club halls

Uses   training and competitions

Heating   ceiling radiator panels
            if necessary underfloor heating
            air heating

Ventilation window ventilation
            mechanical ventilation

Cooling   if necessary air cooling

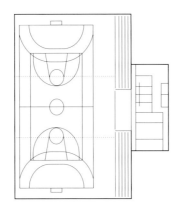

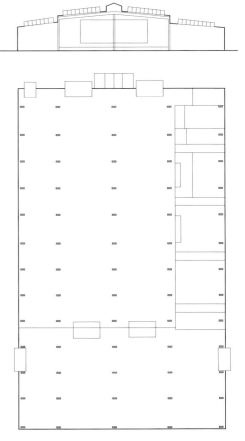

Fig. 4.4.3 **Large halls**
Trade fair and concert halls, multipurpose halls

Uses   trade fairs, conferences, exhibitions,
            seated and non-seated
            concerts

Heating   ceiling radiator panels
            underfloor heating
            air heating

Ventilation mechanical ventilation

Cooling   underfloor heating
            air cooling

Types

Assembly rooms The different sizes and uses of assembly rooms results in a wide range of construction solutions. These types of buildings are all similar in form. They have high headrooms and a large surface area with the fewest possible divisions. If they are to be heated to normal indoor temperatures, halls and meeting rooms must satisfy the requirements of the German Energy Saving Act (EnEV). This is the case for all small public assembly rooms, such as community centres. The external components of larger halls, which are only heated up to 19 °C, must comply with thermal requirements and have adequate thermal insulation.

Small halls Public assembly rooms and small halls are usually heated to normal temperatures and have high requirements for comfort. They usually have mechanical ventilation systems. Depending on use, this can be through windows or in the case of large meetings by means of a ventilation system. Supply air is either introduced through long-range nozzles, which allow event rooms to have fresh air introduced from a central point, or through displacement diffusers in the direct vicinity of the users. Heating can be by radiators, underfloor heating or air heaters. Radiators react to controls quickly and therefore are suitable for small halls not in continuous use. Underfloor heating systems respond sluggishly to controls and therefore the room must be brought to the correct temperature in good time for the start of the meeting. Underfloor heating systems can be used to provide cooling when cooling requirements are moderate in the summer, which represents an efficient dual use of the system.

Sports halls Halls with low occupancy densities, such as sports halls when being used for training purposes, can normally be naturally ventilated. Motor-operated skylights can be operated from a simple switch when ventilation is required during use. To prevent unnecessary heat losses, it is worthwhile to install a time relay to close the vents after about ten minutes during the heating season. Through ventilation is considerably improved if window flaps can be opened on both sides of the hall. Often this type of ventilation is also adequate for indoor sports arenas with spectators, making the installation of mechanical ventilation unnecessary.

If a ventilation plant is installed it must be ensured that it can be regulated to match the actual need. This can be achieved by having different ventilation scenarios or a CO_2 control system. Air heating should be operated with a high proportion of recirculated air and a heat recovery system. Ceiling radiator panels can be retrofitted into existing structures and often installed as part of refurbishment. Almost the whole of the heat released into the hall and felt by the occupants is by radiation. The perceived temperature is therefore several degrees above the actual room air temperature. This means that the room air temperature can be reduced, which leads to considerable energy savings. Ceiling radiator panels respond quickly to the controls. Maintenance costs are less than those for air heating. Underfloor heating systems are always expensive for sports halls as the required elasticity of the floor entails a lot of construction work. Conventional radiators are normally only used in side rooms in sports halls. Due to the risk of injury, radiators must be mounted at least 2 m off the hall floor, which results in part of the heat released not being in the place where it is actually needed. If they are fitted behind cladding then the radiated part of the heat is almost completely blocked.

Large halls Concert halls cannot normally be ventilated through windows during performances because of the noise load on the neighbouring buildings. For this reason and the high occupancy densities involved, mechanical ventilation must generally be installed. It may be possible however to effectively through-ventilate the auditorium quickly during concert intervals by automatic window ventilation. The ventilation system should be able to be regulated to match needs in order to avoid unnecessary energy loss. Heating can be by ceiling radiator panels, underfloor heating or additional air heaters. The normal situation is that events with a lot of participants present from the beginning require little heat even when outside temperatures are low, because of their high heat load. If the surfaces enclosing the room are at high temperature this can be comfortable. A high radiation temperature allows room air temperature to be reduced and consequently leads to savings in heating energy. It must always be borne in mind that for large assembly halls the full volume of the hall does not have to be conditioned; all that is required is to bring fresh air and heat directly into the occupied area.

Fig. 4.4.4 **Design Centre Linz**
Prism panels in the roof of the Design Centre in Linz provide adequate glare-free diffused light to illuminate the exhibition hall.

Illuminance for sports halls [lx]	[lx]
General training	200
General competition	400
Badminton training	400
Badminton competition	400
Table tennis training	300
Table tennis competition	600

Tab. 4.4.1 **Recommended illuminance**
for various sports
Having different preset lighting scenarios can save energy.

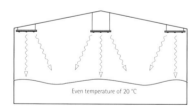

Even temperature of 20 °C

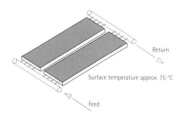

Return

Surface temperature approx. 75 °C

Feed

Fig. 4.4.5 **How ceiling radiator panels are used to heat a hall**

Building services

Lighting accounts for a considerable proportion of the electricity used in halls, a good enough reason for putting in efficient light sources and luminaires. The use of as much natural light as possible should also reduce electricity consumption. Strips of skylights and roof windows are a good method of lighting for large halls. To remain glare-free, white opaque or prismatic glazing can be used, either of which will cut out direct light (Fig. 4.4.4). A control system that reacts to daylight can prevent the unnecessary use of artificial light. In addition, the installation of movement detectors, brightness sensors, and time switches should ensure that after training has ended the lights are turned out even if everyone forgets, as can often happen in sports halls. By adopting different preset lighting levels, the use of full competition lighting can be avoided for training sessions in sports halls (Tab. 4.4.1). It is a good idea to arrange the switching so that all lights in side rooms can be turned off from the hall supervisor's room.

Meeting rooms and halls that are used for different types of events may require different lighting scenarios (Tab. 4.4.2). It is important for switch panels to be simple

Use	Nominal illuminance [lx]	Suitable light source	Light colour
Concert hall, theatre	up to 200	Parabolic reflector lamps Halogen lamps	Warm white
Lecture theatres, auditoriums, assembly rooms	up to 500	Halogen lamps Fluorescent lamps Compact fluorescent lamps	Warm white to neutral white
Sports halls, multipurpose halls and gymnasiums	up to 500	Halogen lamps Fluorescent lamps Metal halide lamps	Warm white to neutral white
exhibition halls	up to 750	Mercury vapour lamps Metal halide lamps	Warm white to neutral white
Industrial hangars	up to 750	Mercury vapour lamps Sodium vapour lamps Metal halide lamps	Neutral white to daylight white

Tab. 4.4.2 **Light sources suitable for meeting rooms and halls**

to operate so that user can select the appropriate lighting concept.

Integration of the building services is very important for halls and meeting rooms. For the most part, the room surfaces should be free of technical installations; therefore ventilation ducts can be located only in the floor or along the ceiling. In sports halls the spandrel areas under the windowsills are available as windows in these buildings do not usually extend to the floor. The area is free for integrating ventilation ducts and displacement diffusers. Lighting installations are mostly visible in the roof construction in exposed or concealed ducts. Water, power and data infrastructure is not normally required in sports halls. On the other hand, trade fair exhibition halls and larger multipurpose halls must be able to be serviced with all media over their whole areas. This is normally done through floor ducts and floor outlets (Fig. 4.4.6). Electrical cables are frequently routed via the ceiling or drawn through ducts. Air ducts are often routed via the ceiling. One disadvantage is the distracting effect in the room of the pipework, ducts and cable trays. This is very undesirable in event halls. The design should provide enough shaft area and an adequate sized network of shafts to avoid this.

Equipment rooms for larger event venues and halls should be located centrally in order to keep the distribution network as short as possible (Fig. 4.4.7). As a rule it is possible to provide services to meeting rooms and halls from an equipment zone positioned along the length of the hall. The cables, pipes or ducts should be placed in accessible installation zones to permit them to be installed later or temporary services provided. Ceiling radiator panels are often used for heating halls (Fig. 4.4.5). A decentralised system of supply is a good solution locally if higher requirements for heating, cooling, ventilation or hot water apply only in certain areas of the building, for example in a cafeteria, changing rooms or special usage areas.

Sports halls have a requirement for hot water as well as heating. Whilst it normally makes good economic and ecological sense to provide hot water from the central heating system, it can lead to problems in summer. When a boiler that is used in winter for providing the whole heat requirement is kept running for hot water only, its efficiency drops drastically. Solar energy systems are therefore a viable option for meeting hot water requirements in summer. The main heating system can be shut down during this time.

Fig. 4.4.7 **Production hall Göttingen**
Main air distribution shaft in a production hall in Göttingen. All supply and exhaust air ducts come together in the ventilation octopus. Distribution takes place at ceiling level, allowing the hall surfaces to be kept free of other installations.

Fig. 4.4.6 **Trade fair exhibition centre Hanover Hall 26**
Ventilation ducts large enough to walk through bring supply air at low speed into the hall.

Fig. 4.4.8 **Industrial monument locomotive shed, Göttingen (photo: GWG)**

Locomotive shed Göttingen

The former locomotive shed was constructed in 1917 and in December 1998 opened as an event and congress centre after about four years of planning and refurbishment works. Trade fairs, sporting competitions, concerts, conferences and congresses now take place there on a presentation area of 8,400 m². With a capacity of 10,000 standing or 3,800 seated visitors, the locomotive shed is a suitable venue for medium to large events. The imposing impression of the space is reinforced by the riveted steelwork with three rows of massive steel piers at 10 m centres. Lighting is through glass roofs. The 0.51 to 1.45 m thick solid brick facade is stepped and has U-values of up to 1.20 W/m²K. The pumice concrete panel roof structure with a thickness of 8 cm has a U-value of approximately 1.30 W/m²K. The roof structure was refurbished and thermally insulated to improve thermal comfort. All the glazing was renewed to improve thermal and sound insulation and meet the latest requirements.

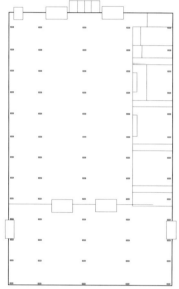

Fig. 4.4.9 **Floor plan**

Construction: 1998
Use: trade fair and concert hall
Client: GWG Göttingen
Architect: Kleineberg & Partner, Brunswick
Energy planning, building services: Ingenieurbüro Hausladen, Kirchheim, Munich
Facade: cleaned solid brick, built in 1900
Energy concept: district heating, ventilation with heat recovery, air heating, rain water exploitation system

Ventilation concept Only limited natural ventilation of the locomotive shed could be provided through windows and skylight openings. The reasons for this are twofold: the high occupancy density for large events and the resulting high CO_2 load, and the sound insulation requirements for concert venues. The hall can be naturally ventilated for trade exhibitions, sports competitions and company presentations. For these events the number of attendees normally does not exceed 1,500, which means that the enormous volume of the space and air infiltration through the building skin is enough to ensure good air quality. No high attendance events are held in the winter garden area and the foyer. The use of the foyer for large events is limited to a period of half an hour. The existing flow of air is adequate to allow mechanical ventilation not to be employed.

Ventilation system A mechanical ventilation system with heat recovery is provided for events with between 1,500 to 9,000 visitors. It is designed for a maximum air requirement of 90,000 m³/h. Heat recovery is by a system connected into a circuit with an effectiveness of approximately 56%. The required airflow was able to be reduced to 10 m³/person (90,000 m³/h) with the agreement of the client. The basis of this reduction was that the enormous air reservoir represented by the hall is available for use and can be introduced as supply air through displacement air outlets in the floor. The visitor would therefore always be in a fresh air zone. The vitiated air rises into the unused space overhead and is extracted. During breaks in the performances, hinged windows may be opened to change the entire volume of air in the hall within 15 minutes.

The ventilation system is not only used for ventilation, it is also there to provide cooling and heating. The cooling concept is based on the premise that events with high internal loads take place in the evening after 8 P.M. At this time of the day the outside air has already cooled enough to be used for room cooling.

The ventilation system provides heating for events with fewer than 1,500 people and heats the hall quickly using recirculated air. The large volume of air in the hall is enough to ensure adequate air quality. For larger events, the system operates using outside air only. The air ventilation system responds to controls quickly and therefore can be adjusted to suit changes in internal heat loads arising from people, lighting or solar radiation.

Air ventilation Displacement ventilation from the floor allows the roof structure to be kept free of distracting installations. Furthermore, former engineering pits can be utilised as supply air shafts (Fig. 4.4.10). The six pits run parallel to the main columns. They were connected by a main positive pressure shaft and extended over the whole length of the shed. Specially cast 15 cm wide concrete beams were laid over the engineering pits with 7 mm gaps between them. Supply air rises through the gaps into the shed over an extensive area. The network of shafts was designed as a pressure chamber and has no control system. The entire supply air duct system can be walked or crawled through and is easy to clean. The shafts also house the supply pipes, ducts and cables for water, heating and electricity. Almost any point in the shed can be fully ventilated for exhibitions and other events.

Heating concept When not in use the shed is tempered by spirally finned tubes near the light cupolas in the roof. They prevent uncomfortable cold air drop during use and provide a thermal shield when outside temperatures are low. They are switched on when outside temperatures are

Events for up to 1,500 people (seated)	Heating output [kW]	Θ_a 0 °C [kW]	Θ_a -5 °C [kW]	Θ_a -10 °C [kW]
Preheating UFH	165			
Recirculated 30,000 m³/h (35 °C)		160	160	160
Radiators		200	250	300
Finned tubes			105	140
Winter garden heated		140	170	
Winter garden tempered				140
Total output		500	685	740

Tab. 4.4.3 Division of the available heat output for small seated events

Events for up to 4,000 people (seated)	Heating output [kW]	Θ_a 0 °C [kW]	Θ_a -5 °C [kW]	Θ_a -10 °C [kW]
Preheating FBH	165			
Recirculated 30,000 m³/h (35 °C)		270	295	320
Radiators		200	250	300
Finned tubes			105	140
Winter garden heated		140		
Winter garden tempered			105	
Total output		610	750	760

Tab. 4.4.4 Division of the available heat output for large seated events

Events for up to 9,000 people (seated)	Heating output [kW]	Θ_a 0 °C [kW]	Θ_a -5 °C [kW]	Θ_a -10 °C [kW]
Preheating FBH	165			
Outside air 90,000 m³/h (28 °C) Outside air 60,000 m³/h (30 °C) Outside air 60,000 m³/h (26 °C)		560	485	450
Radiators		200	250	300
Finned tubes			105	140
Winter garden heated				
Winter garden tempered				
Total output		760	735	750

Tab. 4.4.5 Division of the available heat output for large non-seated events

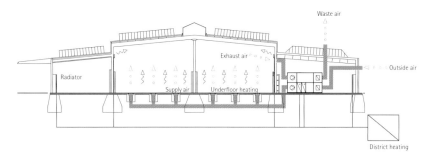

below -5 °C and for seated events involving up to 4,000 people. For larger non-seated events, it can be assumed that the requirements for comfort are reduced.

Some parts of the shed have underfloor heating as additional heating. The runs of pipework are placed at 20 cm centres in the 20 cm thick floor slab between the ventilation pits. The warm surface increases comfort for seated events. For events with lower comfort such as sporting events, heating is provided simply by ribbed tubes and air heating.

The foyer is heated by static heating surfaces near the external walls in front of the columns. Depending on the outside temperature the heat output of the radiators can be increased from 200 to 300 kW. Their operation is independent of the occupancy density of the shed as they are not within the event area. The winter garden is heated by ceiling radiator panels. This system was chosen on grounds of form and function. During the winter months the winter garden is used as an ice rink. The ceiling radiator panels allow the heating to be switched off in the ice rink area, whilst the other areas continue to be heated.

Energy supply The site already had a district heating system, which could be used for heating the shed. The connected load was limited to 760 kW, in order to reduce the basic cost for the connection to the district heating system. The available heat capacity is divided for the different usage scenarios and outside temperatures in accordance with the requirements (Tab. 4.4.3 to 4.4.5).

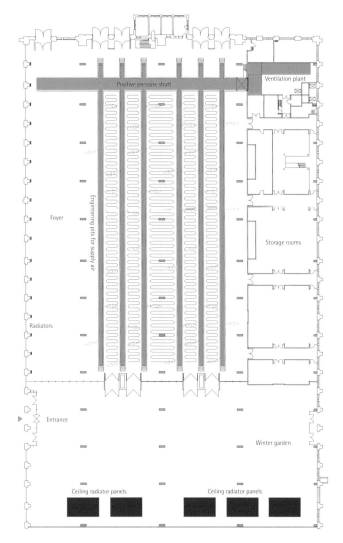

Fig. 4.4.10 **Heating and ventilation concept**
Section through the locomotive shed (above) and plan of ground floor (below)

Arts centre, Puchheim

The arts centre in Puchheim near Munich has a simple
building services concept. In the core zone there is the
building technology area (Fig. 4.4.12). Almost all the
equipment rooms and wet and auxiliary rooms are located in this installation zone, which is only 3 m wide
and extends from the basement to the first floor. The
horizontal distribution of the services is carried out in the
basement. Space is saved because all technical installations are concentrated in this building technology area.
The rooms are heated by underfloor heating. In summer
the underfloor heating system can be used for cooling
and charged with ground water by a heat exchanger. In
addition, the building is naturally ventilated in summer
through skylights on the east side and windows in the
inclined glazing in the west facade and flushed through
with cool night air. In winter the supply air for both
halls and the restaurant is blown into the rooms out of
long-range nozzles, which obtain their air from the main
shafts in the building technology area. The exhaust air is
extracted through concealed openings towards the top of
the main shafts.

Fig. 4.4.11 **Membrane roof on the east elevation**

Fig. 4.4.12 **Plan of ground floor showing
building technology area**
*The elongated hall is divided into three zones
longitudinally. On the west side are the foyer,
restaurant and kitchen, all facing the forecourt.
The hall zone faces east towards the green space.
It contains the council chamber, stage area and a
multipurpose room. All the building services installations are concentrated in the narrow building
services area, which also supplies the ventilation.*

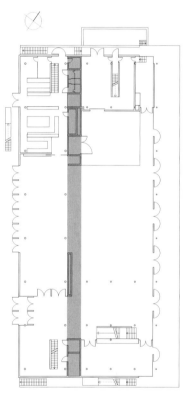

Construction: 1999
Use: arts centre
Client: Puchheim local council
Architect: Lanz Architekten & Ingenieure, Munich
Building services, energy technology: Ingenieur-
    büro Hausladen, Kirchheim, Munich
Facade: mullion and transom construction, larch
Energy concept: ventilated external skin providing
    protection against wind and rain, internal
    skin for light deflection, connection to dis-
    trict heating, underfloor heating, ventilation
    system, seasonal window ventilation, night
    cooling, ground water cooling of floors and
    supply air

"A house is a machine for living in."

Le Corbusier 1887–1965
Vers une architecture (1923)

Residential buildings

House extension Olper Höhe, 1996,
Architects: Kalhöfer Korschildgen
Detached houses are normally found in planning zones designated for housing in the suburbs. The settlement density is low and the A/V-ratio is high. Each house has its own energy supply.

Terraced houses Waldkraiburg, 1996,
Architect: Meck Architekten
Terrace houses allow greater settlement density and are increasingly used in apartment developments. Their compact nature reduces energy consumption and allows integrated energy concepts.

Canal housing in Amsterdam, 1985,
Town planner: Sjoerd Soeters
High development densities achieved with multi-storey apartment buildings are typical. Energy losses are lower and there is flexibility of choice in energy supply. The effects of shadow, road noise and emissions must be taken into account.

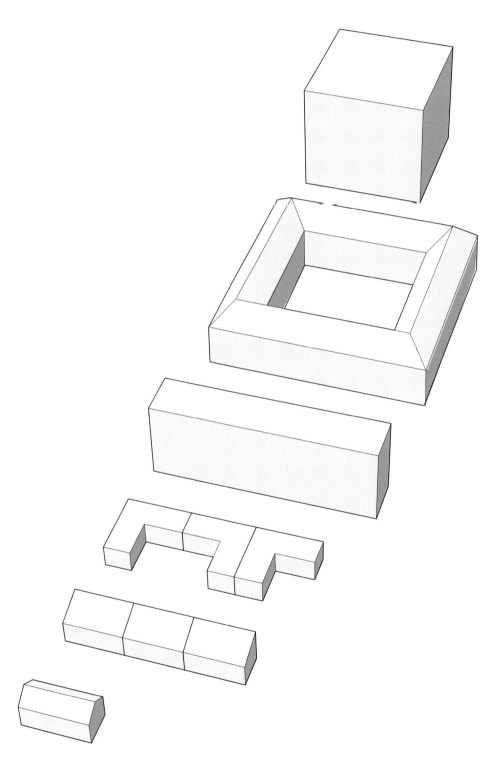

Fig. 4.5.1 **Forms of residential buildings**
*Detached, semi-detached, terraced and courtyard
houses are typical forms of homes for single-
family occupation. In the case of multistorey
construction, typical forms include linear, block
and high-rise developments. The building form
determines the climate characteristics of the
individual homes and the options for the use of
technical building services equipment. The internal
layout of the homes depends to a considerable
degree on the building form and the orientation
of the building.*

Building forms

The various building forms in residential construction influence energy and indoor climate parameters, such as the A/V ratio (ratio of the surface area to the enclosed volume), solar penetration, energy requirement and ventilation. In principle, residential construction can be divided into single-family and multistorey buildings. The basic types for single-family houses are detached, semi-detached, terraced and courtyard houses. Point blocks, linear arrangements and block developments are typical forms of multistorey housing.

Detached house The detached house can be illuminated and ventilated from all sides. The envelope is relatively large because of the unfavourable A/V ratio, hence good insulation is required. The detached house is very flexible in orientation. However, in practice, the direction in which the main rooms face is determined by local considerations such as topography, access, view and shadow.

Terraced house Joining individual houses into a terrace improves the A/V ratio. A high density of development can be achieved. Lighting and ventilation can only be provided from two directions. Terraced houses are normally aligned either north-south or east-west. Greater solar penetration into the depth of the building is possible from both sides with an east-west orientation. On the other hand, the lack of south-facing windows means less useful solar gain in winter and, where the terraces are built too close to one another, shading of one terrace by another. The joining of the individual homes in a terrace lends itself to common energy generation, which could lead to energy savings.

Courtyard house The courtyard house is the densest residential form of construction. Lighting and ventilation are primarily provided from the courtyard and the reduced outside surfaces. The courtyard house can be up to three storeys high but even here illumination of the depth of the rooms is already limited. The direction in which individual homes face has an effect on the ability to add to the courtyard development, as an absolutely northerly orientation must be avoided. This arrangement also makes common energy generation attractive, for the individual rows as well as an entire section of the development.

Linear arrangement Linear arrangement is an oriented form of residential construction with more vertical connection routes. Typically the homes are arranged in pairs so that each home has several window orientations and good through-ventilation. The lines can be aligned north-south or east-west. The decision is normally made based on the local urban planning considerations and shading by other buildings.

Block development Block development is a classic development form in urban areas. The alignment of the buildings is determined by the road system; one side of the building faces the street, the other faces into a courtyard. Typically two homes are connected by a stairwell so that the homes are illuminated from two sides and can be ventilated. The internal courtyard is protected from noise, which means that window ventilation is possible. One disadvantage is that the internal courtyard is in shadow. The orientation is difficult to optimise and is mainly dependent on urban planning considerations.

Point block Point blocks have small main access zones, which are typically placed on the north side and connect many homes. The A/V ratio is good. The layout in plan must take account of the position of the homes in the building, as not all orientations will necessarily be available. The restricted alignment options for the individual homes may give rise to problems with through-ventilation.

Rooms In principle the organisation of the rooms in plan differentiates between auxiliary rooms such as bathrooms, kitchens and storerooms and occupied rooms such as living rooms, dining rooms and bedrooms. In addition, there are the required circulation zones. The individual rooms are arranged according to their use and the orientation of the building. The east side is favourable for bedrooms, a south or west orientation for living rooms. Workrooms can tolerate a fully northern orientation.

For north-south aligned buildings, the auxiliary rooms are normally on the northern side, the circulation zones are in the middle and the occupied rooms face south. With an east-west orientation, living rooms with windows can be positioned on both sides. The auxiliary rooms are mostly in the middle zone. For north-south oriented buildings the facade to the south is usually extensively glazed, whilst to the north it is mainly solid. The sides of the east-west oriented version may have somewhat similarly configured facades. A north-south orientation has advantages from an energy and room-conditioning point of view, as in winter the solar gain can be used to support the heating system. For this to be effective the distance between rows must be large enough. As the rows receive direct sunlight on the south, the depth of the building is less than for the corresponding east-west orientation. To avoid overheating in summer, any large window areas on the east and west sides should be fitted with exterior shading.

Trends in residential buildings

The first purpose of building was to provide somewhere to live. The current housing stock in Germany is around 39 million residential units. Every year there are around 300,000 new residential units built, which represents about 1% of the total stock. Heating of homes accounts for 30% of the primary energy requirement in Germany. Of this, up to 70% could be saved through refurbishments to improve the energy characteristics of building envelopes and install modern heating systems.

Developments in energy Before the beginning of the 20th century, people in Central Europe often lived under very uncomfortable temperature conditions. The only source of heat was the kitchen hearth. Normally this room was the only one in the house to be heated. The widespread adoption of central heating and availability of cheap heating oil certainly led to an improvement in thermal comfort, but the demand for energy rose dramatically. The thermal insulation regulations were intended to reduce heating heat demand in stages from up 400 kWh/m²a to 70 kWh/m²a. Current developments are moving in the direction of a low energy house with a heating demand some 30% below the requirements of the current legal regulations. A current subject featuring in discussions about the passive house, the "house without heating", is controlled house ventilation and the declared target of achieving an energy use of 15 kWh/m²a (passive house standard). There are ongoing experiments, such as the zero energy house or the surplus energy house, which require no external energy or have a surplus of energy available from an extensive active solar system. If the solar energy demand is required to be below 25 kWh/m²a, this leads to higher construction costs and is not economically viable at the moment. However, if the zero and surplus energy house projects are successful they will provide the technological impetus for the future.

Climatic aspects The comfort requirements in residential buildings are very high as they are the most personal of our building types. Energy-optimised buildings reduce not only the energy demand but also increase thermal comfort as improved thermal insulation leads to higher surface temperatures. The acceptance of particular room climatisation conditions in residential construction tends to be greater than in buildings used for commercial purposes as the room climate is generally capable of being adjusted by the user and the occupiers are more likely to agree on the setting. In homes the room in current use changes frequently.

Living and working Advances in communications technology is dissolving the spatial relationship between the desk and the office: "the office is where you are". The spatial relationship between living and working can produce synergy effects, e.g. by extending the energy load curves.

Building control Washing machines with Internet access highlight a trend in which the technical potential of information technology equipment can also be of benefit in residential buildings. To ensure that the equipment is used properly, it must have access to easily comprehensible controls and interfaces. The life cycles of buildings and information technology equipment are extremely different and therefore combining the two technologies is only possible in certain conditions.

Integration of technologies Craftsmen in the building industry tend to be strongly focused on their own trades with the result that in residential buildings there must be tight integration of construction and building services technology. The building services systems are installed as individual components into the existing construction. Complex technical systems should be installed as modules and as far as possible prefabricated in the factory to reduce installation faults and maintenance costs.

Solar energy In relation to solar energy use, active systems can be employed economically for hot water production and where necessary in support of heating during the transition months. Extensive passive use of solar radiation is possible at a glazing fraction of 40%. Solar gain becomes difficult to fully exploit if the glazing fraction is greater than 50%.

Controlled domestic ventilation There are currently two important trends. One is the spread of ventilation systems with heat recovery as absolutely essential to reducing energy consumption. The other is ventilation through windows as a fundamental contribution to the quality of life. With the correct design, planning and operation, ventilation systems can save on energy and improve comfort and air quality.

Architecture and building climate control

Architecture influences the energy demand of residential buildings by means of parameters like compactness, orientation, proportion of window area and the materials used. The urban planning context influences solar penetration, wind exposure and noise load.

Building form Compactness is expressed by the A/V_e ratio, the ratio of surface area to the heated volume. Typical values vary from 0.4 for multistorey buildings or middle terraced houses and 1.1 for bungalows (Fig. 4.5.2). The larger the area of the building envelope, the larger is the energy transmitting area and therefore the A/V_e ratio is an important factor in the calculation of energy consumption. In practice, however, a slightly unfavourable A/V_e ratio can be accepted in favour of a better development concept with advantages in relation to the urban planning structure, plan layout, natural lighting or the economical use of space. A larger building envelope, however, requires thicker insulation and increases the area to be insulated, which puts up construction costs.

Orientation and proportion of window area Maximising the solar energy gain is not a main priority in view of the low heating heat requirement that is already a result of good building insulation. Therefore the influence of orientation should not be overestimated as a planning parameter. Urban planning and usage aspects have a greater influence on orientation than does energy saving. A glazing fraction of 30–50% is an optimum value for the south facade in order to make best use of solar heat gains (Fig. 4.5.3). A larger proportion of window area brings no energy advantage and has the danger of overheating in summer. It is sensible to reduce the proportion of window area on facades not receiving direct sunlight. Improved glass properties means that this rule is not as important as it was in earlier times. In facades on the other sides, the windows should be dimensioned to suit the penetration of natural light, the view and the temperature conditions in the room in summer. Extensively glazed rooms without shading can be prone to overheating. External solar shading should be provided if unpleasantly high temperatures are to be avoided over long periods.

Building envelope The building envelope influences the heat loss from transmission and leaks as well as solar gain. Good insulation of the facade can be achieved with monolithic and multilayered construction. In multilayered construction the U-value is mainly determined by the thickness of insulation. In monolithic outside walls, the materials used must have a very low heat conductivity. As insulation standards are raised, the influence of heat bridges becomes more relevant to total energy consumption. It is of the order of 5 to 20%. Heat bridges must also be avoided as they can lead to structural damage. Condensation forms on surfaces with low temperatures, which creates the conditions for mould to form.

Glazing Innovations in glass manufacture have led to a reduction of transmission loss through the glass by about 70%. U-values could be reduced from about 1.8 W/m²K to 0.5 W/m²K. Now that glass quality is so good, the window frames have become the energy weak point. The thermal transmittance of the window unit should be based on U-values that are calculated by taking proper account of the glass and frame. U-values below 1.0 W/m²K require the use of triple glazing. They have a lower total solar energy transmittance and a lower natural light transmittance but cost more.

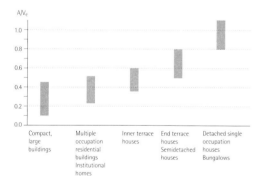

Fig. 4.5.2 **Form factor A/V_e for residential buildings**
A = surface area
V_e = gross heated volume

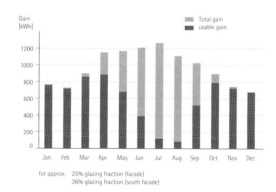

Fig. 4.5.3 **Usable solar energy gain relative to the proportion of window area (after Hellwig)**

Domestic ventilation

Domestic ventilation systems are installed to provide good ventilation. Odours and pollutants, CO_2 and moisture must be removed and conducted away. The fresh air demand depends directly on the period of use and the number of people. During the heating season any air changes involve heat loss. Ventilation heat loss may play a small part in poorly insulated houses but in well-insulated houses it is of the same order as transmission heat loss.

Natural ventilation The simplest way of producing air changes in domestic property is by opening windows. Windows also provide the user with views to the outside. Nowadays tilt-turn windows are in widespread use. This type of window hardware does not allow fine adjustment of air changes and provides too high a rate of air change, in particular during the colder times of year. To optimise the effect of window ventilation in the future, hardware should be used that can be controlled in accordance with various criteria such as indoor climate, outdoor climate or air quality and will allow fine adjustment of the flow of supply air. Ventilation through the external wall does not necessarily have to be through a window. External wall openings can also have opaque ventilation flaps or be slot or lens shaped. The quality of the fresh air with window ventilation can be adversely affected by street noise, dust or pollen.

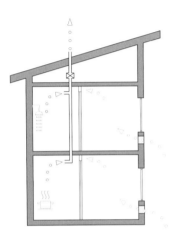
Fig. 4.5.4 **Exhaust air system**
The supply air flows through external wall openings, the exhaust air is extracted through a fan.

Exhaust air systems Exhaust air systems are the simplest form of mechanical ventilation system. They extract the air through mechanical fans from kitchens and bathrooms, where most odours and moisture are created. Supply air flows through external wall openings into the living and sleeping areas (Fig. 4.5.4). Installation costs and the drive energy are reduced as there is only one exhaust airflow. The disadvantage is that the heat removed with the exhaust air cannot be conducted to the supply air and heat recovery is only possible with an exhaust air heat pump. The recovered heat can be used for the production of hot water or for charging a wet heating system. A special form of exhaust air system is the moisture controlled system. This system sets the flow to match the room air humidity and in this way ensures that moisture is removed and conducted away even if the user does not open the windows. The system is less sensitive in its reaction to coincident window ventilation than a supply and exhaust air system and is therefore suitable for apartment buildings.

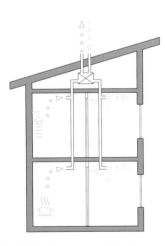
Fig. 4.5.5 **Supply and exhaust air system**
Supply and exhaust airflows are ducted and driven by a fan.

Supply and exhaust air system In a supply and exhaust air system, the supply and exhaust air flows in ducts and is driven by separate fans. Both airflows can be passed through a plate heat exchanger, which can recover up to 90% of the heat. In addition, the heat from the exhaust air is conducted directly into the supply airflow to avoid comfort problems (Fig. 4.5.5).

Window ventilation on top of this usually leads to an increase in energy consumption. This should be borne in mind as the user generally wishes to open the windows for the view, despite the fact that a ventilation system has been installed. The savings in primary energy of a supply and exhaust air system are highly dependent on use. In a single-person household there are normally too many air changes, which can result in less energy saved or even increased consumption. In a home continuously occupied by several people, a supply and exhaust air system may lead to energy savings because of the higher number of required air changes.

Evaluation of ventilation strategies Window ventilation is a simple ventilation method with low capital costs and high user acceptance. The disadvantage is that heat recovery is not possible. If only a low rate of air change is required then controlled window ventilation represents a worthwhile strategy. Humidity-controlled exhaust air systems with heat recovery in combination with a low temperature heating system is a cost effective and technically simple mechanical ventilation solution. The supply and exhaust air system can reduce ventilation heat loss where there is a high requirement for fresh air. Careful planning and design of the system is particularly important as inappropriate operation of the system can lead to considerably higher energy consumption.

Energy generation

The criteria for the selection of the energy generator are the availability of sources of energy, the system temperature of the heat transmission system and the output required by the building (Tab. 4.5.1).

Availability The availability of a source of energy is the first selection criterion. It depends on whether the building is located in a rural or urban area and whether the development zone requires new services infrastructure connections. In rural areas or in newly established development zones with low density of services provision the use of gas as an energy supply is not normally economic. On the other hand in rural areas wood pellets or wood chips are often available at reasonable cost. In development areas that are newly connected, a local district heating system with a central wood-burning boiler or combined heat and power plant could be an attractive alternative. Whether a heat pump can be used depends principally on whether ground water is present or an underground pipe register or boreholes can be installed.

System temperature Another criterion is the system temperature. The temperature of the heat generator and that of the heat transmission system must be compatible. The viability of heat pumps and solar systems installed to support heating systems depends on the system temperature, as their efficiency or energy output drops with increasing system temperature if they are combined with radiator systems.

Output requirement The third criterion is the output requirement. Very good insulation considerably reduces the heating heat demand, which leads to a steep drop in the required heating output. Sometimes this leads to the problem that a heat energy generator may not be able to work efficiently at this small output. This problem can be alleviated by sharing a heat energy generator with several other parties. Another possibility is to smooth the output using an intermediate energy store. The design should also take into account that the heat requirement for hot water production in residential buildings forms a major part of the total heat demand. The hot water requirement of one person is approximately 25 litres (30 °C) per day. The energy required for this is approximately 400 kWh/year.

Combinations of heat energy generation systems
In practice it can be worthwhile to combine two heat generation systems. In doing this you should ensure that the systems have characteristics that complement rather than conflict with one another. If a solar energy system is installed, the conventional fuel-fired heat energy generator can be switched off in summer. In the case of combined heat and power plants or fuel cells, the economic advantage is less because of the shorter annual operating period. In general when planning energy generation systems, it should be borne in mind that simple concepts with fewer components are more reliable in practice, cheaper to maintain and easier for the user to operate than complex systems.

	Combination	System temperature heating system	Suitable heat transfer	Special characteristics
1 Low temperature boiler	5, 6, 7, 8	Feed temperature 40–75 °C	Radiators Radiant panel systems	Economic
2 Condensing boiler	5, 8	Return temperature if possible < 50 °C	Radiant panel systems are particularly suitable	Combustion gas flue, condensate outlet, current standard for gas
3 Wood chips	8	High system temperature possible	Radiators	Buffer store, storage space, transport, operation
4 Wood pellets	8	High system temperature possible	Radiators	Storage space, transport
5 Heat pumps	1, 2, 8	Feed temperature < 40 °C	Radiant panel systems required	Energy from ground water, earth, exhaust air, performance factor should be > 3
6 Small CHP	1	High system temperature possible	Radiators	Maintenance costs high, designed for approx. 20 % of the max. heat demand
7 Fuel cells	1	High system temperature possible	Radiators	Regenerative hydrogen production not yet market ready
8 Solar systems	1, 2, 3, 4, 5	Feed temperature very low	Radiant panel systems required	Mainly hot water, sloping roof

Tab. 4.5.1 **Characteristics of energy generators and combinations of systems**
In the development of energy generation concepts it is important to ensure that system temperatures and the operating periods of the energy generators complement and not compete with one another.

Fig. 4.5.6 Residential and business building
Friedl, Landshut

Residential and business building Friedl, Landshut

In the residential and business block Friedl in Landshut an internal unheated atrium links a north-facing office block with south-facing residential building. The atrium serves as the access zone for the whole building and as a meeting point for residents. Galleries and bridges lead from one part of the building to the other. Vertical access is by a glazed lift. The atrium serves as a supply air space and for lighting the adjacent rooms. At all times of the year the temperature in the atrium is higher than the outside temperature. In order to ensure that temperatures remain above freezing point in winter, the atrium glazing uses insulating glass with a U-value of 1.1 W/m²K. The atrium roof is shaded with internal solar protection to ensure that temperatures remain comfortable in summer. Opening flaps with an area of 10 m² each in the facade and the roof provide good through-ventilation of the atrium. They also function as smoke extraction vents (Fig. 4.5.6). In summer, supply air is brought into the atrium through an earth pipe to achieve a further reduction in temperature. The north facade has large windows. The office area is lit from the atrium through skylights. The building is a low energy design. A well-insulated building envelope in combination with an efficient heating system lowers energy demand.

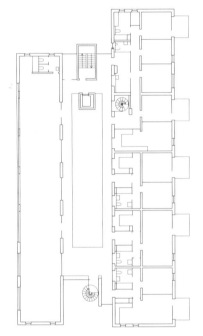

Fig. 4.5.7 Plan of standard floor

Construction: 1998
Use: residential and business building
Client: Friedl Wohnbau, Landshut
Architects: Bauderer, Feigel, Huber, Landshut
Building services: Ingenieurbüro Hausladen, Kirchheim, Munich, Prof. G. Hausladen, J. Bauer
Facade: highly heat insulated building envelope, atrium as intermediate zone
Energy concept: low energy building, decentralised (residential) mechanical ventilation with heat recovery, thermal solar energy system to cover hot water energy demand, earth pipe

Ventilation concept The atrium is used as a supply air space for ventilation. Outside air flows into the atrium through an earth pipe and emerges from an air well. The air for the individual homes is extracted from the atrium by ventilation units with heat recovery. The users can set the rates of air change for their homes to suit their own requirements. Preheated supply air flows into residential rooms and air is extracted from kitchens and bathrooms. The supply air from the earth pipe and heat recovery leads to a low ventilation heat requirement (Fig. 4.5.8).

Heating concept The building is heated by a gas-fired boiler with a total output of 60 kW (Fig. 4.5.10). A thermal solar energy system is installed to cover the hot water energy demand. Flat plate collectors with an area of 40 m² on the part of the roof sloping towards the south charge a buffer storage tank containing 1,500 litres of water (Fig. 4.5.9). The collector system covers about 45% of the hot water demand of the homes. The reduced energy requirement and the thermally optimised outside skin allow radiators to be placed above the doors to the rooms without detrimentally affecting thermal comfort. For this to work, preheating of the outside air is required in addition to the good insulative qualities of the external walls and windows. This is achieved using recovered heat and radiators.

Integration of technologies Throughout the whole building, the installations are installed to be as compact as possible to keep distribution heat losses as low as possible. Horizontal distribution takes place in the atrium under the stairs leading to the first floor and the air is conducted from there to the riser shafts into the offices and homes. The heating equipment room is integrated into the atrium. The heating boiler is situated on the first floor. The solar system buffer storage tank is on the third floor, directly under the solar collectors. Distribution losses are minimised in this way. Heat given off by the heating boiler and the distribution system is of benefit to conditioning the atrium. The ventilation equipment is installed in the entrance areas of the homes. The air ducts are located in the hall along with the heating pipes. The plan layouts allow short pipework lengths. The radiators are positioned above the room doors in order to be able to place the heating pipes together with the ventilation ducts under the hall floor. The external walls remain free from technical installations.

Fig. 4.5.10 **Gas-fired boiler with expansion tank**

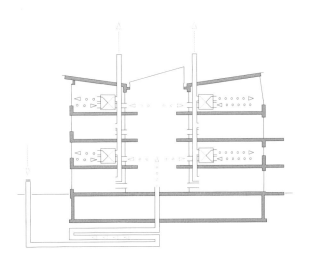

Fig. 4.5.8 **Schematic of the local mechanical ventilation of the individual homes with heat recovery**

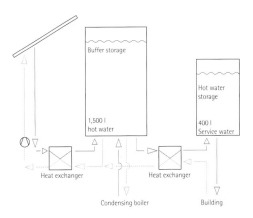

Fig. 4.5.9 **Schematic of the energy concept**

Technologies

You always break out in a sweat at the Olympia Park. On sunny days, you like to cycle to the office. In January this means dressing warmly. You put on a fleece over the jacket of your suit. And, just in case, you put your raincoat on top for good measure. And off you go, with sunglasses, scarf and gloves. The cycle ride through the sunny landscape lifts your spirits, and you take the bend into the underpass under the ring road with panache. Because you are wearing sunglasses, you can only see contours, and you narrowly miss a pothole. Of course, now you have lost your momentum, and it's hard going pulling up the hill on the other side. You're not feeling the cold anymore, and you peel off your fleece. As you pedal along, the cold wind whistles through your thin raincoat. Shivering, you cycle onwards to your office in Schwabing.

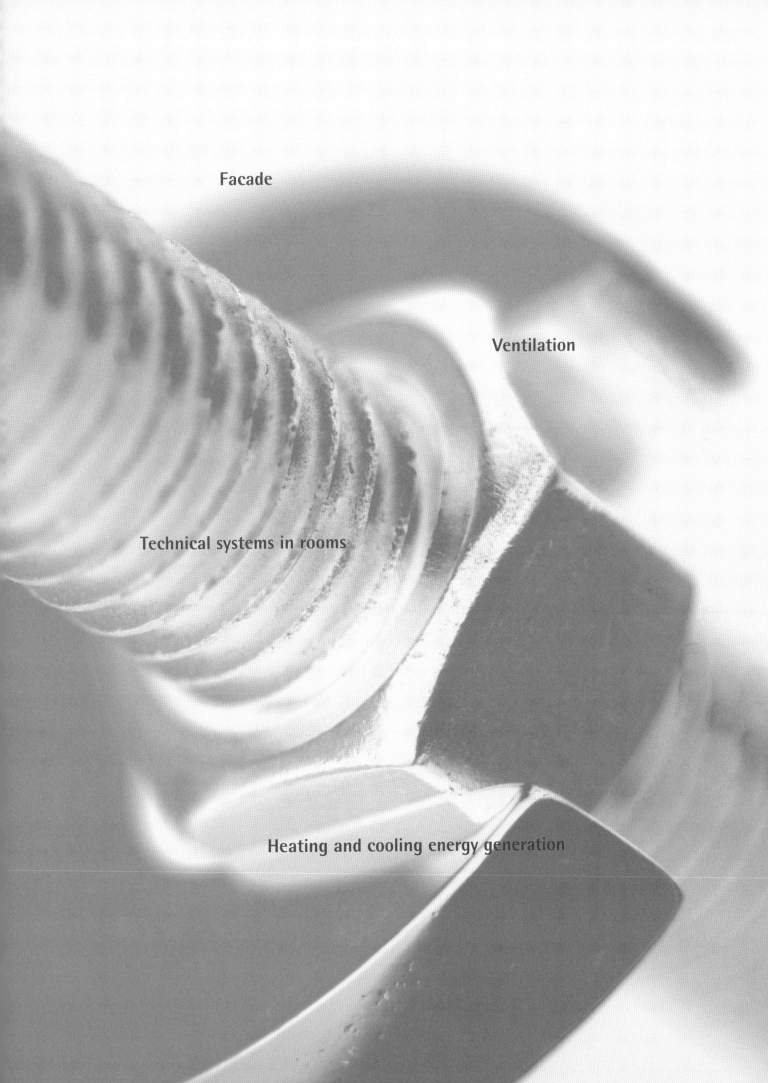

Facade

Ventilation

Technical systems in rooms

Heating and cooling energy generation

Facade

"The best way to light a house is God's way – the natural way, as nearly as possible in the daytime and at night as nearly like the day as may be, or better."

Frank Lloyd Wright 1867-1959

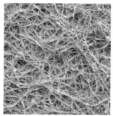
Insulation

Innovative insulation systems

Latent heat storage – PCM

Glass

Variochromic glass

Shading

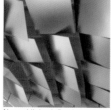
Natural light deflection systems

Insulation

Insulation materials are used to improve the thermal or sound insulation characteristics of buildings. These materials include artificial mineral fibres, foamed inorganic and organic insulation, cellulose and wood, as well as other natural insulation materials. The latter types represent only a very small proportion of the market. A construction material can be described as thermal insulation if its heat conductivity is less than 0.1 W/mK. Heat conductivity increases with increasing bulk density and moisture content (Tab. 5.1.1).

Artificial mineral fibres This product group includes glass, mineral and ceramic fibres. The fibres are made from a silicate melt (e.g. glass, mineral or slag melt, with a high proportion of waste glass or recycled material). Ceramic fibres are mainly used in industrial plant construction and in fire protection. Mineral and glass wool are used for heat, sound and fire protection. Handling fibre insulation materials can lead to dust from the smallest fibres entering the lungs and to irritation of the skin, mucous membranes and eyes by the larger fibres.

Foamed inorganic insulation Foam glass, expanded perlite and expanded clay are used as insulation fill in areas in contact with the ground, as core insulation in construction components or in roofs, as a regulating medium or as an additive in concrete or mortar. The fire protection properties of foamed inorganic insulation are very good. A 10–20% increased thickness must generally be provided compared with the equivalent foamed organic insulation.

Foamed organic insulation This group includes mineral oil-based insulation. Expanded polystyrene foam (XPS) is a rigid closed cell insulation made from polystyrene. Polystyrene granulate is expanded by the addition of a foaming agent into blocks or boards in an extruder. The extrusion process creates large numbers of small closed cells, which give the material a high mechanical strength and tolerance of moisture. Extruded polystyrene foam (EPS) can be manufactured for almost any purpose in construction and consequently is widely used. Polyurethane (PUR) rigid foam boards are manufactured from a reaction mixture of diphenylmethane diisocyanate, polyols and additives. PUR is an insulation material capable of carrying compressive loads and is compatible with all other materials found on construction sites.

Cellulose and wood-based insulation This product group includes cellulose fibres made from waste paper, wood fibreboards made from wood residues and lightweight woodwool slabs. Cellulose fibre insulation consists of newspaper mechanically cut into small pieces and treated with chemicals such as borax to reduce its flammability. In most cases the fibre mass is also mixed with hydrophobic additives. Cellulose fibres are used as fill or blown into voids. Installing this material creates a lot of dust. The particles in wood fibreboard are normally bonded together by binding agents within the wood itself rather than by chemicals. Cement or magnesite can be added to increase the strength. Wood fibreboard is suitable for use as divider panels for loose insulation material or as thermal or impact sound insulation under floating screeds. Lightweight woodwool slabs provide only slight heat insulation properties and are mainly used in refurbishment projects or as plaster baseboards or acoustic boards.

Natural insulation Other insulation materials based on plant or animal products are not widely used. This is partly because of limited resources and the still relatively undeveloped production processes. Insulation materials from renewable sources include cork, coir and flax fibres, reeds and wool. These materials are mainly made into boards or insulation mats.

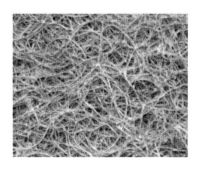

Heat conductivity λ [W/mK]
Heat conductivity is a material property. It is the amount of heat that passes per hour through 1 m² of a 1 m thick layer of a material when the difference in temperature between the two faces is 1 K.

Thermal transmittance U [W/m²K]
Thermal transmittance is a measure of the heat passing through a component taking into account the thermal transmittance of the individual layers of the component and the heat transmitted at the surfaces of the component.

Tab. 5.1.1 **Thermal conductivity groups of various insulation materials**

Insulation	TC
Rock fibre	035–040
Glass fibre	035–050
Foam glass	045–060
Expanded perlite	055
Expanded clay	085–090
XPS	035–040
EPS	035–040
PUR	025–035
Cellulose fibre	040–045
Wood fibreboard	045–055
Lightweight woodwool	090
Expanded cork	045–050
Coir	040–045
Reeds	055–060
Flax fibres	040
Wool (sheep)	040
Cotton	040

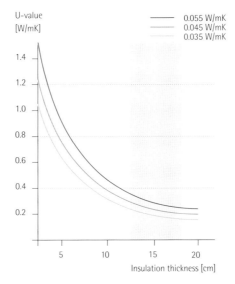

U-value [W/mK]

— 0.055 W/mK
— 0.045 W/mK
— 0.035 W/mK

Insulation thickness [cm]

Fig. 5.1.1 **U-value with respect to thickness of insulation and thermal conductivity [W/mK]**

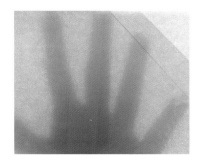

Innovative insulation systems

Translucent thermal insulation and vacuum insulation represent new developments in the field of insulation materials. They allow heat gain from external walls or highly insulated wall elements of very little thickness.

Translucent thermal insulation (TI) Translucent thermal insulation is insulation that allows light to pass through it and has good insulation properties. A wall with translucent insulation can also allow solar energy to be used for heating. Translucent thermal insulation is an insulation material with a high permeability with respect to solar radiation. Hollow chamber structures (capillaries and honeycombs) in plastic or glass have the best properties in relation to light permeability and thermal insulation. Small parallel tubes, perpendicular to the absorber, suppress the convective transmission of heat. The thermal insulation effect comes from the low conductivity of the stationary air in these small tubes. The diameter of the small tubes is approximately 5 mm. Source materials are polymethylmethacrylate (PMMA) or polycarbonate (PC).

There are three basic systems: solid wall, hybrid and direct gain. In solid wall systems, solar radiation passes through the translucent insulation layer and strikes the solid building component behind it made from calcium silicate masonry or concrete, which is normally painted a dark colour to improve heat absorption. The heat store releases heat into the adjacent rooms over time (Fig. 5.1.2). The buffer effect of the absorber wall makes particularly good use of solar gain. External walls insulated with translucent materials have a positive monthly energy balance. The net heat gain is between 50 to 150 kWh/(m²a), depending on the quality of the TI system.

Hybrid systems use a heat exchanger (air or water) to conduct the energy gained through ducts to the building energy supply system.

Solid wall systems and hybrid systems must be shaded in summer to avoid overheating. Ways of doing this include roller blinds within the TI elements or providing the whole TI element with a cover during the relevant seasons. Optical systems that block the high summer sun by means of prismatic panels are being used in trial applications.

Direct gain systems do not rely on heat storage. They are used to provide natural light in skylights and roofs to improve room lighting.

Vacuum insulation panels (VIP) Vacuum insulation consists of a core of microporous materials, such as microporous silica, polystyrene or polyurethane foam, or aerogels, enclosed in a gas-tight welded film. Fine-pored materials (aerogels, fumed silica) also have good insulation properties without vacuum. Enclosing them under reduced gas pressure can increase their insulation effect for the same thickness by five to ten times compared with conventional insulation materials (Tab. 5.1.2). Microporous quartz undergoes no noticeable material aging and is heat resistant. Its long life makes quartz-based VIP insulation ideal for use in buildings.

VIP is preferred to conventional insulation because of its low thickness, especially in older buildings. It is used as thermal insulation inside buildings, for external wall insulation as well as ceiling and floor insulation where room heights are low. Vacuum insulation panels embedded between glass panels can be integrated into facades as spandrel panels.

VIPs can be manufactured to any shape and size. For reasons of cost a uniform standard size is normally used. VIPs cannot be cut and therefore connections to conventional EPS boards have to be manufactured. This may mean that heat bridges have to be tolerated as a result. When used as external or internal insulation the panels are attached to the walls with adhesive mortar or a system of rails. For internal insulation a plasterboard partition wall must be built to support the vacuum insulation layer so that the insulation panels are not visibly damaged by screws or nails. Vacuum panels are delivered with a foam surround to protect them from damage on site.

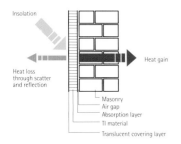

Fig. 5.1.2 **How TI works in a solid wall system**
Solar radiation striking the absorber wall is released over time into the room.

Tab. 5.1.2 **Physical characteristics of TI systems and vacuum insulation panels**

TI system	U [W/m²K]	g [-]	Thickness [mm]
Solid wall system	0.8	0.59	131
Direct gain system	0.8	0.63	49

VIP thickness [mm]	U_{intact} [W/m²K]	$U_{ventilated}$ [W/m²K]	λ [W/mK]
4	0.140	0.40	0.006
6	0.100	0.29	0.006
8	0.072	0.22	0.006

Latent heat storage – PCM

In contrast to conventional heat storage, the temperature of which can be felt to increase, phase change materials (PCM) are able to store latent energy. When temperature rises, the temperature of a latent heat store does not increase but the medium changes from one physical state to another and by this means it stores energy. Therefore the take up of energy cannot be detected by touch. The temperature only rises detectably after a complete change of phase has taken place (Fig. 5.1.3). When a change takes place, the latent heat involved is equal to the heat of melting or crystallisation of the storage medium. The advantage of PCM is that large amounts of heat or cold can be stored within small temperature ranges, the storage taking place under conditions of constant temperature. In buildings this enables smoothing of temperature fluctuations and load peaks.

The characteristics of PCM are usually created using water with additives, salt hydrates or paraffins. The phase changes from solid to liquid and therefore a PCM cannot be used for structural purposes. They have to be encapsulated in small containers or mixed with conventional construction materials. Organic latent heat storage based on paraffins are normally micro-encapsulated. They are made up of tiny stable capsules, the contents of which fully melt or crystallise when the phase changes. One problem of paraffin-based PCMs is the flammability, which must be given particular attention in buildings.

Area of application In buildings latent heat storage is mainly of interest in summer for heat protection. For this reason, paraffins have been developed with melting points of between 24 and 26 °C. One of the ways these paraffins can be integrated into buildings is by mixing with dry mortars. Buildings constructed with lightweight elements often lack thermal storage mass. Internal loads and solar radiation quickly lead to overheating of the building. PCMs can be used to counteract this effect. Large amounts of heat can be stored in a small space. PCMs can be used in office rooms to shift the daily maximum temperature. PCMs can greatly improve the summer conditions in buildings when used in conjunction with night cooling.

PCMs can also be effective in separate heat and cold storage, but this requires additional components such as fans, pumps and a control system. The advantage of this type of system is that the stored heat can be used in specific ways. When PCM granulate is integrated into floors, its storage properties can allow savings of up to 50% of the thickness of a conventional screed. As latent storage has a higher storage density and a constant temperature, it can be very effective when integrated into solar air systems. It is used in absorber units in solar air collectors and facades, supply air heating, hypocaust heating and additional storage.

Use in facades The main use of PCMs in facades at the moment is as an additive to mortar and plaster. A new trend is the integration of PCM into glazed facades. Sunlight melts the PCM. A layer of PCM only a few centimetres thick can store as much heat as a thick brick wall and release it overnight (Fig. 5.1.4). The PCM material is translucent and allows diffuse light to enter the room.

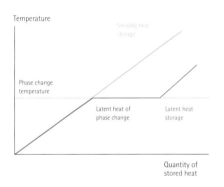

Fig. 5.1.3 **Heat storage of sensible and latent heat storage devices**
When the phase change temperature is reached, the temperature stops increasing in the latent storage until the phase change is complete. Then the temperature starts to rise again by a detectable amount.

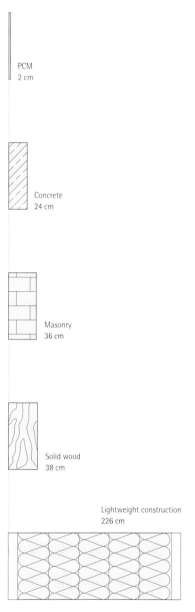

PCM
2 cm

Concrete
24 cm

Masonry
36 cm

Solid wood
38 cm

Lightweight construction
226 cm

Fig. 5.1.4 **Heat storage capacity of PCM compared with other materials**
For a heat storage capacity of 1.6 kWh/m² and a temperature increase of 10 °C, 36 cm of masonry, 24 cm of concrete, 38 cm of solid wood and 226 cm of lightweight construction would be required. A 2 cm layer of PCM is adequate to provide the same effect (after Dörken).

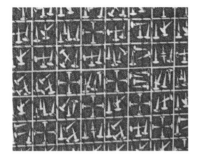

Glass

Glass should allow as little heat and as much light into the room as possible. The total solar energy transmittance g should be as high as possible if the primary requirement is solar heat gain in winter. A low g-value is required for good room climate in summer. In addition to this, good sound insulation is necessary at noisy locations. Glazing should not add or subtract from the true colours of the outside environment and not appear reflective from the outside. Low U and g-values generally lead to a reduction in natural light transmittance   (Tab. 5.1.3). The very low U-values of glass in use nowadays means that window frames have become the thermal weak points of facades. Much attention is therefore required to the form of the frame.

Heat insulation glass Heat insulation glass reduces heat transmission in two ways. A thin skin of transparent silver coating on the outside of the internal pane reduces some of the heat emission so that almost no radiation interchange takes place between the panes. In addition, an inert gas filling prevents heat exchange by conduction. The gas is often argon or krypton. two-pane glazing can achieve U-values as low as 1.0 W/m²K, with three-pane this goes down to 0.5 W/m²K. These very low values also allow extensive glazing at reasonable energy cost. Thermal comfort is improved because of the higher surface temperatures and alleviates the problem of cold air drop, which often occurs with tall glass panels.

Solar control glazing Special coatings on the inside of the external pane of solar control glazing allow a lot of visible light but only a very small proportion of the energy of the rest of the spectrum into the room. The spectral composition of the proportion of light admitted is altered and the result is a colour shift in the room. The coating's effect is the same throughout the year and hence solar gain in winter is reduced. In summer additional measures are generally needed to ensure shading and solar protection. The glass achieves g-values down to 0.15. The low total solar energy transmittance also reduces the admission of natural light (Fig. 5.1.5) and the external surface has a mirror-like appearance, and therefore solar control glass is only suitable for special functions or for use on parts of buildings. Offices can be completely glazed with glass with g-values as low as 0.30.

Printed glass Printing on glass is one way of reducing its g-value whilst preserving a transparent appearance. The view out is retained to a certain extent depending on the amount and structure of the printing. From the outside, printed glass has an opaque appearance, which prevents people from looking in. Other ways of treating the surface of glass include etching or sandblasting. These techniques also prevent people from seeing into the room and allow only diffuse light to enter.

Sound insulation glazing The sound insulation effect of glazing increases with the weight, elasticity and distance between the panes. Other factors include the gas filling and the construction of the panes. Having panes of different thicknesses improves sound insulation. Sound protection glazing achieves a weighted sound reduction index R_W of up to 55 dB. In selecting the glass it should be remembered that glass satisfying the requirements for sound insulation provides less heat insulation.

Safety glazing Safety glazing must be installed where there are increased requirements for intruder protection or resistance to bullets, in high facades and overhead glazing. Types include toughened glass and laminated safety glass. The pane is thermally prestressed for toughened glass. It has a higher bending strength and when fractured it breaks into many grains of glass with no sharp edges. When this happens the glass no longer defines the room boundaries. Laminated safety glass is composed of two or more sheets bonded together by an elastic film. The robust lamination of sheets and film ensures that if part of the glass breaks the rest remains in place to form the boundary to the room and no large, dangerous splinters are detached.

Light transmittance R_W [dB]
The light transmittance t represents the amount of visible radiation between the wavelengths of 380 to 780 nm, a range relating to the light sensitivity of the human eye.

Total solar energy transmittance g [-]
The total solar energy transmittance of glazing indicates how much solar energy in the wavelength range 320–2,500 nm is allowed to pass through.

Light transmittance τ [%]
The light transmittance t represents the amount of visible radiation between the wavelengths of 380 to 780 nm, a range relating to the light sensitivity of the human eye.

Fig. 5.1.5 **Light transmittance   shown with respect to total solar energy transmittance g**

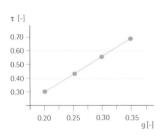

Tab. 5.1.3 **Typical values for various types of glass**
Total thermal transmission coefficient U_g, total solar energy transmittance g, light transmittance τ and sound reduction index R_W

	U_g [W/m²K]	g [-]	τ [-]	R_W [dB]
2-pane heat insulation	up to 1.1	0.55–0.65	0.8	30–31
2-pane heat insulation	up to 0.5	0.5	0.7	32
Solar control glass	up to 1.1	0.3–0.45	0.4–0.7	34
Sound insulation glass	up to 1.1	0.5–0.65	0.7–0.8	36–50

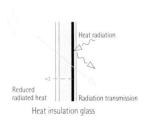

Fig. 5.1.6 **Operation of heat insulation glass, solar control glass and sound insulation glass**

Variochromic glass

Controllable glazing allows the user to vary the amount of light and radiation transmitted through it and therefore offers a solution to one of architecture's most basic problems, namely, it provides a highly efficient and weather-protected way of controlling the amount of shading. Active systems change their optical and thermal characteristics at the press of a button, whilst passive systems work automatically (Tab. 5.1.4). In combination with TI elements it provides an additional option whereby heat input can be specifically controlled. Variochromic glass systems are at the testing stage and almost ready to be introduced to the market.

Electrochromic glass Electrochromic glass is an active system. It requires controls and switches. An active coating in the form of a film is embedded in laminated glass between two sheets. After being switched on or off the glass changes colour gradually. With electrochromic glass, even when switched on, you can still look through the glass. Additional glare protection is therefore not required. The glass appears slightly blue in operation.

Gasochromic glass Gasochromic glass is also an active system. The cavity between the panes is connected to the control device outside the glazing unit. Colour change is brought about by contact with a gas. The view through the glass is retained but the colour is distorted. The co-

louration appears slightly blue. Glare protection must still be considered.

Thermotropic glazing Thermotropic glazing is a passive system. The cloudiness occurs automatically once a certain threshold temperature is exceeded, which is determined during manufacture by the mixture of materials. The user cannot intervene in or control this process, the threshold temperature is fixed. As the temperature rises the glass goes from being clear and transparent to being opaque, thus diffusing the light. The glass no longer allows clear visibility and is therefore mainly suitable in skylights or in combination with transparent panes.

Photochromic coatings Photochromic coatings combine the functional aspects of electrochromic coatings and electrochemical solar cells. An external voltage is required only for the decolourising process. As long as the switch is open, the coating turns blue under the action of sunlight. In winter, when colouration may not be desirable, it can be removed by applying an electric charge.

Other systems PDLC glass (PDLC = Polymer-Dispersed Liquid Crystal) works in a similar way to thermotropic glass. As long as the correct voltage is applied, the liquid crystals are uniformly aligned and the visibility is clear. The system is used where visibility needs to be controlled or as an indoor switchable projection surface.

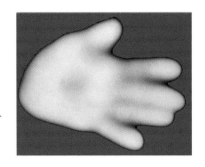

Electrochromic glass
The system normally consists of five layers: two conductive transparent electrodes, an ion storage layer and an active layer, usually of tungsten oxide. An electrical voltage is applied to this galvanic element. The ion exchange causes the colouration to take place.

Gasochromic glass
A thin catalysing layer is placed on a layer of tungsten oxide. Atomic hydrogen, in a mixture at low concentration with a carrier gas, e.g. nitrogen, is introduced into the glazing cavity and diffuses into the tungsten oxide layer. This produces the colouration. Raising the oxygen concentration reverses the process.

Thermotropic glass
Two coatings with different refractive indices are mixed. The plastics in the polymer blend mix well or less well according to the temperature and separate as the temperature rises. Light striking the layer is refracted, diffused or reflected to different degrees. With hydrogels, the polymer dissolves in the gel at low temperatures; at higher temperatures they separate and become cloudy.

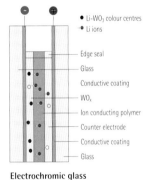

Electrochromic glass

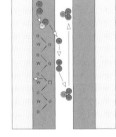

Gasochromic glass

Thermotropic glass

Fig. 5.1.7 **The principles of variochromic glazing**

	Total solar energy transmittance g (example) [-]		Light transmittance (τ) (example) [-]		Switchable visibility	Optical impression	Controllability	Requires electricity	Disadvantages
	Not switched	Switched	Not switched	Switched					
Thermotropic	0.5	0.15	0.74	0.16	No	Clear-white	No	No	No visibility Not controllable
Gasochromic	0.5	0.15	0.6	0.16	Yes	Neutral-blue	Yes	Yes	Glare risk Switching by absorption
Electrochromic	0.36	0.12	0.5	0.15	Yes	Neutral-blue	State switchable	Yes	Glare risk Switching by absorption

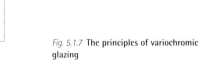

Tab. 5.1.4 **Comparison of variochromic glazing**

Shading

The amount of solar radiation admitted through the facade is determined by the reduction factor of the shading and the total solar energy transmittance of the glazing. The shading must allow enough daylight into the room. The ideal systems are those that also deflect light. The shading can be external, internal or within the facade cavity (Fig. 5.1.8).

External systems External shading is the most effective system because the solar radiation is blocked before it reaches the facade. However, its exposure to weather and wind requires higher capital and maintenance costs and a drive to control the shading. The system cannot operate in strong winds and therefore additional glare protection is necessary. Another way is to install moving elements that allow a clear zone to be maintained for visibility. External Venetian blinds made from aluminium, plastic or wood achieve sun shading reduction factors F_c as low as 0.1. Disadvantages with respect to natural light use can be redressed by having differentially adjustable Venetian blinds in the skylight area. They can also deflect light. On southern facades the steep angle of incidence of the sun means that fixed systems, such as balconies, projections or loggia can also be considered.

Internal systems Internal shading is protected from the weather, can be operated in all wind conditions and provides antiglare protection. The shading effect is considerably less than external systems.

Internal shading could also be in the form of film roller blind or highly reflective Venetian blinds. Solar protection films allow some visibility, with the effect that some relationship with the world outside can be maintained. The solar protection effect is based on reflection away from the building and therefore interacts with the absorption and reflection properties of the glazing. Internal systems can achieve FC-values as low as 0.3. Values measured in practice are often higher than this because of dirt. From the point of view of thermal comfort the heating up of the internal solar shading can be a source of discomfort as the hot shading behaves like a radiator.

Systems in the glazing cavity Movable systems in the plane of the glazing are highly efficient and not affected by wind. The drive motors for the moveable shading in the gazing cavity are prone to breakdowns and when they fail the whole glazing unit needs to be replaced. In addition, the cost of provision is high.

Reflective louvres within the cavity of double glazing achieve g-values as low as 0.5. Shading can be fixed or movable. Fixed systems such as light-diffusing coatings, prints, surface textures or louvres reduce visibility and the entry of light. They are only suitable for areas where visibility is not required. Movable systems consisting of lamellae inside the glazing cavity can be actuated manually or electrically and therefore are easier to adjust to suit user requirements and radiation conditions. The lamellae act as shading and as antiglare measures.

Reduction factor of the shading system F_c [-]
The F_c-value is the reduction factor of the shading system and is used to calculate the total energy transmittance.

Total energy transmittance $g_{tot} = g \cdot F_c$
The total energy transmittance g_{tot} is the product of the total solar energy transmittance g of the glass and the reduction factor F_c of the shading.

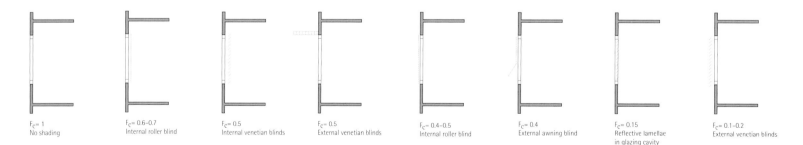

F_c= 1
No shading

F_c= 0.6–0.7
Internal roller blind

F_c= 0.5
Internal venetian blinds

F_c= 0.5
External venetian blinds

F_c= 0.4–0.5
Internal roller blind

F_c= 0.4
External awning blind

F_c= 0.15
Reflective lamellae
in glazing cavity

F_c= 0.1–0.2
External venetian blinds

Fig. 5.1.8 **Arrangement and F_c-values of typical shading systems**

Natural light deflection systems

Good use of natural light cuts down electricity consumption, reduces cooling loads and leads to improved comfort. The objective is to improve lighting conditions, particularly in the depth of the room. For this to happen, a large proportion of light must be deflected deep into the room. The lighting of the area near the window is reduced to the benefit of the depth of the room. This reduction has hardly any significance for workplaces near the window. Efficient light deflection requires light, reflective painted surfaces or reflector elements. Undesirable reflections and glare can be reduced by good daylight deflection systems.

Reflector systems Reflector systems work on the principle that the angle of incidence equals the angle of reflection (Fig. 5.1.9). They can be constructed as light-deflecting Venetian blinds, light shelves or heliostats. Light-deflecting Venetian blinds can achieve good light deflection into the interior of the room. With two-part blinds, the upper blind in the skylight area deflects light into the depth of the room. The lamellae of the lower blind act as shading. Light deflection Venetian blinds allow the user to match the light conditions to his needs. Light shelves provide direct light deflection and even room illumination. They are attached outside in front of the skylight zone of the facade and do not interfere with visibility. This light deflection system is rigid and cannot be guided. On the south side, light shelves act as fixed shading for the summer months. Heliostats, mirrors guided on two axes, can deflect direct sunlight over long distances. Typical areas of application include the improvement of lighting conditions in internal courtyards, vertical light wells or atria.

Prismatic systems Prismatic systems rely on the principle of total reflection (Fig. 5.1.10). They provide selective shading by retro-reflecton outwards and light deflection into the interior of the room. Direct light from certain angles is blocked or aimed into the room. Prismatic panels can be attached in front of the facade, in the facade cavity of double-skin facades, in the glazing cavity or inside the room. Systems fitted into the glazing cavity are maintenance-free. Prismatic systems can be fixed or guidable. They are translucent; visibility is not possible.

Holographic systems Another means of deflecting or aiming natural light is to use holographic films (Fig. 5.1.11). Laser light is used to create a holographic interference pattern. The holographic film is embedded into laminated glass between the two glass sheets. Sunlight striking at a certain angle defined by the interference pattern of the hologram is either deflected or reflected. Diffuse light can pass unobstructed through the transparent elements. The deflected light is neutral in colour (white light hologram). The crucial advantage is that visibility from inside the room is permitted. The holographic film is transparent and has only a slight light-scattering effect. The system is maintenance free thanks to the position of the film in the glazing cavity. Laminated glass with embedded holographic film can be installed either as light deflection lamellae in front of the window or in conjunction with any other desired type of glass in the window. A disadvantage is the high costs.

Daylight factor D = E_p / E_a [%]
The daylight factor D is the ratio of the horizontal illumination of a point in the room (E_p) and the horizontal illumination outside under an overcast sky (E_a).

Tab. 5.1.5 **Comparison of natural light systems**

	Principle	Arrangement at the facade	Shading
Light deflecting venetian blinds	Reflection	Internal, external or in glazing cavity	Yes
Light shelf	Reflection	Internal or external	Partial
Heliostat	Reflection	Internal and external	No
Prismatic system	Retro-reflection, light deflection	Internal or external in Glazing cavity	Selective
Holographic system	Retro-reflection, light deflection	Glazing cavity	Selective

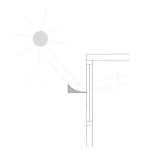

Fig. 5.1.9 **Reflecto**
Light deflection by Venetian blinds, light shelves or heliostats relies on the principle that the angle of incidence equals the angle of reflection.

Fig. 5.1.10 **Prismatic panel**
Prismatic systems provide selective shading. Direct solar radiation within a certain range of angle is deflected and reflected. Zenith light is deflected into the room.

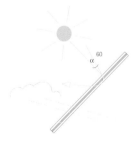

Fig. 5.1.11 **Hologram**
Holograms selectively block sunlight striking them or deflect it into defined areas within the building. Holograms work by bending light. Special photography techniques can minimise spectral scattering of light so that the bent light appears white.

Ventilation elements

"And the jessamine faint, and the sweet tuberose,
The sweetest flower for scent that blows."

Percy Bysshe Shelley 1792–1822
The Sensitive Plant (1820)

HVAC – systems

HVAC components

Air supply elements

Heat recovery

h,x - diagram

HVAC systems

Heating, ventilation and air conditioning systems supply and condition air. They normally consist of several components arranged in series to supply, filter, heat, cool, humidify and dehumidify the air. A heat recovery system is usually incorporated. It is normally advantageous to heat and cool rooms with water-operated systems, as otherwise large volumes of air are required.

Design of HVAC systems All HVAC systems can be expected to replenish and filter room air. In addition, they may also heat, cool, humidify or dehumidify the air. HVAC systems can be subdivided into the ventilation, partial air conditioning and full air conditioning systems. Ventilation systems do not perform any other air treatment functions, except perhaps some heating of the supply air. Partial air conditioning systems perform combinations of two or three thermodynamic air conditioning functions, such as heating and cooling. Air conditioning systems perform all four thermodynamic functions in the treatment of air (Fig. 5.2.1).

HVAC systems can be categorised as low- or high-pressure systems (Tab. 5.2.1). In low-pressure systems, supply air is conducted at low pressure (or velocities) through a duct. In high-pressure systems, air flows through the duct system at very high velocities of between 10 and 25 m/s. To avoid draughts, the velocity is reduced in terminals before the air enters the room. Although they have larger duct cross sections, low-velocity systems have the advantage of using less powerful fans than those required for high-velocity systems.

Induction systems Induction air conditioning systems have air ducts that conduct air to induction devices below windows. These induction devices are combinations of air outlets and heating and/or cooling registers. The registers are connected to cold and hot water networks. The thermodynamic treatment of the air is carried out in a central ventilation plant and in decentralised induction devices. The induction effect draws additional room air into the heat exchanger and conditions the air as required. In this way a higher cooling capacity can be obtained for a given rate of flow of fresh air. Induction devices usually involve a high technical content.

Volume flow In controlled systems with variable volume flows the cooling load for the room and part of the heating load are transported by means of air. All that is required to control temperature is a volume flow regulator. The disadvantage of the system is that the amount of air used is greater than that required for hygienic air changes.

		Air velocity [m/s]	Duct cross section [cm²]
Low pressure system	External ventilation slats	2–3	840–560
	Main duct	4–8	420–210
	Secondary duct	3–5	560–330
	Exhaust air grill	2–3	840–560
High pressure system	Main pipes	15–25	110–67
	Secondary pipes	15–20	110–83
	Connector pipes	< 10	> 175

Tab. 5.2.1 **Comparison of ventilation cross sections**

Boundary conditions
Room area	100 m²
Room height	3 m
Room volume	300 m³
Air changes	$n = 2h^{-1}$
Air flow	600 m³/h

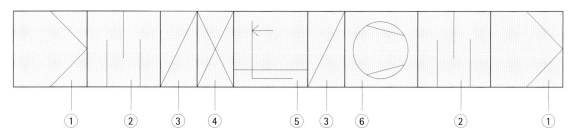

Fig. 5.2.1 **HVAC system, schematic**

Construction of a typical HVAC device for a full air conditioning system with the ability to filter, heat, cool, humidify and dehumidify air
1) Filter
2) Silencer
3) Air heater
4) Air cooler
5) Spray humidifier
6) Fan

HVAC components

Heating, ventilation and air conditioning systems are made up of various components for supplying, treating and filtering air. The components should be selected so that pressure loss is low. Regular servicing and cleaning are required to avoid a reduction in air quality.

Fans Fans are used in equipment rooms and in local ventilation units. The output of a fan can be read off the fan performance curve in which differential pressure is plotted against speed (rpm). There are axial and radial fans. Air flows through axial fans along the fan blade axis. Axial fans are used for small fans as well as in large HVAC equipment rooms. In hybrid ventilation concepts an axial fan can be integrated into a naturally driven supply air-flow as air can still pass through it even when stationary. The fan can be called upon to support natural ventilation if the supply airflow ceases to be adequate. Blade angle and speed (rpm) can be selected to suit the desired output.

Air filters Air filters remove dust and other particles. The filter effect is produced by passing the air through a fibrous material that retains particles greater than a certain size. These particles are categorised as coarse dust, fine dust or submicron particles (Tab. 5.2.2). The particle size retained defines the class of filter. Another means of removal is by an electrofilter, which charges the dust particles and collects them on electrically charged plates. Fibrous filters can be in the form of filter belts or as pockets. Filter belts are wound on automatically as soon as they become clogged and a predefined differential pressure is exceeded. Filter pockets have the advantage of a

greater surface area. Filters must be changed at correct intervals otherwise pressure loss rises and air quality is reduced.

Heating/cooling registers Supply air can be heated or cooled using a heating or cooling register. This involves feeding air into a heat exchanger that has a circulating liquid heating or cooling medium. If the air is cooled below the dew point, condensation forms and the supply air is dehumidified. Heating/cooling registers must be designed to cause low pressure loss and yet have a high air transfer capacity. Higher capacities require more space for heating or cooling registers.

Air humidifiers Especially in winter it may be necessary to humidify the supply air. If this is not done, the heating of the cool outside air reduces its relative humidity and may lead to loss of comfort. Increasing the humidity of air can be done in various ways. Steam can be introduced or water sprayed into the airflow. The evaporated water is taken up by the supply airflow. Ultrasonic atomisers can also be used for humidification. These devices create extremely small particles of water vapour which are carried along by the airflow. It is important to maintain systems properly, otherwise micro-organisms can flourish where air is humidified.

Ventilation registers Ventilation registers are required to open and close junctions in the ducts or to divide the airflow. They are also used to control airflow rates. They can be provided as louvre grills, flaps or sliding gate valves. Typical applications include switching of bypass ducts and the disconnection of areas of a building. Fire dampers are used at the boundaries of fire protection compartments.

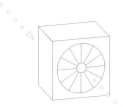

Fan

Filter

Register

Humidifier

Flap

Fig. 5.2.2 **Components of HVAC systems**

	Filter class	Application
Coarse dust filter	G1–G4	Prefilter for coarse dust and prefilter for fine dust filter
Fine dust filter	F5–F9	Prefilter for sub-micron filter, filter for restaurants, halls, hospital wards etc. and prefilter for clean rooms
Sub-micron filter	EU 10–EU 17	Filter for high and highest demands, filtering of finest sub-micron particles such as tobacco smoke, soot, viruses; filters for operating theatres, clean rooms in the chemical and pharmaceutical Industries

Tab. 5.2.2 **Classification and use of filters**

Air supply elements

The air is distributed horizontally and vertically throughout the building from the ventilation equipment room and introduced into individual rooms through supply air openings. Volume flow regulators can be installed in the ducts to regulate airflow. Fire dampers are required where the ducts pass between fire compartments. Overflow openings are required if an atrium is used as a means of conducting the air.

Air ducts The air is distributed through shafts and ducts. Sheet metal ducts are adequate for the vertical distribution of small airflows. Larger airflows can be conducted through masonry or concrete shafts. Horizontal distribution can be done by exposed folded spiral-seam pipes, in flat ducts or in sheet metal ducts integrated into the suspended ceiling. The floor can be specially designed as a double floor to conduct the air. This can give rise to problems of hygiene, however.

Supply air elements Supply air elements are used to introduce air into the room. These elements are designed to suit the type of ventilation, and the use and geometry of the rooms. The most common supply air elements are displacement diffusers, swirl diffusers and long-range nozzles (Tab. 5.2.3). Supply air elements usually mix the supply air with the room air, limit the airflow velocity or direct the air within the room.

Displacement diffusers allow the air to enter the room at low velocity over a wide area, with the effect that the lowest possible amount of mixing with the room air occurs. Swirl diffusers, on the other hand, achieve a powerful mixing with the room air, which means that supply air at a lower temperature than the room air can be introduced into the room with no loss of comfort for the user. Long-range nozzles blow the air in specific directions into the depth of the room. In addition, diffusers draw in room air using the induction effect, which results in a more thorough mixing. They may also improve air distribution by creating airflows close to the ceiling by means of the Coanda effect.

Diffusers can be rectangular, round or slotted. They are often fitted with a valve or flow controller to allow the airflow to be set in each room. Diffusers can be integrated into cupboard walls, suspended ceilings, double floors or, in high occupancy public rooms such as lecture theatres, cinemas or theatres, even in the seating. If the supply air is introduced directly into occupied areas where people are standing or sitting, care must be taken to reduce the air velocity quickly so that no draughts are caused.

Volume flow regulators These devices are used to introduce the required flow of air directly into the duct and can be controlled by a building management system or manually.

Overflow openings If the ventilation concept covers several rooms this would involve overflow openings. At the simplest, they can be slots or grills. Overflow openings must be very carefully designed in relation to sound and fire protection.

Exhaust air elements Removing exhaust air from rooms is much less critical than the introduction of supply air as in general it is not associated with thermal discomfort. Exhaust air elements can be configured like supply air elements or may be simple grills or masked openings. They may be specially integrated into luminaires. These units extract the air through the light fittings. The heat generated by the lamps is taken directly out of the room. The lights do not contribute to the cooling load.

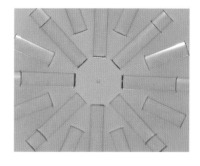

Coanda effect
If the introduced airflow is close to a wall or a ceiling this can give rise to the Coanda effect: The airflow follows the wall or ceiling closely due to a zone of reduced pressure.

Diffuser	Air velocity on exit [m/s]	Diffuser size [cm²]	Volume flow [m³/h]
Displacement diffuser	0.2	1,000	70
Displacement diffuser	0.2	2,000	145
Displacement diffuser	0.2	5,000	360
Swirl diffuser	1.5	250	135
Swirl diffuser	1.5	350	190
Swirl diffuser	1.5	800	430
Slot diffuser	3.0	75	80
Slot diffuser	3.0	150	160
Slot diffuser	3.0	225	240
Long-range nozzle (range 10 m)	4.0	450	650
Long-range nozzle (range 10 m)	8.5	450	1,375
Long-range nozzle (range 10 m)	21,0	450	3.400

Tab. 5.2.3 **Comparison of types of air outlet elements**

Swirl diffuser

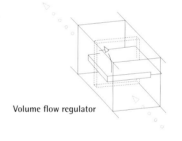

Volume flow regulator

Induction diffuser

Overflow opening

Fig. 5.2.3 **Air supply elements in HVAC systems**

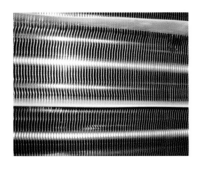

Heat recovery

Heat recovery involves removing the heat from the exhaust air and conducting it into the supply air or heating system. The heat energy introduced for supply air heating is therefore reused. Heat exchangers have different degrees of effectiveness and can be classified according to their design and their method of conduction of supply and exhaust air (Tab. 5.2.4). By the inclusion of an upstream humidifier, the heat recovery system can be used for adiabatic cooling in summer. The exhaust air heat pump is a special form of heat recovery device. The exhaust heat pump abstracts the energy from exhaust air at a higher temperature and it is then conducted into a water-operated system.

Plate heat exchanger A plate heat exchanger is made up of thin parallel aluminium plates spaced at a distance of between 2 to 10 mm. Supply and exhaust air flow through these gaps separately from one another in two cross-flows. There are other types in which the flows take place in opposite directions. The separation of the supply and exhaust airflows ensures that air quality is not detrimentally affected. Plate heat exchangers are very efficient. Supply and exhaust airflows must be brought to a central equipment room.

Rotating heat exchanger A rotating heat exchanger has a slowly rotating wheel between the supply and exhaust airflows that takes up heat from the exhaust air and after rotating through 180° gives up that heat to the incoming cooler supply air. The rotor has axial honeycombed air passages. By using a suitable material for the rotor, a rotating heat exchanger can also dehumidify the air. A disadvantage of rotation heat exchangers is that they may transfer odours and particles, as the airflows cannot be completely kept apart. Their advantage is that they are highly efficient. The supply and exhaust airflows must be brought to the same place.

Heat pipes Heat pipes are evacuated ribbed pipes, in which a refrigerant vaporises and liquefies at a particular temperature. In the bottom half of the pipe, the heat in the exhaust air vaporises the refrigerant whilst the cold of the outside air condenses the refrigerant in the top half of the pipe, which drops into the bottom half again. The exhaust air is cooled and the outside air heated. The system is compact and low maintenance. Industrial heating processes can also use this system.

Liquid coupled systems In liquid coupled systems the supply air and exhaust airflows each have a heat exchanger. These heat exchangers have a liquid storage medium flowing through them. The medium is circulated by a pump. The storage medium takes up heat from the exhaust air duct and then is pumped to the outside air duct, where it gives up its heat to the cold outside air. This has the advantage that the outside air inlet and the exhaust air outlet do not have to be adjacent to one another. There is no detrimental effect on air quality. The disadvantage is the system's low efficiency.

Exhaust air heat pump With this system, heat is extracted from exhaust air and, in higher temperature conditions, transferred to the supply airflow or a radiator system. Supply and exhaust airflows do not have to be brought to the same location and air quality is not detrimentally affected. Additional energy is required for driving the compressor. Efficiency depends very much on the temperature of the exhaust air and the required temperature of heat transfer. A particular area of application is in heat recovery from exhaust air systems that have no supply air feed. The waste air can be cooled below the temperature of the outside air using the exhaust air heat pump.

Plate heat exchanger

Rotating heat exchanger

Heat pipe

Liquid coupled system

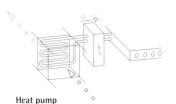

Heat pump

Fig. 5.2.4 **Heat recovery systems**

	Efficiency [%]	Mixing of media	Air flows to be brought to single place in building	Comment
Plate heat exchanger	45–65	No	Yes	Low maintenance
Rotating heat exchanger	65–80	Yes	Yes	May transmit noise
Heat pipe	35–70	No	Yes	Industrial application
Liquid coupled system	40–70	No	No	Low space requirement
Exhaust air heat pump	System dependent	No	No	Heat recovery in exhaust air system possible

Tab. 5.2.4 **Comparison of heat exchangers**

h,x – diagram

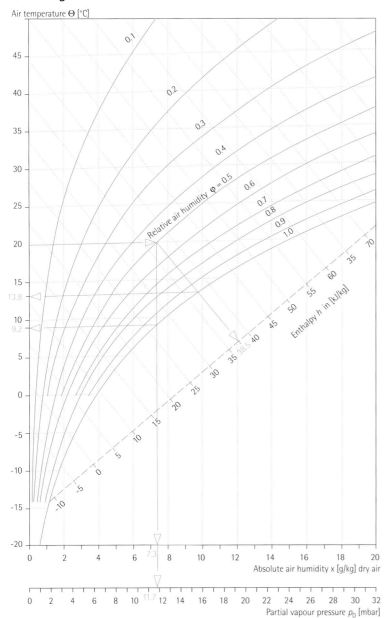

Air temperature Θ [°C]

Relative air humidity φ = 0.5

Enthalpy h in [kJ/kg]

Absolute air humidity x [g/kg] dry air

Partial vapour pressure p_D [mbar]

Fig. 5.2.5 Properties and changes of state of moist air in an h,x diagram (at 1013 mbar)
The h,x diagram can be used to represent or read off parameters and changes of state of moist air. The x-coordinate gives the absolute humidity of the air x [g/kg] and the partial vapour pressure P_D [mbar], whilst the y-coordinate gives the air temperature [°C]. The lines of constant temperature (isotherms) rise slightly from left to right. The various curves in the diagram run through points of constant relative humidity [-]. The curve with the value 1.0 is the saturation curve, i.e. the case where the air is 100% saturated with water. The saturation curve divides the area of unsaturated air (above the curve) from that of oversaturated air (below the curve). The lines of enthalpy h [kJ/kg], the total heat content of the air, are the vertical straight lines.

The dew point temperature p, absolute air humidity x and partial vapour pressure P_D can be read off the diagram for a given temperature (e.g. 20 °C) and relative humidity (e.g. 50%). Follow the appropriate isotherm across to the right (in this example the 20° isotherm). Where this intersects the 50% relative humidity curve, project a straight line vertically downwards. The intersection point with the saturation curve gives the dew point temperature (in this example 9.2 °C). In addition, the x-coordinate gives the absolute air humidity (in this example 7.3 g/kg) and the partial vapour pressure (in this example 11.7 mbar). To determine the enthalpy of the air, take a line from the intersection of the isotherm with the relative humidity curve at right angles to the enthalpy axis. In the example the value of the enthalpy is 38.5 kJ/kg. The intersection of this line with the saturation curve gives the wet bulb globe temperature f. This value represents the lowest possible temperature that can be achieved by humidifying the air. In this example the value is 13.8 °C.

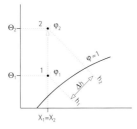

Fig. 5.2.6 Mixing process
If, for example, colder outside air is mixed through in winter (outside air temperature Θ_a, absolute air humidity x_a) with warm inside air (inside air temperature Θ_i, absolute air humidity x_i), this creates a new state of mixed air (mixed air temperature Θ_M, absolute air humidity x_M). The new relative humidity Θ_M is on a straight line between φ_a and φ_i.

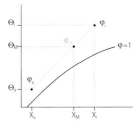

Fig. 5.2.7 Heating process
The temperature rises ($\Theta_2 > \Theta_1$) and whilst the absolute air humidity x remains constant ($x_1 = x_2$), the relative air humidity drops to a lower value ($\varphi_2 < \varphi_1$). The enthalpy rises as the air is supplied with energy in the form of heat ($h_2 > h_1$).

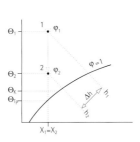

Fig. 5.2.8 Cooling process
If a room is cooled and the absolute humidity x is kept constant ($x_1 = x_2$), the relative humidity rises to a higher value ($\varphi_2 > \varphi_1$). As a result the enthalpy drops ($h_2 < h_1$). To avoid condensation forming on the cooling surface when cooling takes place, the cooling surface temperature Θ_K should always be above the dew point temperature Θ_{Tp}. If the cooling surface temperature Θ_K is below the dew point temperature Θ_{Tp}, then the air must be dehumidified first to prevent condensation from forming.

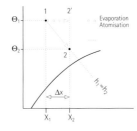

Fig. 5.2.9 Humidifying process
If the air is humidified by vaporisation ($x_2 > x_1$), the enthalpy of the air rises whilst the temperature remains the same. With pure evaporation or atomisation enthalpy remains constant ($h_1 = h_2$) and the air is cooled ($\Theta_2 < \Theta_1$). Follow the lines at right angles to the enthalpy axis to determine the new state of the air.

Technical systems in rooms

"Technology ... the knack of so arranging the world that we need not experience it."

Max Frisch 1911-1991
Homo Faber (1957)

Heat transfer systems

Cold transfer systems

Decentralised unit

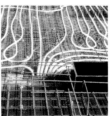
Concrete core activation

Night cooling

Sprinkler systems

Building automation

Lamps

Luminaires

Heat transfer systems

The heat lost from a room must be made up by the heating system. The heat is usually generated centrally, transported to the room by water or air and dissipated into the room by a heat transfer system. In exceptional circumstances, the heat can be generated in the room and dissipated directly by the heat source, e.g. gas radiators for large halls, domestic fireplaces or electrical heaters. Heat transfer systems differ from one another in the method of releasing heat, viz. either radiation or convection (Fig. 5.3.1), the required feed temperature and the method of regulation (Tab. 5.3.1). Heat dissipated by radiation is more comfortable for the user because it avoids the discomfort associated with air movements. Heat transfer systems can compensate for cold air drop and radiation asymmetry.

Radiant panel heating Underfloor, wall or ceiling heating gives off its heat mainly by radiation. Large heat transfer surfaces allow low feed temperatures for which low temperature energy generators may be used. Radiant panel heating may give rise to cold air drop near the facade. Closer pipe spacing in the facade area can overcome this. Due to their thermal inertia, radiant panel heating systems are difficult to regulate effectively. The surface temperature for underfloor heating should not exceed 29 °C. A special form of radiant panel heating is the ceiling radiator panel, which is operated at a higher feed temperature and is suitable for heating high halls by radiation.

Flat radiators These large area radiators release heat mainly by radiation. They contain only a small volume of water and hence respond quickly to controls.

Radiators These ribbed radiators release heat by radiation and convection. The convection proportion increases with depth. Radiators are often used to raise the temperature of supply air provided by natural ventilation to a comfortable level. They require medium feed temperatures and hence respond quickly to controls.

Convectors Convectors release heat mainly through the air flowing past them. They respond quickly to controls and they are relatively small. They are often used as underfloor convectors in front of facades to counteract cold air drop. Their high feed temperatures and the build up of dust between the convector plates are two disadvantages, which can lead to dust particle charring. Convectors can also be used as blower convectors with an integral fan or as supply air induction units by connection to a central supply air system. Heating exclusively by convection is not found as comfortable as heat released by radiation.

Air heating With a good standard of insulation it is possible to provide the required heat along with the air changes that proper hygiene demands. The air can be heated by a heating register centrally or individually for each room. Air heating responds quickly to controls.

Heat radiation
Heat transport by electromagnetic waves. Heat exchange is not possible in the shadow of another object.

Convection
Heat transport is by means of a moving medium. Convection takes place only within a liquid or gas.

Heat conduction
Heat transport within solid bodies. The heat is transferred from molecule to molecule.

	Specific output [W/m²]	Feed temperature [°C]	Controllability	Radiation / convection	Comment
Underfloor heating	40–50	30–35	low	90 / 10	Cold air drop possible
Ceiling heaters	30–60	30–35	good	100 / 0	Can be uncomfortable
Thermoactive ceiling	40	25	low	90 / 10	Self-regulating effect
Ceiling radiator panels	80	80–120	good	100 / 0	For halls
Flat radiators	75	35–55	good	70 / 30	Suitable for refurbishments
Radiators	75	45–65	good	50 / 50	
Convectors	75	60–90	good	20 / 80	Possible hygiene problems
Induction devices	75	30–60	good	0 / 100	Possible hygiene problems
Air heating	50	30–40	good	0 / 100	

Tab. 5.3.1 **Characteristics of different heat transfer systems**

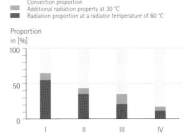

I   Panel radiators (single), no convector plate
II Radiator (pipe radiator)
III Panel radiators (double), three convector plates
IV Ribbed pipe radiator

Fig. 5.3.1 **Proportions of heat transferred by radiation and convection for different types of radiators at a room temperature of 20 °C**

Cold transfer systems

Active cooling is required if the internal and solar loads of a room exceed the outflow of energy by transmission and ventilation. The cold can be conducted to the room by water or air and introduced by various transfer systems. Cold transfer systems can be classified according to their specific capacity, the way they release the cold and the feed temperatures (Tab. 5.3.2). The temperature must remain below the dew point otherwise condensate pipework is required.

Chilled ceiling panels Chilled ceiling panels can be incorporated into the plaster on the soffit of a ceiling, as suspended ceilings or as larger chilled panel "sails". The cold is released mainly by radiation, which means that a higher level of comfort is achieved. Depending on their form of construction, suspended systems can interact with the surrounding room air to achieve a considerable convective effect (Fig. 5.3.2). Some form of dew point-based control to restrict the cooling output and hence prevent water from condensing on the chilled ceilings when there is a condensation risk will be required. For this reason chilled ceilings are often combined with mechanical ventilation and dehumidification equipment. Chilled ceiling panels can also be used with higher feed temperatures, which allows regenerative sources of cooling energy to be exploited.

Downdraught convectors Downdraught convectors positioned close to the ceiling have cold water flowing through them. They create a falling convection current. Condensate pipework is required as the temperature is below the dew point. Downdraught cooling is often positioned behind a facing on a wall with the effect that convection accelerates and the air thus emerges near floor level. Another form of construction is as a chilled beam, which is suspended from the ceiling and often combined with luminaires. These devices sometimes have a fan, which increases the through-flow of air and the cooling capacity without an increase in noise.

Induction devices Centrally preconditioned supply air is conducted through ducts to induction devices. There it is further cooled in a cooling register. The induction effect removes air from the room and cools it, thus increasing the cooling output.

Recirculatory air coolers Room air is extracted by a fan, cooled in a water-operated cooling register and blown back into the room to recirculate. Recirculatory air coolers can achieve high cooling outputs. They can be combined with decentralised refrigeration equipment.

Air conditioning systems The air is cooled and dehumidified centrally and conducted to the room. Large quantities of air are required to achieve higher cooling outputs. High air velocities and large temperature differences require careful design of the way supply air is introduced into the room.

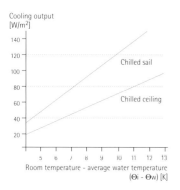

Fig. 5.3.2 **Performance chart for cooling sails and solid chilled ceiling panels**

	Cooling output [W/m²]	Feed temperature [°C]	Controllability	Cooling transfer	Comment
Chilled ceiling	80–120	10–16	very good	Radiation	Dewpoint regulation
Thermoactive ceiling	35–45	16–20	low	Radiation	No suspended ceiling
Downdraught cooling	60–100	6–10	good	Convection	Condensate pipework may be required
Induction devices	60–100	6–10	good	Convection	Condensate pipework may be required
Recirculatory coolers	80–120	6–10	very good	Convection	Condensate pipework may be required
Air conditioning systems	80–120	6–10	good	Convection	Higher installation cost

Tab. 5.3.2 **Typical characteristics of cold transfer systems**

Decentralised equipment

The current trend is towards decentralised ventilation equipment integrated into the facade. The reasons for this lie in the overall reduced technical content, the wish to bring air in directly through the facade, the minimisation of shaft and duct space inside the building and the increased technical flexibility. Decentralised ventilation equipment takes in outside air directly at the facade, heats or cools it, and then introduces it after filtering into the room. Space is saved by locating the equipment close to the facade because ventilation installations are not required elsewhere inside the building. This allows the room height to be reduced and the thermal storage masses kept relatively free. Decentralised ventilation equipment can either be used as supply air devices with a central exhaust air system or as supply and exhaust air devices (Figs. 5.3.3 and 5.3.4).

Ventilation Decentralised ventilation equipment provides ventilation through the facade largely independently of the weather conditions. Air changes are defined whilst the supply air can be preheated in winter and precooled in summer and therefore be introduced into the room in a way not detrimental to comfort. Depending on the arrangement of the equipment, the supply air can be introduced into the room by displacement ventilation or by mixed flow ventilation. Setting the equipment airflow can help avoid discomfort due to high air velocities. Cold air drop in winter can be counteracted by positioning the units under windows. One problem with decentralised ventilation equipment is the interaction with the pressure conditions at the facade. Too high a pressure or suction can lead to the rate of air change being too high or too low. With double-skin facades, this problem can be alleviated by ensuring that air is taken in from the facade cavity under neutral pressure conditions. However, it should be borne in mind that sometimes the air in the cavity may be at quite a high temperature.

Room conditioning Whilst the heating output can be fairly high the cooling output is limited by the dew point (Tab. 5.3.3). A condensate pipe system will be required for higher cooling outputs. This usually results in higher installation costs. A condensate pipework system that outfalls directly to the outside away from the facade is not usually permitted. Depending on the design of the equipment, it may have an integrated heat recovery system. If decentralised ventilation equipment is the only form of installation, then the cooling output will be low and the amount of solar radiation admitted needs to be strictly limited. An attractive option is to combine a decentralised ventilation system with concrete core activation, which allows the combined limited performances of both systems to provide an adequate total output.

Flexibility The advantage of decentralised systems is their great flexibility with regard to technical equipment. The flow of air and the heating and cooling outputs can either be matched to the conditions of use of the room by operating the appropriate devices or by varying the number of devices in operation. This option can also be implemented after the building has passed into use if the appropriate openings have been provided in the facade.

Maintenance The disadvantage of decentralised facade ventilation equipment is the very high maintenance costs, as each device must be separately maintained. This disadvantage can be lessened by adopting a modular design with the maintenance-intensive parts placed together in one block that can be replaced relatively easily. Cleaning the equipment is also simplified so that the maintenance time and the associated disruption of the normal functioning of the offices can be limited to a few minutes. If decentralised ventilation is adopted, the required openings in the facade have to be designed in some detail. In particular, condensation problems at thermal bridges must be avoided.

Equipment type	Cooling output [W]	Heating output [W]
Window sill device at 120 m³/h	600	1200
Underfloor device at 120 m³/h	800	1500

Tab. 5.3.3 **Typical performance data of decentralised equipment**

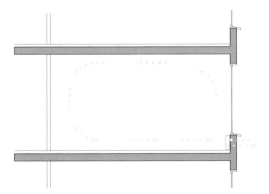

Fig. 5.3.3 **Supply and exhaust air equipment with mixed flow ventilation**

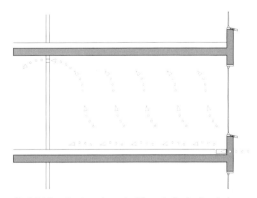

Fig. 5.3.4 **Supply air equipment with centralised exhaust air**

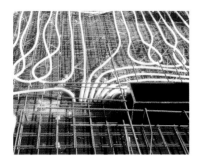

Concrete core activation

In recent years thermoactive ceilings have become very popular. They offer a pleasant room climate, are simple and cost-effective to install and have several benefits in terms of energy consumption. In contrast to chilled ceilings or underfloor heating, thermoactive ceilings temper the whole ceiling construction. The concrete acts as a thermal storage mass and enables a thermal phase shift to be exploited without great expense. In effect this allows cold night air or a chiller not required at night to be used for cooling during the day. Load peaks also can be smoothed out so that a reduced cooling capacity can be installed. The large energy transfer surface allows very small differences between room temperature and the heating or cooling water temperatures. This means that regenerative heat and cold energy generators can be used efficiently and the energy release can be set using the system's self-regulating properties (Fig. 5.3.5).

Construction The pipework is located in the area of the neutral axis of the ceiling construction or in the monolithic screed (Fig. 5.3.9). Location in the monolithic screed simplifies the construction process and any damaged pipes can be simply repaired. In special cases, the screed is placed on impact sound insulation and the ceiling and screed are tempered with two separate pipework systems. This ensures good impact sound deading properties and a

better controlled system. Suspended ceilings and double floors should not be installed as they could interfere with the release of heat energy. This restricts the options for room acoustics and limits technical flexibility.

Controllability The high thermal inertia and the release of heat energy upwards and downwards makes the control of individual room climates somewhat difficult. Room temperatures cannot be adjusted quickly. In practice control devices are oriented towards the sky in order to respond to changes of solar radiation. Energy release in winter and the transition months takes advantage of the system's self-regulating properties. The ceiling temperature is kept at a constant temperature of approximately 23 °C. If the room temperature is above this value the ceiling cools; if the room temperature is below this value it acts as a heater. The transition between heating and cooling is smooth. In summer, the feed temperature is determined by the source of cooling energy and the dew point.

Performance The thermal inertia of the system means that rapid adjustment of the temperature is not possible. Therefore the minimum ceiling temperature should be limited to 18 °C for cooling to avoid the risk of condensation forming. This gives a cooling output of about 40 W/m². The amount of energy transferred every day is somewhere between 300 to 350 Wh/m²d.

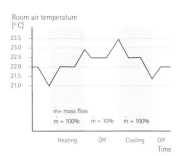

Fig. 5.3.5 Control strategy for a thermo-active ceiling

m= mass flow
$\dot{m}$ = 100% $\dot{m}$ = 10% $\dot{m}$ = 100%

Heating   Off   Cooling   Off   Time

Pipes in the structurally neutral zone of the RC ceiling slab

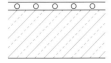

Pipes in screed

Pipes in screed and in the RC ceiling slab

Fig. 5.3.6 Location of the pipes in the thermoactive ceiling

Boundary conditions for Fig. 5.3.7

Facade area	13.5 m²
Office area	22.5 m²
Glazing fraction	70%
Glazing	g = 0.58
Shading external	F_c = 0.20
Internal walls	lightweight
Loads	2 Pers. + 2 PCs
Ventilation 8:00–18:00 hrs	n = 2.0 h⁻¹
Infiltration 18:00–8:00 hrs	n = 0.5 h⁻¹
Climate	Würzburg
Concrete ceiling	25 cm, exposed
Pipes	18/20 mm
Pipe centres	200 mm
Flow	continuous
Mass flow	15 kg/m²h
Feed temperatures	16/18/20/22 °C

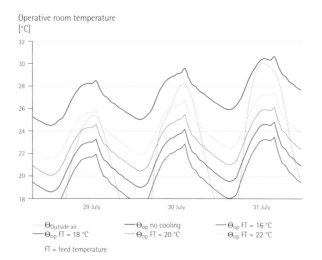

Operative room temperature [°C]

—Θ Outside air   —Θop no cooling   —Θop FT = 16 °C
—Θop FT = 18 °C   —Θop FT = 20 °C   —Θop FT = 22 °C
FT = feed temperature

Fig. 5.3.7 **Graphs of the operative room temperatures with building component cooling on three hot summer days in relation to the available feed temperature**
At feed temperatures of 20–22 °C, e.g. from recooling plants, concrete core activation can offer a noticeable improvement of comfort in summer. If feed temperatures of 16–20 °C are available, then very good conditions can be achieved in summer. This assumes that the amount of solar radiation admitted into the room is limited.

Night cooling

Night cooling exploits the lower temperatures experienced during the night to cool the exposed thermal storage masses in the building. Night cooling therefore offers an effective means of cooling at no additional construction cost. Climatic fluctuations make any guaranteed temperature limits impossible.

Constraints and conditions Night cooling is particularly suitable for parts of the world with high temperature differences between day and night. It is favourable if night-time outside temperatures drop to about 15 °C. The ceilings must be made from concrete and there must be no suspended ceiling or hollow floors. Ideally the internal walls should be solid. Acceptable room temperatures are created if the rate of air change is at least $n = 4 \text{ h}^{-1}$ (Fig. 5.3.8). Large ventilation openings are required for this and they must be protected from the weather and intruders.

Controlled night ventilation Controllable ventilation openings allow cooling to be optimised and overcooling avoided in the transition months. On the other hand they give rise to extra costs for fittings and controls. In practice this is only economically justifiable if controllable

openings were necessary in any case, e.g. for controlled natural ventilation or smoke removal. Thermal or wind-induced flow of air through the building improves cooling, hence the building should have either vertical shafts or opposing facade openings. Overflow openings must comply with the fire protection requirements. If there are no special facade openings or safety aspects that preclude the flow of air through the building then this could also be done mechanically. The disadvantage is the cost of auxiliary energy and the preheating of the supply air by fan waste heat and the duct network. In practice, rates of air change of up to 3 or 4 h^{-1} are quite feasible as long as the ventilation system is already designed to accommodate such high values.

Performance Night cooling can dissipate heat loads of between 200 and 250 $\text{Wh/m}^2\text{d}$. This is enough for a moderately thermally loaded room to have good climatic conditions in summer. Higher loads can be handled in favourable climatic conditions and with extensive thermal storage masses. Temperatures in the morning may be considered to be too low. Low rates of air change are not conducive to achieving optimum conditions but there will still be a noticeable improvement in room air. Adequate thermal storage mass can also be created with phase change materials (PCM).

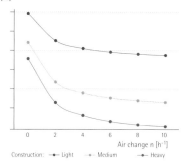

max. operative room temperature [°C]

Fig. 5.3.8 **Influence of usable thermal storage and the rate of air change n on the maximum operative room temperature after several hot summer days**

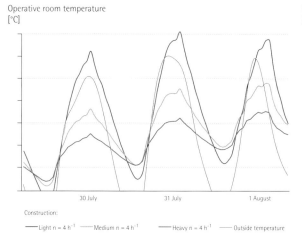

Operative room temperature [°C]

Construction:
— Light n = 4 h^{-1} — Medium n = 4 h^{-1} — Heavy n = 4 h^{-1} — Outside temperature

Fig. 5.3.9 **Influence of the usable thermal storage mass on room climate**
Thermal storage mass is essential for efficient night cooling. The building must be at least of medium weight construction.

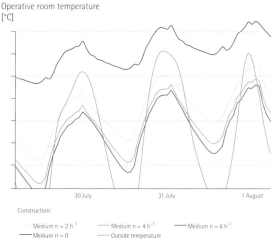

Operative room temperature [°C]

Construction:
— Medium n = 2 h^{-1} — Medium n = 4 h^{-1} — Medium n = 6 h^{-1}
— Medium n = 0 — Outside temperature

Fig. 5.3.10 **Influence of rate of air change n on room climate**
Even low rates of air change will produce a considerable improvement in room climate. Good conditions require a rate of air change of at least 4 h^{-1}.

Boundary conditions applicable to Figs. 5.3.9 and 5.3.10 unless varied as a parameter

Construction heavy:
Internal walls solid, no double floors,
No suspended ceiling

Construction medium:
Internal walls lightweight, no double floors,
No suspended ceiling

Construction lightweight:
Internal walls lightweight, double floors, suspended ceiling

Night cooling 18:00–8:00 hrs   n = 0 to 10 h^{-1}

Office area	22.5 m^2
Facade area	13.5 m^2
Glazing fraction	70%
Glazing	g = 0.58
Shading external	F_c = 0.20
Loads	2 Pers. + 2 PCs
Ventilation 8:00–18:00 hrs	n = 2 h^{-1}
Climate	Würzburg

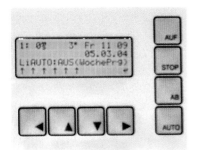

Building automation

Building automation uses instrumentation, measurement, and control devices to ensure that the technical systems in the building operate as required by the conditions. It allows the building to be operated with cost and energy savings. Building management technology provides for the automatic systems to be centrally monitored, adjusted and assessed (Fig. 5.3.11). Fault messages can be transmitted to the responsible servicing and maintenance companies. Today's buildings generally have manufacturer-specific automatic systems optimised for their specific operating needs. This reduces the degree of flexibility and integration. Open systems allow data exchange across all systems in the company and can be extended using non-proprietary equipment.

Modes of operation Building automation can be considered on three levels: the management level with monitoring and operating functions, the automation level with regulating and control programs and the field level with sensors to determine physical parameters such as pressure, temperature, air quality and with interfaces for actuating dimmers, relays, fans and motors.

With conventional electrical installations a circuit is formed from a light and switch. Operating the switch either opens or closes the circuit. If the switch or the light is moved the whole circuit must be reinstalled. With a bus system the situation is different. Instead of a switch there is only a button. Pressing the button causes a processor integrated into the button housing to issue a message and transmit it on the bus system. The light also has a processor, which analyses the messages arriving on the bus. If a message is recognised as intended for the light then it is switched on or off depending on the detail contained in the data.

There are a number of other applications. Measured data can be transmitted, alarm signals sent to a central computer and an SMS or e-mail dispatched. All sorts of devices may be connected to the bus. In general terms, there are units that just send messages (buttons), actuators (lights) that just receive and others that have interfaces that can send and receive (PC).

If the building layout is reorganised, reprogramming the buttons is all that is necessary for them to be able to send their messages to another actuator. There is virtually no limit to the complexity of installations connected to a bus. Conventional electrical installations can also be replaced by a bus system. Advantages include lower cabling costs and greater flexibility. Extensive automation concepts can be implemented quite easily.

Bus systems Bus systems are used by the building automation system to exchange data in a similar way to a computer network. Typical bus systems include the EIB (European Installation Bus), BACnet (Building Automation and Control Network) and LON (Local Operating Network). The European Installation Bus is a decentralised installation system for field-level mode. The EIB transmits energy and information separately. The Building Automation and Control Network is a communications protocol for the management and automation levels. It is specially designed for the requirements of building technical services. It is suitable for use in complex building automation and management systems. The Local Operating Network, like the EIB, is a decentralised installation system for field level. In addition, equipment attached to the bus may have its own software, which results in increased intelligence of the automation at field level. LON is suitable for more complex control and regulation functions.

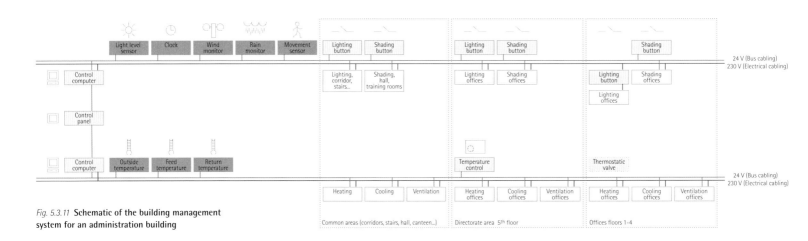

Fig. 5.3.11 **Schematic of the building management system for an administration building**

Sprinkler systems

Sprinkler systems are autonomous fixed fire-extinguishing systems. They provide protection to people and property. Sprinkler systems may also compensate to some degree for departures from the fire protection regulations. They can be used to detect fires at an early stage and fight the fire locally in a targeted way, to limit the fire or even extinguish it. They consist of the protected area, the alarm and the water supply (Fig. 5.3.12).

The protected area is the whole area of the sprinkler-protected parts of the building. The alarm device is based on an alarm valve, which indicates that the system has been triggered by sounding a water-driven bell or an electrical siren. In parallel to the acoustic signal, the triggering of the system must be indicated by sending a signal to a continuously manned location. The extinguishing water supply comes from a storage tank, pumping station or the public water supply.

Wet pipe systems The entire pipework behind the alarm valve in wet pipe systems is kept full of water. If the triggering devices on one or more sprinklers are affected by thermal loads this causes water to be released from the sprinkler heads. If pressure falls in the pipework system, the alarm valve is opened, the alarm activated and the water supply brought into operation. Wet pipe systems are adopted in locations where frost or overheating is unlikely, for example in offices and administration buildings.

Dry pipe systems In dry pipe systems the pipework behind the alarm valve is kept filled with compressed air. Air flows out of the pipework first when a sprinkler is triggered. The fall in pressure opens the alarm valve and the pipework is flooded with water. Dry pipe systems are adopted for areas in which frost is a real danger or where temperatures could exceed 100 °C. They are typically found in underground public car parks.

Quick-acting dry systems are a combination of a dry pipe system and a fire detection system. Smoke detectors or similar devices in the fire detection system cause the pipework to be filled with water before the first sprinkler is opened. Fire extinguishing can start without delay. These systems are used in areas where frost is a danger and a rapid spread of fire is anticipated.

Other special variations include pre-action dry pipe systems, which are also a combination of a fire detection system and a dry pipe system. The extinguishing starts only after triggering of the fire detection system and a sprinkler. This type of system is mainly used in places where a high number of defective sprinklers can be anticipated, e.g. in rail stations, or in places where inadvertent triggering of the sprinkler system could cause a lot of damage to property.

Tandem systems Tandem systems are combinations of wet and dry pipe systems. One or more dry pipe systems are built on to the pipework of a wet pipe system. The alarm is triggered by the pretriggered wet pipe system. Tandem systems are mainly used where frost is a risk in small areas or where local high temperatures are anticipated, e.g. in a canopy or open entrance hall.

Gas fire-extinguishing systems In addition to water-operated systems there are also systems that use gases to extinguish the fires. They are used for protecting particular rooms or equipment. With the exception of a few chemically active extinguishing media, the principle of gas fire-extinguishing systems is based on displacing or diluting the oxygen required for the combustion process to form a non-ignitable mixture of gas and oxygen. The extinguishing medium may be CO_2, an inert gas or halogenated hydrocarbon. Typically these systems are used for electrical switchgear or storage rooms for inflammable liquids. It is important to remember when designing gas fire-extinguishing systems that most of the extinguishing media are hazardous to health and therefore an adequate warning time must be incorporated before the system is triggered. In addition, the walls enclosing the protected area must be able to resist the increased pressures and there must be adequate pressure compensation vents into the open air to conduct the fire or extinguishing gases away without causing damage.

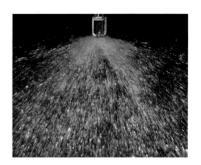

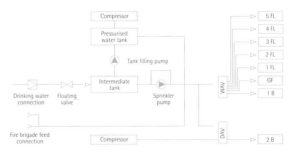

Fig. 5.3.12 **Schematic of a sprinkler system**
On the triggering of a sprinkler head the pressure drops in the wet (WAV) or dry (DAV) alarm valve. Water flows from the pneumatically pressurised water tank, which is kept at a constant air pressure. The pressurised water tank is refilled from a buffer tank. The fire brigade can provide additional water if necessary.

Lamps

Lamps are sources of artificial light and can be classified depending on how they generate their light as either thermal radiators or as discharge lamps. Thermal radiators such as incandescent lamps and halogen lamps give off light from a heated material. Discharge lamps produce light by means of the electrical discharge of gases and vapours. These lamps are divided into low-pressure lamps, such as fluorescent lamps and compact fluorescent lamps, and high-pressure lamps such as metal halide lamps. Light-emitting diodes (LED), on the other hand, belong to a group called electro-illuminescent radiators. They rely on a semiconductor circuit that converts electrical current into light. In some cases the various lamp types have very different characteristics with respect to luminous efficacy, switch-on behaviour and replacement life (Tab. 5.3.4). With this in mind, the selection of the lamp type must take into account the conditions of use and the particular requirements of the room.

Incandescent lamps Incandescent lamps are the most common form of artificial light source. They are thermal radiators and obtain their light from a tungsten filament, which is made to glow by an electric current. Incandescent lamps produce very natural colours. The lower colour temperature of the radiated spectrum gives a pleasant warm light, similar to evening sunlight. They are mainly used in the domestic environment. The disadvantage of incandescent lamps is their very low luminous efficacy (5%) and a relatively low replacement life (approx. 1,000 operating hours). Dimming greatly increases lamp life.

Halogen lamps These lamps work on the same principle as incandescent lamps. The difference is that the glass cylinder contains a small amount of a halogen, which delays the vaporisation process of the filament and therefore permits operation at higher temperatures. Luminous efficacy and replacement life can be as much as doubled,

which means the lamps are more economic. Low-voltage halogen lamps are becoming more and more popular. They are distinguishable by their high light output and very compact design.

Fluorescent lamps In Germany around 80% of artificial light is created using fluorescent lamps, which find their main use in factories and offices. In contrast to thermal radiators, in these lamps pre-excited gas atoms provide the light energy. Different fluorescent materials can be used as lamp fillings to obtain a wide range of colour and brightness. Lamps in general use are those that give off something like natural light. They are very economic with a luminous efficacy of almost 50% and a replacement life of up to 15,000 operating hours. Operation with an electronic ballast reduces power consumption and provides a steady non-flickering light.

Compact fluorescent lamps, also known as energy-saving lamps, are a further development of fluorescent lamps. Like incandescent lamps, they are mainly used in the home. Compared with incandescent lamps, they consume only a fifth of the energy and last eight times as long with a replacement life of up to 8,000 hours. However, the quality of their light does not match that of an incandescent lamp.

Metal halide lamps These lamps are termed mixed light lamps. Like incandescent lamps, when switched on a tungsten wire heats up and after a short time all the radiation is produced from mercury discharge. Metal halide lamps are notable for their very high luminous efficacy and replacement life of up to 9,000 operating hours.

Luminous efficacy / efficiency

This term is the ratio of the luminous flux to the connected electrical load. The luminous efficacy of a lamp is measured in lumen per watt (lm/W). It is used mainly in the context of administration buildings as an indication of economy.

Colour temperature

This describes the colour of the light from a light source. The colour spectrums of the different groups: warm white (ww), neutral white (nw) and daylight white (dw), render the illuminated object differently. Whilst the colour temperature of a thermal radiator is almost the same as the actual temperature of the heated filament, the colour temperature of a discharge lamp is given in terms of a reference light source.

Colour rendering

Lamps radiate different spectrums and therefore vary in the quality of their rendering of the original colour of an object. The colour rendering index Ra and the colour rendering level express the amount of deviation from the reference light source. The ideal value is 100.

Tab. 5.3.4 **Typical values for various lamps**

Lamp type	Luminous efficacy [lm/W]	Colour rendering index R_a, Soll = 100	Colour temperature	Replacement life [h]	Examples of use	Comment
All purpose lamps (A)	10–20	100	ww	1,000	Living areas, gastronomy	Dimmed operation considerably extends the replacement life
Halogen lamps (QT)	15–25	100	ww	1,500–2,000	Shop windows, museums, galleries, restaurants	Dimmed operation extends the replacement life
Low voltage halogen lamps (QT, LV)	25			2,000–3,000		Dimmed operation extends the replacement life
Fluorescent lamps (T)	up to 100	90 and above	ww, nw, dw	8,000–15,000	Industry, office	Operation with an electric choke considerably extends the replacement life, dimming is possible but it does not extend replacement life
Compact fluorescent lamps (TC)	50–85	90 and above	ww, nw, dw	8,000–12,000	Living areas, commercial and corporate image premises	Operation with an electric choke considerably extends the replacement life, dimming is possible but it does not extend replacement life
Metal halide lamps (HIT)	up to 100	60 – 70	ww, nw, dw	5,000–9,000	Outdoor lighting	Dimming from 70 W power consumption possible but does not extend replacement life

Luminaires

Luminaires distribute and filter artificial light and are necessary to accept, support, protect and supply energy to lamps. Glare and economic efficiency are the most important criteria in administration buildings. There is a variety of luminaires available for all types of lamps. There are two basic types. Stationary luminaires such as downlights, uplights, louvre luminaires and washlights are in permanent position and radiate in a given direction. Movable luminaires such as spotlights, on the other hand, are used mostly in groups or tracks and are usually flexible in their direction of radiation. Light effects are produced from the interaction of lamp, luminaire and the lighting environment.

Downlights Downlights are normally fixed to the ceiling and are directional, usually pointing downwards (Fig. 5.3.13). Narrow-beam downlights illuminate relatively small areas and create less glare than wide-beam types thanks to their greater cut-off angle. Darklight technology works with a very narrow light cone and identical cut-off angles for the lamp and reflector.

Uplights Uplights are normally integrated into the floor or walls. They radiate light upwards and provide indirect room lighting or accentuated wall lighting using grazing light.

Louvred luminaires These luminaires were designed for linear light sources such as fluorescent lamps and energy-saving lamps. They have covers consisting of grids that cut off the light, deflecting mirrored reflectors or prismatic panels. Installation can be flush or surface mounted or as suspended luminaires. Louvred luminaires have wide-beam symmetrical light distribution curves and are therefore mainly used to illuminate areas. Cut-off grids can affect the beam direction and with that the amount of direct light. Computer monitor desk louvred luminaires can be fitted with highly effective reflectors so that the light distribution and glare cut-off can be adjusted to suit the requirements of the user. Direct-indirect louvred luminaires give out light downwards. At the same time they direct light upwards and illuminate the ceiling to give an overall indirect diffuse light.

Washlights Washlights are used to give an even light over an area. Wall washers are mounted on the ceiling and illuminate walls and sometimes parts of the floor. Ceiling washers provide additional illumination of the ceiling to give an overall diffuse light (Fig. 5.3.14). Floor washers are installed in the lower part of a wall and used mainly to illuminate corridors and circulation zones.

Spotlights Spotlights are movable luminaires. Their narrow-beam light distribution is suitable for the direct illumination of objects and accent lighting. Narrow-beam types (spots) and wider beam distribution types (floods) have different beam angles. The defined narrow beam requires compact lamp types such as incandescent lamps, halogen lamps or compact fluorescent lamps. Point light sources such as metal halide lamps provide a particularly concentrated beam of light.

Intelligent luminaires These luminaires allow changes of illumination level and lighting colour. Individual control means lighting conditions can be adjusted to suit actual activities or personal mood or can be based on stored illumination levels. For larger rooms with little natural light, lighting can be made to follow particular cycles and match the dynamics of natural light.

Lighting control Different environments and uses demand flexible lighting systems. Separate switching of individual luminaires is essential. Electronic storage of different lighting scenarios is useful for complex lighting systems. Remote control receiver modules in individual or groups of luminaires on the same circuit or distribution boxes respond to infrared signals to switch on or dim the connected luminaires.

Luminous intensity distribution curve
The luminous intensity distribution curve is a section through the 3-D luminous intensity distribution graph that shows the luminous intensity of a light source for all room angles. For rotationally symmetrical light sources, the distribution of luminous intensity can be represented by a single curve. Two or more curves are required for axially symmetrical light sources.

Luminous intensity
Luminous intensity is the spatial distribution of luminous flux. It represents the luminous flux of a light source per solid angle and refers to a particular direction. Luminous intensity is measured in candela (cd).

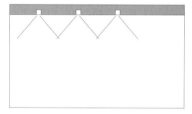

Fig. 5.3.13 **Direct lighting**

Fig. 5.3.14 **Indirect lighting**

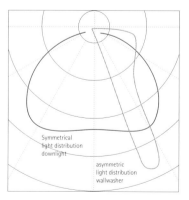

Symmetrical light distribution downlight

asymmetric light distribution wallwasher

Fig. 5.3.15 **Luminous intensity distribution curves of downlights and wall washers**

Tab. 5.3.5 **Light output ratios of various luminaires**

Lamp type	Luminaire operating efficiency [%]
Non-directional luminaires	approx. 90
Reflector luminaires	approx. 50–70
Luminaires with transparent plastic covers	approx. 60
Suspended luminaires	approx. 70

Heating and cooling energy generation

"Solar Architecture is not about fashion – it is about survival."

Norman Foster

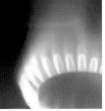

Conventional heating and cooling energy generation

Heat pumps

Power-heat coupling (PHC), combined heat and power plant

Fuel cells

Renewable fuels

Energy from ground water and earth

Solar collectors

Absorption and adsorption chillers

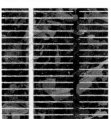

Photovoltaics – solar electricity generation

Air-earth heat exchanger

Energy storage

Conventional heating and cooling energy generation

The boiler is the most popular form of heat generator. Energy sources such as oil, gas or solid fuels can be burned in boilers. The heat released is given up to the heat transmission medium (water) in a heat exchanger. The lower the waste gas temperature, the higher the efficiency. Cooling energy is normally used in combination with room air treatment systems or chilled ceilings. The most widespread cooling system is a compression chiller in combination with a heat recovery plant.

Low temperature boiler These boilers can be operated continuously with return temperatures of 35 to 40 °C with no danger of corrosion from condensing water. Ribs or more than one wall skin prevent the surface temperature from falling below the dew point. The temperature can be gradually allowed to drop, to an extent that depends on the boiler design. The boiler can be shut down at night to reduce standby losses and hence operating costs. In two-stage operation the boiler operates at its higher output on days of extreme frost only. On all other days it can be run at the lower output. Multistage or infinitely adjustable low temperature boilers can also be operated at a feed temperature of 90 °C. They are suitable as replacements for old standard boilers.

Gas circulatory water heaters These heaters were originally developed to heat service water and as a compact means of generating hot water. Hence they are suitable for heating single floors or for small residential properties. The upper limit of their performance is between 24 and 35 kW, which is generally adequate for providing heating and warm service water in one- or two-unit dwellings. The cost of the equipment is low and the space requirement minimal, no need for heat or fuel storage. Gas circulatory water heaters are suitable for low and high temperature operation.

Condensing boilers The condensing boiler represents a further step in low temperature technology with respect to the cooling of combustion gases. Condensing boilers are designed to continuously condense a large proportion of the steam in the combustion gases. When steam is condensed to give water a lot of energy is released. This is latent heat. In condensing boilers the hot combustion gases are cooled by the return water feed until condensation forms. This takes place in a secondary stainless steel combustion gas heat exchanger. Sensible heat as well as latent heat is transferred from the combustion gases into the return water flow by this process. Expressed in terms of the net calorific value n.c.v., an efficiency of 110% can be achieved. For a condensing boiler to work the return flow temperature must be below the dew point of the

steam in the combustion gases. Depending on the CO_2 content of the combustion gases, the dew point lies between 45 and 57 °C. Low temperature heating systems are suitable for operation with condensing boilers. Gas is the usual fuel as its combustion gases contain less sulphur than those of heating oil and have a higher dew point.

The combustion gases leave the condensing boiler at a temperature so low that the thermal draught in the chimney needs to be supported with a fan. The chimney should be lined with a gas-tight condensate-resistant internal liner. Stainless steel, glass or fireclay are suitable materials for the liner. Plastic liners are also permissible. The condensate from the condensing boiler is moderately to strongly acidic and is conducted into the sewer system.

Compression chillers Their construction is identical to that of compression heat pumps. Adopting the reverse of heat pump principle, these chillers use the latent heat of evaporation to cool the cold water feed. The heat arising in the condenser has to be conducted away in a separate cooling circuit so that the refrigeration process works. It is beneficial in terms of energy savings to use the unwanted heat energy for warming service water or heating. This assumes that there are concurrent cooling and heating requirements. This is seldom the case in normal offices.

Recooling plants These plants cool the warmed water emerging from the condenser in a chiller. If the outside temperature is low, air can be used as the coolant. Recooling plants are normally one of three types. With open recooling plants, the cooling water trickles in a thin film over the surface of a heat exchanger, is cooled by the flow of air and evaporation and is then returned to the cooling circuit. Fresh water must be continuously added to top up losses caused by evaporation and spray. With closed circuit recooling plants, the cooling water circuit is separated from the airflow by a heat exchanger, which is cooled by trickling water applied in a spray. Closed-circuit recooling plants require larger cooling towers than open systems. Dry cooling towers function as closed systems without trickling water. Cooling towers are normally located on roofs.

Latent heat
Latent heat is the quantity of heat evolved or absorbed at a change of physical state. The term 'latent' applies because this taking up or release of heat is not accompanied by a change in temperature of the medium. The heat is "hidden". Examples: latent heat of evaporation, fusion or crystallisation.

Sensible heat
Sensible heat can be felt and detected by a change in temperature of the material.

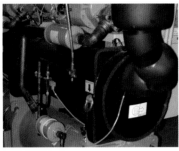

Heat pumps

Heat pumps work on the fact that every body contains a certain amount of energy. A heat pump draws heat from the surroundings at a lower temperature and releases it at a higher temperature into the heating system of a building.

Functional details A heat pump basically consists of four components: an evaporator, a compressor, a condenser and an expansion valve (Fig. 5.4.1).

The refrigerant is evaporated in the evaporator at a pressure of about 3 bar. This draws sensible heat from its surroundings but does not increase the temperature of the refrigerant as the heat is absorbed as latent heat of evaporation. The compressor then compresses the refrigerant to about 12 to 22 bar, with the increase in pressure the temperature of the refrigerant rises. The compressor requires energy to operate. This is normally electrical energy. The high pressure sharply raises the condensation point of the refrigerant so much that heat can be transferred on the consumer circuit (in this case the heating circuit). This could be, for example, the feed of a hot water heating system at a temperature of 30 to 45 °C.

The refrigerant under high pressure is condensed in the condenser and releases its heat in the consumer circuit. This takes place mainly through the transfer of latent heat. Then the refrigerant flows through the expansion valve. The pressure loss sharply cools the refrigerant and it is able to absorb heat from the surroundings again in the evaporator.

The smaller the difference in temperature between the surrounding heat and the heating circuit, the more efficient the heat pump works. Heating systems with low feed temperatures operate very well with heat pumps.

Heat sources Earth, air or water can be used as heat sources. The heat is normally transferred on a water-operated circuit.

The water can be surface, ground or waste water. An important prerequisite for the use of lake or river water is that it is at an adequately high temperature all year round. The temperature of surface water follows the outside temperature with a slight time shift. The water temperature must not fall below freezing point for a cooling of 4 to 5 K otherwise the heat exchanger could ice up. Ground water has an almost constant temperature of about 10 °C all year round. The water is abstracted from a well, taken through the evaporator and then returned to the ground down an injection well. Ground-water heat pumps can be used effectively even in the depth of winter. Waste water from industrial plants and commercial equipment (e.g. coolant water, sewage treatment water) likewise offers a constant potential heat supply.

The outside air is an easily accessed potential source of energy, although its temperature is subject to large fluctuations. The air temperature is at its lowest in winter when the heating requirement is at its highest. The waste air at a constant temperature from a ventilation plant is much more suitable.

A system of pipes or boreholes is necessary to exploit the earth as a heat source. The pipes are buried over an area approximately 2 m deep in the earth. A mixture of water and glycol is pumped through them, which then releases its heat in the evaporator. Moist loamy soils are very suitable. The area required is 2.5 to 3 times the heated area. Boreholes are suitable for smaller pieces of land or for retro-installation as part of a refurbishment project. At a depth of 15 m, the earth temperature is constant throughout the year at between 10 to 14 °C. Usually a plastic pipe is installed in the ground and a mixture of water and glycol pumped through it.

Operation If a heat pump is the only equipment used for heating, this is termed monovalent operation. In bivalent alternative operation, the heat pump supplies heating when the outside temperatures are high and is switched off when they are low. A conventional heating boiler then takes over the task of heating. In bivalent parallel operation, a conventional heating boiler is switched on when heating demand is high and the heat pump runs in parallel.

Energy efficiency factor and season energy efficiency factor

The energy efficiency factor ε is the ratio of the usable heat energy Q_h and the energy required to drive the compressor P_{el}

$$\varepsilon = \frac{Q_w}{P_{el}}$$

The value of ε varies between 2 and 4. This means that between 2 and 4 kilowatt hours can be extracted from the surroundings for each kilowatt hour of electricity used in extracting it. The average energy efficiency factor over the whole year is the seasonal energy efficiency factor β.

Fig. 5.4.1 **How heat pumps work**

1 *The refrigerant evaporates and in doing this absorbs heat from its surroundings.*
2 *The compressor compresses the refrigerant to between 12 and 22 bar, as a result of which its temperature and condensation point rise.*
3 *The condenser condenses the refrigerant under high pressure and releases its heat to a consumer circuit.*
4 *The expansion valve produces a pressure drop and leads to a cooling of the refrigerant and dropping of the condensation point*

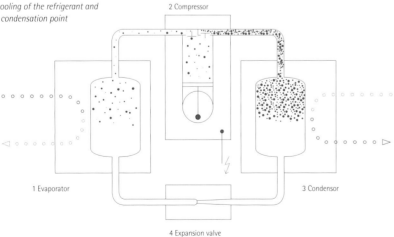

2 Compressor

1 Evaporator

3 Condensor

4 Expansion valve

Power-heat coupling (PHC), Combined heat and power plant (CHP)

The processes involved in power-heat coupling are just as common in central power plants as they are in decentralised combined heating and power plants. They generate electricity and heat at a high temperature. This heat can be used for heating or as process heat. This dual use results in better use of the primary energy source (Tab. 5.4.1). Power-heat coupling is therefore always viable where there are steady and coexistent demands for electricity and heat. In Germany the heating demand in summer is only 10% of that in winter. The demand for electrical power on the other hand is relatively constant over the whole year. In summer it still amounts to 85% of the electricity demand in winter. Power-heat plants are therefore normally designed on the basis of heating heat demand. Plants with power-heat coupling should be used for more than 5,000 hours per year in order to work efficiently.

District heating In power-heat plants the heat is decoupled from the steam turbine process and fed into a district heating system. The distribution of heat is mainly by hot water and high pressure. Each house has a heat transfer station in which a heat exchanger releases heat to the domestic system.

Power-heat plants are therefore only viable if there is a high requirement for heat in the locality (within a radius of about 10 km). The heat created centrally is distributed over an extensive district heating network, which is responsible for high costs and heat losses of between 8 and 15%. The excess of heat energy in summer can be used to generate cooling energy by means of absorption or adsorption chillers.

Combined heat and power plant (CHP) These power plants use internal combustion or diesel motors to drive a generator. Combined heat and power plants may also use fuel cells. The most common fuel is natural gas; others include heating oil, landfill or biogas. The waste heat of the motor created during combustion can be used by waste gas heat exchangers and coolant water heat exchangers for heating (Fig. 5.4.2). CHPs usually supply heat at a temperature of 80 to 90 °C. The heat is distributed over a district heating network.

Combined heat and power plants are typically used outside conurbations. Small CHPs with capacities of up to 5 kW electrical output (kWel) are suitable for use in apartment blocks. Large CHPs with marine diesel motors with outputs of up to 10,000 kWel can be used for the production of electricity and heat for residential areas and factories. Viable areas of use for CHPs with concurrent relatively constant heat and electricity demands include, for example, hospitals, swimming pools, and commercial premises with high process heat requirements.

Used mainly in residential and office buildings, CHPs are designed for approximately 50% of the maximum heat output. The proportion of the total heat produced is therefore about 80%. Peak outputs are achieved by using additional conventional heating boilers with short annual operating periods. Normally several units (modules) are installed. At any one time the demand is covered by one or more modules. Further modules can be added in a cascade arrangement if the designed heat requirement increases. The excess of heat energy in summer can be used to generate cooling energy by means of adsorption chillers.

Power plant type	Primary energy efficiency η [%]
Nuclear power	34
Gas turbine	38
Coal	42
Gas/steam turbine	55–60
Combined heat and power	80
Power-heat coupling	85–90
Hydroelectric	95

Tab. 5.4.1 **Efficiency of different types of power plants**

Fig. 5.4.2 **Layout of a district heating network with a combined heat and power plant**

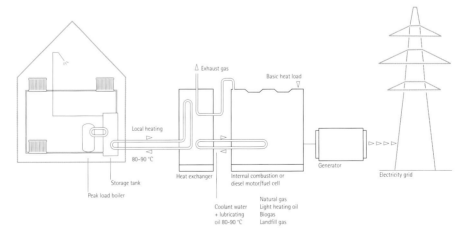

Fuel cells

In fuel cells chemical energy is converted directly into electrical energy. They work continuously, as long as they are fed with fuel and an oxidising agent. Applications range from vehicle drives, domestic heating and large-scale power plants to mobile phones and notebooks. Fuel cells create electrical power with an efficiency of between 40 and 70%. Waste heat can be used as process heat or for heating purposes. Fuel cells can cope with fluctuating loads without significant loss of efficiency. Their efficiency reaches maximum by the time they are loaded up to half capacity.

Functional details In fuel cells an energy source containing hydrogen (hydrogen, methane, natural gas) is converted directly into electrical energy in a catalytic combustion process. Heat is generated as a by-product. The fuel cell reverses the process of electrolysis by which water is split into hydrogen and oxygen with the help of electrical energy. Fuel cells are relatively simple to construct. The cell consists of two electrodes, the anode and the cathode, and between them the ion-transporting electrolyte. The electrodes are made from platinum and act as catalysts. They trigger an oxidisation process that does not actually involve combustion in the traditional sense. The anode is supplied with the hydrogen fuel, the cathode with the oxygen oxidising agent (Fig. 5.4.3).

The fuel cell generates direct current at a voltage of between 0.6 and 0.9 volts. To arrive at usable volt-ages, multiple cells are connected in series in what are called stacks. The stacks of cells can produce voltages of up to 200 volts. The strength of the electrical current is proportional to the area of the electrodes and can reach 0.1 to 1 A/cm^2, depending on the cell type and operating conditions. The direct current is converted into alternating current by an inverted rectifier. Stationary plants normally use atmospheric oxygen and natural gas. Before the combustion process, the natural gas is reformed into a hydrogen-rich synthesis gas.

Cell types Fuel cells are grouped according to their type of electrolyte. Fuel cells can be low temperature (up to about 200 °C) or high temperature (up to about 1,000 °C).

The polymer electrolyte membrane fuel cell (PEMFC) finds the widest use. With a temperature of up to 120 °C, the PEMFC is a low-temperature fuel cell. It is very flexible and simple to operate for anything from mobile phones and power-heat power plants to vehicle drives. Its range of output extends from less than 1 kWel up to 1 MW_{el}. PEM plants for smaller buildings with an output ranging up to 5 kW_{el} are being developed. The PFM fuel cell boasts low weight combined with high power density and requires atmospheric oxygen instead of pure oxygen as its reaction gas. The output of a PEM fuel cell responds well to controls. It is suitable for mobile use and decentralised energy supply.

High temperature fuel cells are mainly used in power plants. Their range of output is between 1 kW_{el} and 10 MW_{el}. Their temperature range is between 600 and 1,000 °C.

Fuel cell reaction

Hydrogen and oxygen are converted into electrical current in a fuel cell. The reaction can be considered as two separate reactions. Water is produced as a by-product.

Anode reaction
$$2 H_2 \rightarrow 4 H^+ + 4e^-$$

Cathode reaction
$$O_2 + 4 H^+ + 4e^- \rightarrow 2 H_2O$$

Total reaction
$$2 H_2 + O_2 \rightarrow 2 H_2O$$

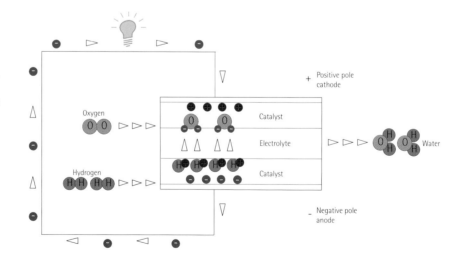

Fig. 5.4.3 **How fuel cells work**
In a conventional hydrogen-oxygen cell a wafer-thin membrane of electrolyte allows only protons to pass (positively charged hydrogen ions (H^+). The electrons of the hydrogen atoms are separated by the catalyst and are held back whilst the hydrogen ions react with the oxygen ions on the other side. The excess electrons on the hydrogen side and the deficiency of electrons on the oxygen side of the electrolyte form a positive and negative pole. These free electrodes flow over an external circuit to the cathode and thus create an electrical potential. Electrons flow continuously from the anode to the cathode with a closed external circuit and a constant supply of fuel.

Renewable fuels

Land and aquatic plants convert around 0.1% of radiated energy into biomass by processing carbon dioxide. When organic material is burned it releases the bound carbon dioxide into the atmosphere again. Biomaterials are therefore CO_2-neutral (Fig. 5.4.4). Biomaterials are considered in three different groups in the context of heating: solid fuels (wood, straw), liquid fuels (plant oils, alcohol) and gaseous fuels (biogas).

Wood In Europe wood is the renewable raw material most often used for the generation of energy. It is supplied mainly as a by-product from forestry (thinnings) and the wood processing industries. There is still great potential in the use of straw residue and wood energy from cultivation of short-term rotational crops with growing periods of between one and four years (poplar, reeds, miscanthus). Wood is burned as logs, wood chips or pellets. Wood-chip heating is suitable for auxiliary heating (fireplace or tiled stove) and for central heating of individual homes. Wood chips come direct from forestry operations. They require greater storage space and a mechanised fuel feed. They are very suitable for larger heating plants. Wood pellets are formed under high pressure out of sawing waste. They are very easy to handle and store. Pellets are supplied in bags or by tanker. Charging can be fully or partially automatic (for single furnaces). Pellet heating is most suitable for central heating. A store of about 0.9 m³ is required for each kilowatt of heat output. A temporary heat buffer is necessary so as not to waste any heat produced at a time when it is not wanted.

Plant oil Rape is the most common type of oil plant cultivated in Germany. Each hectare yields between three and five tonnes of rape seed. Natural plant oil is used as fuel for combined heat and power plants (CHP) in duotherm motors (Elsbett process) or in conventional indirect injection diesel motors.

To make plant oil the seeds are ground and then cold pressed and filtered. Unlike biodiesel, pure rape oil is not chemically produced. Biodiesel is made by heating rape oil and methanol (earlier known as wood alcohol) in the presence of a catalyst (sodium hydroxide). The chemical transformation process causes glycerin and methanol to change places and the result is three individual fatty-acid methylester chains and a glycerin molecule.

Biogas Like natural gas, biogas also consists mainly of methane. Methane is odourless and inflammable. It is always formed when biological materials undergo bacterial decay in anaerobic conditions. In Germany biogas is mainly produced from agricultural waste and production residues from the food industry. The chemical conversion takes place in four stages. Various types of bacteria break up the raw waste in a processing tank (digestor, fermenter) into methane, carbon dioxide and water. The residue from the fermentation process can be used as manure by the local farmers. Biogas is normally used in combined heat and power plants locally to generate electricity and heat. About 30% of the heat evolved is necessary for the biogas process itself, the remainder can be used for heating in a district heating system. The electricity is fed into the public grid. Further similar waste methane-containing gases include sewer gas or fermentation gases from sewage treatment works, fire damp from mines or landfill gases from refuse tips.

Fuel	Calorific
Wood pellets	5.0 kWh/kg
Wood chips	3.8 kWh/kg
Logs	4.2 kWh/kg
Rape oil	10.0 kWh/kg
Biodiesel	10.2 kWh/kg
Diesel	11.9 kWh/kg
Biogas	6.0 kWh/m³
Natural gas	10.0 kWh/m³
Hydrogen	3.0 kWh/m³

Tab. 5.4.2 **Calorific values of different regenerative and conventional fuels**

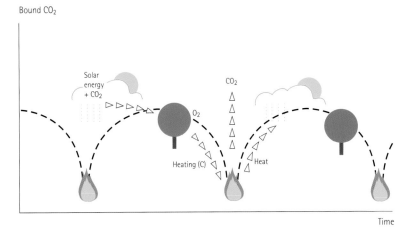

Fig. 5.4.4 **The CO_2 balance of biomaterials is neutral**
The amount of CO_2 bound in the growing phase is equal to the amount released during combustion.

Solar collectors

Germany has between 900 and 1,200 kWh/m² of available solar energy per year. For thermal use of this potential energy source, solar collectors convert the sunlight into heat in absorbers. The overwhelming majority of thermal solar collectors are used for heating potable water. Depending on the design, an annual average of 50 to 70% of the energy required for heating water could be saved. In well-insulated buildings such as low-energy houses, thermal solar installations can also be used to supplement heating. As an annual average the optimum collector direction is between 30 to 40° south. The yield is only slightly sensitive to small deviations in inclination and orientation.

Types The simplest form of thermal solar collector is the absorber. It consists of black plastic hoses laid out on open surfaces or roofs. Absorbers are particularly suitable for installation in open-air swimming pools, where maximum availability of solar energy coincides with the period of maximum use. The water in the pool is heated directly as it is pumped through the absorber. This system achieves water temperatures some 20 °C above the outside air temperature.

Higher temperatures can be achieved with glazed collectors. Absorber plates connected to a pipework system are fitted into a well-insulated housing with a glass cover. A heat transfer medium, incorporating suitable protection against frost, such as a water-glycol mixture, is pumped through the pipework. Flat plate collectors can achieve temperatures of about 50 °C and efficiencies of 50 to 60%. Metals like copper or aluminium are normally used as absorber materials and can be given special coatings to maximise the absorption of solar energy and prevent radiation losses. Antireflective glass can be used to cover the collectors, which increases the amount of radiation admitted to between 90 and 95%. Flat panel collectors are also available in the form of vacuum panels. The

vacuum inside the collector reduces the heat losses due to convection.

Vacuum tube collectors offer improved efficiencies and higher temperatures. The evacuated glass tubes contain absorber strips. The vacuum provides ideal thermal separation and keeps convection heat losses to a minimum. The vacuum tube is connected at one end to a manifold and from there the solar energy is carried by the pumped heat transfer medium to the thermal store. A dry connection by a heat pipe can enable damaged vacuum tubes to be replaced even whilst the system is running. Vacuum tube collectors can achieve temperatures of up to 70 °C above the outside temperature. Vacuum tube collectors are particularly suitable for auxiliary heating and process heat.

Heat storage Typical systems for heating service water consist of a two-circuit system, which keeps the solar heating circuit separate from the service water circuit. The solar heating circuit charges a service water tank by means of a heat exchanger. Controls are designed to start up the circulatory pump as soon as the collector temperature reaches a few degrees above the storage temperature. In summer the heat gained is usually sufficient for heating service water. In winter the water is preheated by solar energy and then fully heated by a conventional boiler.

A two-storage tank system is normally used to provide auxiliary heating (Fig. 5.4.5). A large buffer storage tank provides heated service water and acts as buffer supply for days without sunshine. The service water tank has priority. A conventional boiler heats the upper part of the storage tank (the stand-by volume) as required. Heat is also taken from the standby volume. Energy costs are minimised because the whole of the storage tank volume is not heated. There are temperature layers within the storage tank that the charging process should not be allowed to disturb. This is ensured by adopting low flow velocities, heat pipes and baffle plates on the cold water feed.

Hot water	
Collector surface	Plate collectors: 1.0-1.5 m²/Person Vacuum tubes: 0.8-1.2 m²/Person

Hot water and heating support	
Collector surface	Plate collectors: 2.0-3.0 m²/Person Vacuum tubes: 1.5-2.5 m²/Person

Storage tank	
Plate collector	60-80 l/m² collector surface
Vacuum tube collector	75-100 l/m² collector surface

Tab. 5.4.3 **Values for guidance in the design of solar energy systems for various uses**

Fig. 5.4.5 **Schematic showing details of a combined solar system for room and service water heating with two-storage tanks**

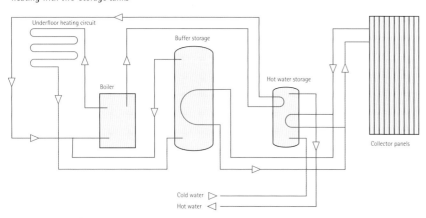

Photovoltaics – solar electricity generation

Solar cells are used to generate electricity. They are normally integrated in modules into the roofs or facades of a building. The optimum arrangement of modules depends on the orientation and latitude of the site. A southern orientation of the modules and an inclination angle of about 30° provides the best results over the whole year. A vertical position on an east or west facade can capture about 60% of the radiation. A tracking system is not normally economic in central Europe because the proportion of diffuse light is about 50%.

Functional details Solar cells are semiconductors. Most solar cells are made from silicon. Mono- and polycrystalline silicon cells enjoy about 80% of today's market. They are sawn out of crystal blocks as 0.3 mm thick, 10 cm wide plates and have a high efficiency (Fig. 5.4.6).

With a thickness of only a few thousandths of a millimetre sputtered on to a substrate, amorphous silicon cells use less material, but their effectiveness is clearly lower (Tab. 5.4.4).

The voltage created by a single photovoltaic cell is about 0.6 volt. The electron flow, termed the current strength, is proportional to the intensity of radiation and the area of the cell. A 10 x 10 cm cell with an irradiance of 900 W/m² produces a current strength of about 3 amps.

To obtain a useful amount of output, 20 to 40 separate cells are normally connected into 1.0 x 0.5 m modules. In solar modules the cells are connected in series in strings to increase the voltage. The strings are connected in parallel to increase the current strength. In series the solar cells with the lowest light intensity determine

the output of the whole module. Hence even very small shadows have a very negative effect. Various loss factors mean that the effectiveness of an ordinary solar module drops below 20%. Some of these factors are physical and cannot really be reduced. A sudden leap in efficiency should therefore not be expected.

Autonomous and networked operation Photovoltaic systems can be operated autonomously or in a network.

Applications for stand-alone solutions include supplying electrical power to mountain huts and refuges, radio relay stations or parking ticket machines. Autonomous systems require rechargeable batteries to store the electricity. Lead accumulator batteries are normally suitable for stationary solar systems. The charging efficiency of a lead battery can be expected to be about 90%. An electronic charge/discharge controller ensures that the battery is charged in the proper manner. The controller switches the charging current off when the end of charge voltage is reached and then on again when the voltage drops below the minimum. An electronic deep discharge load control protects the battery from being drained of too much charge.

In parallel networked operation the current produced by the solar generators is fed into the public grid. The solar inverter is the connection between the solar cells and the alternating supply network. The inverter converts the direct current from the modules into a 230-volt alternating current synchronised with the public grid. Systems coupled with the network use the public grid as storage. If the solar supply produces more than the house requires, the excess is fed into the public grid. If the opposite is the case in poor weather or during the night, the house draws current from the public grid.

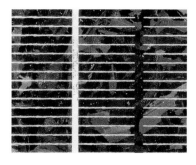

Semiconductors

A semiconductor is a substance with conduction properties between those of a conductor and an insulator. Unlike conductors the resistance of a semiconductor is reduced as its temperature (or insolation) rises. The electrons in a semiconductor are only weakly attached to their atoms. The introduction of energy can break this attachment. The conductivity depends on the introduced energy and the physical properties of the substance.

Solar cell type	Cell efficiency [%]
Monocrystalline silicon	15–17
Polycrystalline silicon	14–15
Amorphous silicon	5–7

Tab. 5.4.4 **Typical efficiency of solar cells**

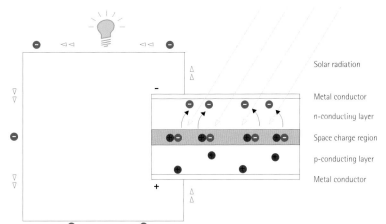

Solar radiation

Metal conductor

n-conducting layer

Space charge region

p-conducting layer

Metal conductor

Fig. 5.4.6 **The principle of a solar cell**
When solar radiation strikes a semiconductor it creates two differently charged layers. The "n-conducting" layer has a higher number of electrons. The "p-conducting" layer has "holes" where electrons are missing. A boundary layer forms between the two layers. An electrical field is created in this boundary layer, the space charge region. The electrons dislodged from their bonds within the atom by solar radiation and any free electrons are accelerated by the charged field to the top surface. Positively charged holes accumulate on the bottom. A voltage builds up between the top and the bottom surfaces. The excess electrons can pass through metal contacts on the top and bottom surfaces from the top to the bottom of the semiconductor and fill the electron holes there.

Energy from ground water and earth

Earth, because of its great mass, has considerable energy that can be used for the cooling of buildings in summer. In winter the warmth of earth can be extracted by a heat pump and used for heating. This potential source of energy can be extracted through piles or buried systems of pipes or boreholes (Tab. 5.4.5) or directly by using the groundwater. This approach is worth considering where relatively small cooling loads are involved. In contrast to air-earth heat exchangers, which contribute to cooling the building only through the ventilation system, water-operated systems can supply thermoactive ceilings, floors or chilled ceilings with cooling energy. Boreholes and piles can be used to take advantage of the seasonal sequence of earth temperature to use the heat stored as a result of cooling in summer for heating in winter by means of heat pumps. Continuous warming of the earth can be avoided in this way, even where natural ground-water movements are small.

Ground water If ground water is used for cooling the building, the ground water pipes must be large enough to be able to deliver the required quantities of water. The determination of geotechnical properties such as soil permeability, the direction and speed of ground water flows is necessary to calculate the spread of the temperature fields and the required distance between the abstraction and injection wells. Ground water should be chemically analysed to ensure compatibility with the evaporator in the heat pump. The ground water is taken from an abstraction well and transferred to the building's system

through a heat exchanger. To avoid the effects of possible fluctuations in ground water levels the abstraction well should be terminated about 5 to 6 m under the actual ground water level. The heated water is returned to the earth down an injection well (Fig. 5.4.7). If the direction of ground water flow is unknown, the injection well should be about 15 m from the abstraction well so that any interaction between them can be prevented. If the direction of flow is known, the injection well should be downstream of the abstraction well. The water temperature varies with the season between 8 and 12 °C, and therefore a design feed temperature of 10 to 12 °C can be assumed. Cooling the building with ground water must be agreed and approved by the local water authorities.

Piles and boreholes Piles may be part of a piled foundation required for structural reasons. They extend 20 to 30 m into the ground and offer many options for constructing earth heat exchangers. Locations where piled foundations are required often have high groundwater levels and good thermal conductivity. The pipes are fixed into the reinforcement cages and concreted into the foundations.

Boreholes on the other hand are bored deep underground to a depth of between 30 and 150 m and can be installed at any time. The boreholes may consist of several individual pipes or a coaxial double pipe. The outside pipe in the coaxial arrangement is in contact with the earth and carries the water from the building, whilst the inner pipe takes the cooled water into the building. Boreholes may be vertical or inclined. The minimum distance between vertical boreholes should be 8 m.

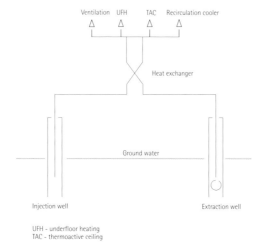

UFH - underfloor heating
TAC - thermoactive ceiling

Fig. 5.4.7 **Principles of ground water use**

Design parameters for boreholes	Cooling	Heating
Average output	30–40 W/m	40–50 W/m
Output with ground water flow > 0.5 m/day	40 W/m	> 50 W/m
Output without ground water flow: poor thermal conductivity of the ground (dry sand)	< 30 W/m	25–30 W/m
Output without ground water flow: good thermal conductivity of the ground	< 30 W/m	30–35 W/m
Average heat and cold energy storage		60–80 kWh/m
Maximum extraction temperature (summer)		ca. 20 °C
Minimum extraction temperature (winter)		ca. 2 °C

Tab. 5.4.5 **Simplified guide values for the design of earth piles and boreholes**
The above heating and cooling outputs are given per 1 m length of borehole or pile (in accordance with EMPA).

Absorption and adsorption chillers

Absorption and adsorption chillers (or refrigeration machines) are used instead of conventional electrically driven compression refrigeration machines for cooling. They are driven by hot water made available from the excess heating potential of district heating plants or waste heat from combined heat and power plants. Combined heat and power plants can operate for longer in the year and at a greater efficiency by making this heat available. Absorption and adsorption chillers are closed systems installed as main units for buildings or parts of buildings. Like compression refrigeration machines, absorption chillers use the sensitivity to pressure of the boiling point and dewpoint of a refrigerant. Instead of the compressor a sorbent absorbs and condenses the refrigerant vapour in the absorber. Through the introduction of heat the refrigerant and sorbent are separated and both substances can be fed back into the circuit (Fig. 5.4.8). The required temperature range of the heat used to drive the system is 80 to 120 °C for single stage absorption chillers. If larger temperature differences are required the compression takes place in two stages, which needs a higher drive temperature of between 140 to 160 °C (Tab. 5.4.6). Nowadays absorption chillers are mainly used in large systems with outputs of 200 to 300 kW. Gas may be used to drive absorption chillers directly as an alternative to hot water.

The absorption chiller is an example of this most widespread thermally driven refrigeration technique. Adsorption is the reversible taking up of gas molecules into the pores of a highly porous adsorption medium, such as silica gel. The system does not work continuously because of the solid adsorption material but switches periodically between cooling and generation. To operate continuously adsorption chillers require at least two separate chambers with adsorption medium. Whilst one of the chambers adsorbs the refrigerant vapour created in the evaporator the other chamber regenerates (Fig. 5.4.9). Adsorption chillers are larger and more expensive than single stage absorption chillers and have no moving parts inside the process chambers. There is also no risk of the sorbent crystallising therefore no limit to the coolant water temperature. Maintenance costs are lower. A cold water tank can be installed to smooth out the fluctuating temperatures caused by the changing of the chambers (Tab. 5.4.6).

Absorption
Take up of gases by liquids.

Adsorption
Take up and physical binding of gases, vapours and liquids at the surface of a substance.

COP Coefficient of Performance [–]
The COP is defined as the ratio of the cooling output and the driving heat required for this.

Tab. 5.4.6 **Overview of the most important processes for producing cooling water with heat**

Process	Absorption chiller			Adsorption chiller
Number of stages	1	2	1	1
Sorbent	Lithium bromide	Lithium bromide	Water	Silica gel
Refrigerant	Water	Water	Ammonia	Water
Drive temperature	80 110 °C	140–160 °C	80–120°C	60–95 °C
Driven by	Hot water	Hot water, steam, direct heating	Hot water, steam, direct heating	Hot water
Efficiency COP	0.6–0.8	0.9–1.2	0.3–0.7	0.4–0.7

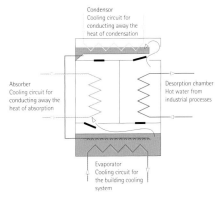

Fig. 5.4.8 **Schematic of an absorption chiller**
The refrigerant vapour formed in the evaporator is sucked into the absorber. The refrigerant vapour is absorbed by the solution. The solution pump delivers the enriched solution to the generator. The absorbed refrigerant vapour is driven out by the introduction of heat. The solution is regenerated and fed back to the absorber. The refrigerant vapour flows into the condenser. The condensed refrigerant flows into the evaporator where it is able to take up heat from the cooling circuit of the building again.

Fig. 5.4.9 **Schematic of an adsorption chiller**
The refrigerant is vaporised in the evaporator and in doing this takes up heat from the cooling circuit of the building. After a certain pressure has been reached, the refrigerant vapour flows into the adsorption chamber, where the refrigerant is adsorbed with the release of heat. This continues as long as the adsorber is able to take up refrigerant. Heat is introduced into the desorber chamber, which causes the adsorbed refrigerant to be driven out of the silica gel. The refrigerant flows into the condenser and is condensed there. When the desorption and adsorption cycle has been completed, the chambers are interchanged.

Air-earth heat exchanger

Air-earth heat exchangers, sometimes called earth pipes or cooling tubes, precondition the outside air drawn from the neighbourhood of the building. This reduces the ventilation heat or cooling energy requirement. Air-earth heat exchangers make use of the temperature of the earth, which at a depth of about 3 m at our latitudes fluctuates between 6 and 15 °C. Air-earth heat exchangers consist of individual pipes or systems of pipes placed horizontally into the ground, which are then used as air ducts. Outside air is drawn through these ducts and prewarmed or precooled. They require mechanical ventilation to work. In residential buildings in winter, air-earth heat exchangers normally only contribute to reducing the ventilation heat losses. The energy gain from the air-earth heat exchanger can prevent icing of the ventilation equipment in winter with heat recovery. If properly designed an air-earth heat exchanger can allow a ventilation plant to operate without a preheating register. In heating mode the earth pipe can raise the air temperature by up to 20 K or drop it by as much as 12 K for cooling (Fig. 5.4.10).

Design Normally in the sizing of a ventilation system the required airflow is set. The length and diameter of the pipe for an air-earth heat exchanger depends on the site, the weather, the height of the ground water level and the thermal and moisture properties of the soil. Soil properties have the greatest influence on the performance of an air-earth heat exchanger. It is often the case that the soil properties are not accurately known in the initial planning phase.

A high soil density and moisture content and a high ground water level all contribute to an increased performance. Surface water soakaways in the ground above the air-earth heat exchanger and short heating and cooling periods have positive effects on its performance.

Performance can also be improved by selecting a pipe of the right size. Low air velocities, long pipe lengths, pipework systems with large pipe spacings and depth are important beneficial factors. If the pipe diameter is too small this can result in increased pressure loss in the pipe system for a given flow, which in turn means much higher electricity consumption for the fan. For large airflows the pipes are usually large enough to walk through, which makes maintenance and cleaning easier.

The pipes must have sealed joints in areas where the ground water level is high to prevent the entry of water. Condensation may form in earth pipes in summer. The pipes must therefore be laid at a fall of 1 to 2% to allow the condensate to run away and seep into the ground at a soakaway or outfall into the waste water system. The design should also incorporate inspection shafts.

Layout The simplest arrangement is to place the pipes in the excavation around the building. A double basement wall can be used for conducting the air. It is important to avoid heat from the building affecting the air-earth heat exchanger.

Pipework systems can also be installed under open area or beneath floor slabs. Additional excavation is necessary for placement under open areas and therefore this option is not usually economic.

PVC is normally suitable for small diameter pipes. For larger diameters concrete or fibre-reinforced cement is more cost effective than plastic.

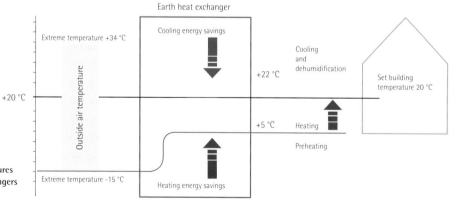

Fig. 5.4.10 **Influence of outside temperatures on the operation of air-earth heat exchangers** *(after Dibowski)*

Energy storage

To be able to use energy sources such as solar energy that are available only at certain times, the energy must be stored in the form of heat or electricity for a while. Ordinary solar systems for heating service water have a storage tank that can retain the heat for a few days. If the system is used as auxiliary heating, a much larger heat store is required to retain enough heat energy for several days of heating. Seasonal energy storage accumulates energy in summer and makes it available in winter.

Phase change materials can also be used to store heat. These latent heat stores have undergone rapid development in recent years. Thermochemical heat storage achieves even higher heat densities. This relies on a reversible chemical reaction. The storage of electrical current can be in batteries or by using hydrogen (Tab. 5.4.7).

Seasonal hot water storage Large insulated tanks can store heat over longer periods. Water, with its high heat capacity, is very good as a storage medium. The temperature level inside a tank containing water fluctuates during the year. A hot water storage tank should be designed to be as compact as possible and have a small surface area. For installation inside a building the tanks are usually made of insulated steel and can be charged and discharged in layers. Outside storage is mostly provided as aquifer storage. Aquifer storage is insulated and filled with gravel and water. Charging and discharging is through pipes at several levels. Effective storage management can optimise the charging and discharging process.

Latent heat storage Latent heat storage exploits the fact that a change of phase, e.g. when a substance melts, is accompanied by the release of a great deal of heat without an increase in the temperature of the substance. These types of substance are also called phase change materials (PCM). Salt hydrates are used for storing heat or cold energy in the temperature range 5 to 130 °C (chemically combined water). Paraffins can also be used for the same temperature range. Paraffins have an energy density comparable to salt hydrates and are often preferred because of their simpler handling. Sugar alcohols are being developed for the temperature range 90 to 130 °C.

The advantages of latent heat storage lie in their higher energy density, and consistent temperatures of release and take up of heat. The feasibility of integrating latent heat storage into buildings as additional thermal storage mass in order to mitigate temperature fluctuations of the building is currently being investigated. PCM can be integrated into gypsum plaster, floors and ceiling systems as well as facade elements.

Ice-storage systems are another option for storing cooling energy. The system is charged with a conventional refrigeration machine operating on cheaper off-peak electricity. The cooling energy is then made available over the day, which reduces the required cooling energy requirement.

Thermochemical storage The crucial advantage of thermochemical storage systems is the almost loss-free heat storage over a long period and the high energy density. Thermochemical storage relies on introducing heat to produce a process of chemical change in the storage medium, for example to desorb water from the medium. When the process is reversed and water added, steam is released from which the heat can be recovered. Silica gel or zeolite is used as the storage medium as they have a larger internal surface area and can bind a great deal of water. Silica gel is a porous glass-like substance. It is particularly suitable for charging with solar collectors. Zeolites are water-containing metal aluminium silicates. They require higher operating temperatures (100 °C) for the desorption process to work but during the discharging process they supply at higher temperatures. Zeolite storage systems have been used to even out the loads on district heating networks in pilot projects. Sorption storage systems are undergoing practical trials as a means of seasonal energy storage to supply buildings.

Batteries as electricity storage The type of battery in most widespread use is the lead battery. With a weight of 350 kg, it supplies about 11 kWh of electricity, which is the equivalent of a litre of heating oil. Sodium sulphur batteries and zinc-air batteries have greater capacities and are being tested as prototypes. Battery storage of electricity from solar systems is only recommended where no main electricity supply is available (Tab. 5.4.8).

Hydrogen as electricity storage Hydrogen electricity storage technology is still in the development stage. It must overcome high costs and technical content as well as large energy losses in generation, transport and use. Electrolysis splits water into hydrogen and oxygen with the help of an electrical current. The gases can be stored in pressure tanks and changed back into electricity again in a fuel cell on a seasonal basis.

Energy density [Wh/kg] [Wh/m³]
Energy density is the amount of energy that can be stored related to mass and/or volume.

Storage type / Storage medium	Energy density / Working temperature
Sensible / Water	approx. 60 kWh/m³ < 100 °C
Latent / Salt hydrate Paraffins	up to 120 kWh/m³ ca. 30–80 °C ca. 10–60 °C
Thermochem. / Metal hydride Silica gels Zeoliths	200–500 kWh/m³ approx. 280–500 °C approx. 40–100 °C approx. 100–300 °C

Tab. 5.4.7 **Physical properties of different storage media**

Battery type	Energy density [Wh/kg]	Cycle strength[1]	Efficiency
Lead-acid (sealed)	20–45	200– 2000	70–80
Lead-acid (gel)	10–30	500	70–80
Ni-Cd	15–45	>5000	60–75
NiMH	40–60	3000– 6000	80–90

Tab. 5.4.8 **Characteristics of different battery types for energy storage in photovoltaic systems**
[1] Cycles with a discharge depth of 60 to 80%

Planning

Without orientation
Reit im Winkl, Mühlengasse 3
9:30 A.M.
*The postman brings the parcel with the competition documents,
which are going to ensure you a major breakthrough. Admittedly
it is not going to be an easy task, but you have always had a soft
spot for energy-optimised construction. Especially since you have
already renovated the old mill in which your apartment and office
are housed ecologically. So why shouldn't you be able to do it again
just on a larger scale? You place the envelope on the occasional
table next to the T-square. Now, you just have to finish planning
your neighbour's winter garden.*
6:30 P.M.
*At first glance you see that the plot for the competition is too nar-
row and pointed and too small. The building line lies along a heavily used road and the alignment, although plausible from the point
of view of urban architecture, would face westwards.*
8:30. P.M.
*You grab your sketch roll and give your creative powers full rein.
You want it to be innovative, with harmonic spaces, natural ventilation and plenty of daylight. But the cost should not be so outra-
geous that the whole project would fail. On the contrary, clever
design should allow savings in building technology.*
10:30. P.M.
*You have just discovered a suitable shape and now you are con-
sidering what the building should look like from the outside, and
already you are facing a series of problems that put your ecological principles to a tough test. What was that again? North-facing
offices are better than east- or west-facing offices, both from
the point of view of daylight and with regard to the conditions in
summer. But don't you get a much more dynamic start to the day
when your office catches the morning sun? Is it possible to cast the
building lines prescribed by the local authority to the wind in order
to get optimum alignment of the building for the air conditions in
the rooms within? And while we are on the subject of wind, will it
be possible to have natural ventilation for the building if it aligns
across the direction of the prevailing winds, or will the staff find
that the wind blows their papers from their desks if they open the
windows? And does this mean that the building needs an expensive
double-skin facade, or will it be enough simply to have a double
facade on the side facing the heavily trafficked street?*
4:15 P.M.
*You come to the conclusion that you can always solve all these
problems at some later point. As the deadline is imminent, you concentrate on your main business, and for just 20 euros, the officer
behind the counter turns the date stamp back one day.*

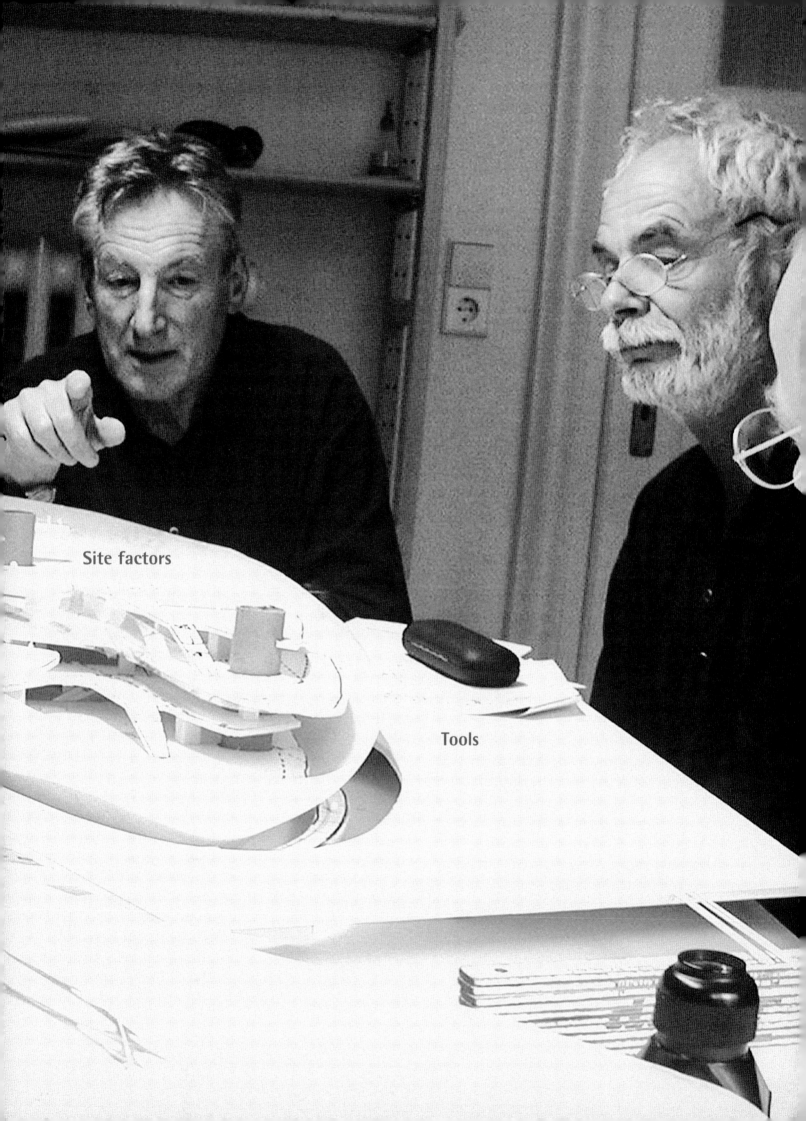

Site factors

Tools

"Study nature; love nature; stay close to nature. It will never fail you."

Frank Lloyd Wright 1867-1959

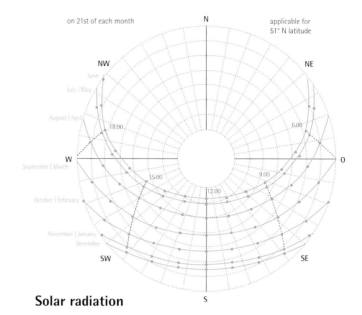

Solar radiation

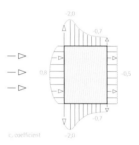

Wind

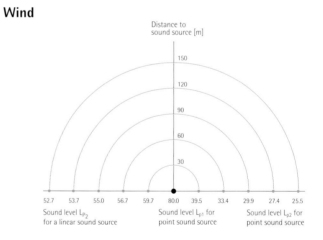

Sound

Site factors

The site of a proposed building is characterised by the climate of the region, the local climate and the microclimate in the immediate surroundings of the building. Therefore climate and the urban context exercise considerable influence on the energy and room climatisation aspects of planning a building. Energy can be saved and the comfort of the user improved by fine-tuning the building concept to suit local circumstances.

The integration of the building with its urban surroundings usually determines orientation and layout and therefore its insolation and exposure to wind and noise. The neighbouring buildings, surfaces and vegetation have their effects on shade, reflection and microclimate.

The quality of the foundation soils and the strata beneath them may permit their use in the heating or cooling of the building. The moisture content of the earth is the critical factor in its thermal exploitation; the ideal situation is flowing ground water. The temperature graph at a depth of 3 m follows the average monthly outside temperature with a delay of two to three months. From a depth of 6 m it follows the average annual temperature. The ground water is at a temperature about 10 °C all year round and can therefore be used directly for cooling and, with a heat pump, for heating. Earth can release or take up energy through the floor slab or piles depending on the form of the foundation. Boreholes reach depths of between 70 and 150 m underground and can be installed at any time in the life of the building. If the building has a ventilation system, the earth can precool or preheat the supply air in an earth pipe.

Insolation causes paved surfaces to heat up severely. Planted surfaces on the other hand are at much lower temperatures; vegetation shelters the surface from solar radiation and evaporation means that it heats up less, creating a positive effect on the microclimate. Deciduous trees provide seasonal shade. In winter some solar radiation can find its way through them. Vegetation also reduces the speed of locally generated wind currents. Areas of water have beneficial effects on thermal comfort as they moderate temperatures in summer by taking up heat or cooling the area by evaporation.

Congested roads or industrial operations create pollution, dust, odour and noise loads. The arrangement of air intakes needs special care in highly polluted areas. Window ventilation is not recommended here.
The noise intensity at a location influences the design for the layout and whether natural ventilation is possible. The seriousness of the noise load depends on the particular source and its distance. Buildings, trees or the topography can suppress noise propagation.

The following effects are noticeable with increasing altitude: Average air temperatures fall by approximately 0.5 K per 100 m and strong winds occur more frequently. The amount of received solar energy is greater at higher altitudes as there is less dust and fog occurs less often. At the same time, temperature differences between day and night are greater, which in turn is beneficial to night cooling. Higher locations have increased requirements for heat insulation but solar energy gains are also higher. Thermal conditions in valleys give rise to mountain and valley winds with directions and strengths which change in the course of the day according to air temperature and solar radiation. At night and in the morning these winds blow out of the valley, from noon to late afternoon into the valley. Cold air fluxes have a positive effect on urban ventilation and carry away emissions. Lack of wind at heating boiler flues can result in stagnant emission zones. In summer the trapped heat increases temperatures, whilst in winter low wind velocities encourage the formation of pools of cold air and mist.

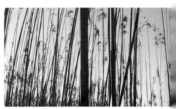

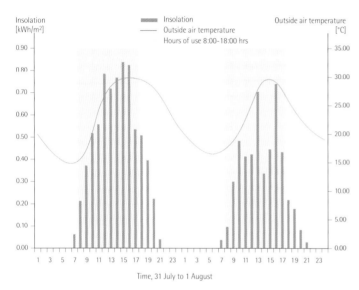

Fig. 6.1.1 **Temperature and radiation over two days shown for an occupancy period of 08:00 to 18:00 hrs for the test reference year in Würzburg**

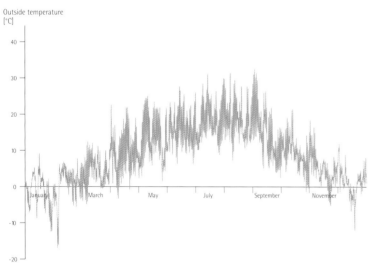

Fig. 6.1.2 **2 Outside air temperature graph over a year for the test reference year in Würzburg**

Climate

The most important parameters affecting climate are solar radiation, air temperature, wind conditions and precipitation. The determinant factors are the geographic coordinates, the height above sea level, the proximity to areas of open water and topography. The tilt of the Earth's axis produces the seasonal cycle of climate, the main engine of this effect being the change in insolation. The earth's rotation produces the sequence of day and night. As latitude increases, the differences in the seasons and day lengths are more pronounced. Coastal regions have a more moderate climate (maritime climate) because of the thermal storage capacity of the sea; regions remote from the coast, on the other hand, are subject to considerable seasonal fluctuations and experience hotter summers and colder winters (continental climate).

The climate in Würzburg represents that of Germany as a whole relatively well. Hence weather data for the test reference year for Würzburg are often used for dynamic simulations.

Outside temperature Outside temperature depends on insolation and the temperature of the incoming masses of air. Outside temperature influences transmission and ventilation heat losses in winter as well as the amount of unwanted incoming heat and options for cooling in summer. Efficient night cooling requires low night temperatures (Fig. 6.1.1). The frequency distribution curve of the number of days of extreme weather is very important to building behaviour. The curve has consequences on the effectiveness of passive cooling and design of technical systems.

Average outside temperatures in summer in Germany are approximately 20 °C, whereas in winter they are around 0 °C (Fig. 6.1.2). Local influences and the immediate weather conditions can be the cause of considerable deviations from average temperatures. Day-night fluctuations generally average between 5 and 10 K.

Humidity In discussing humidity we differentiate between relative and absolute humidity. Absolute humidity is the water content of the air. Its value depends on the season, time of day and weather. It is important when considering the dehumidification of rooms. Relative humidity relates the actual water content of the air to the maximum possible water vapour content of the air at the same temperature (the saturation moisture content). The saturation moisture content increases with temperature. Absolute humidity changes with the season whereas relative air humidity undergoes little variation. The average relative humidity is between 50 and 70%, with no great differences between the seasons.

Solar radiation

Solar radiation is a crucial design parameter as it can reduce heating energy demand and has a considerable influence on room climate in summer (Fig. 6.1.4). The solar angle of incidence changes as the inclination of the Earth's axis changes and this produces the variation in day length. When the sun is low in the sky the solar radiation has a longer path through the atmosphere. The intensity of the solar radiation is also determined by the turbidity of the atmosphere. The insolation on the outer atmosphere of the Earth is 1,360 W/m² (solar constant); in Germany on the Earth's surface the maximum figure is 1,000 W/m². The global solar radiation on the Earth's surface is composed of direct beamed solar radiation and diffuse scattered radiation. Global radiation on a horizontal surface in Germany under a clear sky and low turbidity in summer is up to 8.0 kWh/m²d; the corresponding value in winter is 1.2 kWh/m²d (Tab. 6.1.1). In Germany the daily average number of hours of sunshine in winter is 1.0 hour (out of a possible 7.6 hours), the corresponding values in summer are 7.8 and 16.8 hours respectively. These values deviate in different cities in Germany by between one hour in winter and three hours in summer. The number of hours of sunshine is between 1,400 and 1,800 hours per year. The solar angle of incidence at midday is calculated in spring and autumn as a = 90°- latitude, in summer as a = 90°- latitude + 23.5° and in winter as a = 90°- latitude - 23.5° (Fig. 6.1.3).

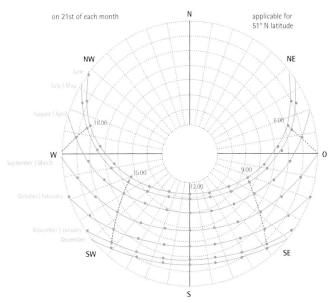

on 21st of each month   N   applicable for 51° N latitude

Fig. 6.1.3 **Sun path diagram over the day for various times of the year, applicable for latitude 51° N**
The celestial hemisphere is represented in terms of polar coordinates. The current position of the sun (height above the horizon and azimuth angle) is shown for each month (sun path) and hour (point). At noon the sun is positioned due south (local solar time).

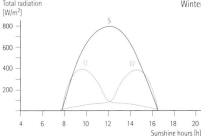

Fig. 6.1.4 **Graph of insolation on surfaces with different orientations in summer, autumn, spring and winter in conditions of low turbidity**

Orientation		Spring/ March	Summer/ June	Autumn/ September	Winter/ December
Horizontal	G_r	2.68	5.54	3.53	0.65
	D_r	1.57	2.95	1.85	0.46
90° South	G_r	2.53	2.81	3.11	1.03
	D_r	1.09	1.96	1.38	0.28
90° East / West	G_r	1.75	3.21	2.29	0.45
	D_r	1.03	1.94	1.28	0.29
90° North	G_r	0.93	2.18	1.14	0.27
	D_r	0.93	1.87	1.14	0.27

Tab. 6.1.1 **Daily insolation, average global solar radiation G_r and diffuse radiation D_r [kWh/m²d]**
The values refer to wall surfaces with different orientations on sunny days in spring, summer, autumn and winter.

Wind

The prevailing wind conditions at the proposed location of the building play a significant role in its design. Important aspects in this are the positive and negative pressures acting on the building envelope. The wind load on a building depends on the predominant wind effects, building form and the surroundings. Positive and negative pressure zones can be used for natural ventilation. The position of supply and exhaust openings must be aerodynamically efficient.

Wind velocities in Germany Average wind velocities in winter are higher than in summer. Wind velocities inland are much lower than those reached at the coast. In northern Germany the average wind velocity is about 5 m/s, in southern Germany about 2 m/s. Wind velocities in summer and winter are less than those in the transition months. Very cold weather is associated with low wind velocities (3 to 8 m/s). High wind velocities of around 20 m/s mainly occur with average outside air temperatures (Tab. 6.1.2). Wind mainly comes from a westerly direction. Very cold winds come mainly from an easterly direction. The reference height for wind data is 10 m. From an aerodynamic point of view, wind flowing over an urban landscape does so in a boundary layer over a rough surface, driven by the undisturbed wind above it (Fig. 6.1.6).

Tab. 6.1.2 Estimated peak wind velocities shown in relation to height above ground

Height above ground [m]	Wind velocity [m/s]	Wind velocity [km/h]
0–8	28	102
8–20	36	129
20–100	42	151

Equation used for the calculation of wind pressure in Fig. 6.1.5

$$p = c_p \cdot \frac{\rho}{2} v^2$$

p   wind pressure [Pa]
c_p wind pressure coefficient [-]
ρ   density of air (1.18 at 25 °C) [kg/m³]
v   wind velocity [m/s]

Equation used in Fig. 6.1.6 for calculating wind velocities in the boundary layer profile
All wind velocities in the wind profile can be calculated for different densities of development using the reference wind velocity at a height of 10 m.

$$v(h) = v(10) \cdot \left(\frac{h}{10}\right)^{\alpha}$$

v(h)   wind velocity at height h [m/s]
v(10)   reference wind velocity at 10 m height [m/s]
h   height [m]
h_G gradient height (surface roughness influence effective up to h_G)
α   roughness coefficient, depends on density of building development

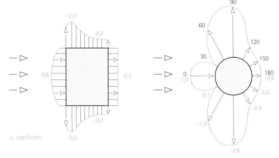

Fig. 6.1.5 **Formation of positive and negative pressure zones when wind flows around rectangular and circular bodies**
The pressure coefficient c_p can be used with the wind velocity to calculate positive and negative pressure loads.

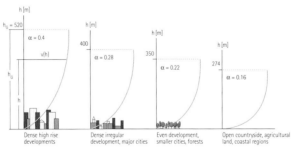

Fig. 6.1.6 **Boundary layer wind velocity profiles and roughness co-efficients for different types of countryside surfaces**
(after Ruscheweyh)

Friction and turbulent shear forces create a wind velocity profile. The thickness of the boundary layer depends on the roughness of the ground. For a level landscape, the boundary layer thickness is approximately 300 m, for higher but irregular development approximately 400 m and for dense high-rise development approximately 500 m.

Pressure distribution on buildings Aerodynamically, buildings are rather stubby, unstreamlined bodies. The flow around buildings depends on the shape of the building, the prominence of its corners, surface roughness of its facade and the shape and slope of its roof. In addition, wind and the anticipated peak velocities increase with height. Wind flow also depends on the wind direction, wind profile and gustiness. When wind flows around a building, it creates a positive pressure on the windward side and a negative pressure on the leeward side which are relatively constant on the whole facade surface. On the sides parallel to the wind the flow separates at the edge facing the wind, which leads to the formation of a negative pressure peak. This negative pressure decreases in the same direction as the wind. The pressure distribution on the facade also creates a gradual drop in pressure inside the building from windward to leeward sides. The pressure differences cause compensatory flows which vary in their intensity, depending on the permeability of the building envelope and the resistance to the flow of air through the inside of the building. The aerodynamic coefficient c_p is used to calculate the pressures (positive and negative) on a facade. This coefficient can be used with the wind velocity at the location to estimate the positive and negative pressures at any point on the facade (Fig. 6.1.5).

Effect of the surroundings The surroundings of buildings affect wind flow. The type of landscape, the shape and separation of neighbouring buildings and local vegetation play a role. The wind flow only reforms itself at ground level some distance behind a building. This means that there is a pronounced turbulent wake in the lee of a building, the size of which depends mainly on the velocity profile and the turbulence of the arriving wind flow. The second building experiences lower wind pressures if is separated from the first by a distance less than the length of the wake. The lower part of the building may even experience negative pressures. The neighbouring buildings can produce a nozzle effect, which increases wind velocities.

Sound

The communicative and aesthetic aspects of sound, speech and music are just as important in the design as noise. Developments in society and advancing technology are leading to increased traffic and industrialisation with an accompanying increase in noise emissions. People are becoming more sensitive to interference in their environment and are annoyed by stray noise. Loud continuous noise can lead to damage to health. It is important to design the type and shape, orientation, internal zoning and facade of the building with sound insulation in mind in order to stay within the limits for noise set out in DIN 4109.

Types of sound Sounds differ in their type, duration and propagation. There are point and linear sound sources (Fig. 6.1.7). A trafficked street is an example of a linear sound source; a crowded school yard is a point source. In duration a sound can be continuous, intermittent or cyclic. Cyclic noise can have a greater effect on the human ear than other types of sound. It is characterised by short peaks of sound above the general level of noise. The propagation of sound may be through the air, directly or reflected, or through solid objects (structure-borne sound), e. g. through building components, machine parts or pipework.

Sound sources External sound sources include road, rail and air transport and industrial noise The outside noise level used for assessing the required sound insulation is determined outside in front of the building. The most frequent source of noise is traffic. The number of vehicles per hour, the gradient of the road, surfacing, speed limit and the distance of the building from the road influence sound levels (Tab. 6.1.3). In the absence of other information, such as statutory noise requirements, development plans or noise maps, average values for traffic noise can be calculated in accordance with DIN 4109. For sound emission calculations on the side of a building facing away from the traffic a value of 5 dB (A) can be subtracted for a low density development area and 10 dB(A) for high density development. The result gives the sound insulation requirements of the outside components.

Sound insulation measures On the one hand, the shape of the building, its height and the orientation in combination with the internal zoning affect the level of noise admitted. On the other hand, the design of the facade, such as the incorporation of sound insulation windows, baffle panels or a double-skin facade, can have an influence on the propagation of sound in the building. The design should always ensure that living and sleeping rooms are affected to the least possible extent by outside noise. If a U-shaped building complex is closed by glass panels to form a protected courtyard, along with the effect of the reduced entry of noise, this solution can offer additional interior quality space. Other influential factors are the density of development, vegetation and the prevailing wind direction on the site. Noise from existing roads can be reduced by noise abatement schemes. These often incorporate sound protection walls or embankments (Fig. 6.1.8).

Tab. 6.1.3 **Average noise level for different roads**

Type of road	Average noise level
Heavy traffic	80
Medium traffic	70
Low traffic	55

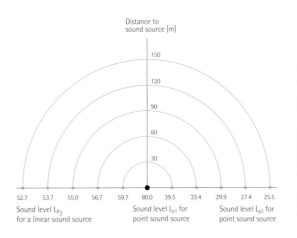

Fig. 6.1.7 **Sound pressure in relation to the type and distance of the sound source in open conditions**

Distance to sound source [m]

150
120
90
60
30

52.7 53.7 55.0 56.7 59.7 80.0 39.5 33.4 29.9 27.4 25.5

Sound level L_{P_2} for a linear sound source

Sound level L_{p1} for point sound source

Sound level L_{p2} for point sound source

Equation used in Fig. 6.1.7 to calculate the reduction in sound for a linear sound source

$$L_{P_1} - L_{P_2} = 10 \cdot \lg \frac{d}{d_0}$$

L_{P_1} sound level of sound source [dB(A)]
L_{P_2} sound level [dB(A)]
r, d distance to sound source [m]
$r_0 = 0.282$ m, $d_0 = 0.282$ m

Equation used in Fig. 6.1.7 to calculate the reduction in sound for a point sound source

$$L_{P_1} - L_{P_2} = 20 \cdot \lg \frac{r}{r_0}$$

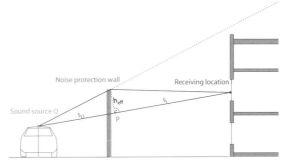

Fig. 6.1.8 **Reduction of sound level by a noise protection wall**
The effective wall height h_{eff} is the main factor in the determination of the reduction in sound achieved by a sound insulation wall.

Equation used in Fig. 6.1.8 to calculate the reduction in sound achieved by a noise protec-

$$D_z = 10 \cdot \log (3 + 6 \cdot 10^{-2} \cdot f \cdot z)$$

whereas:

$$z \simeq \frac{h_{eff}^2}{2} \cdot \left(\frac{1}{S_Q} + \frac{1}{S_I}\right)$$

D_z noise level reduction [dB]
f frequency [Hz]
z sound path length [m]
h_{eff} effective height of the noise protection wall [m]
S_Q distance of sound source to P [m]
S_I distance of emission location to P [m]

"Now there is one outstandingly important fact regarding Spaceship Earth, and that is that no instruction book came with it ..."

Buckminster Fuller 1895-1983
Operating Manual for Spaceship Earth
(1969)

Measurements on prototypes
Mock-up
Climate laboratory

Model measurements
Artificial sky
Wind tunnel

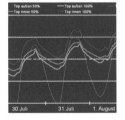

In situ measurements
Blower door test
Measuring luminance
Thermography

Dynamic processes
Lighting simulation
Thermal simulation
Flow simulation

Tools

There are a great number of tools available for planning and optimising a building. They can be used in all phases of a project. Sketches and models are useful for developing three-dimensional geometries. Static methods of calculation can provide estimates of energy quantities and outputs in the case of simple concepts. Dynamic methods of analysis such as computer-aided simulation of light, energy or flows are required when additional transient parameters like time, temperature or flow are introduced into the development of a concept. If the limits of mathematical models or available computing time are exceeded, then wind tunnel tests or measurements in a climate laboratory or on a 1:1 scale model may prove to be the answer. The final stage of building and testing of prototypes has an important role to play in facade design. Planning tools can be generally categorised as either computer analysis or metrological processes. Computer analyses can be static or dynamic.

These methods of investigation may be applied to the planning of live projects or to parametric studies. Parametric studies provide basic knowledge to assess typical questions like whether light deflection systems are effective or natural cooling strategies are efficient. This knowledge forms the basis for a quick and demonstrable preselection of concepts.

As the design of the building progresses the scope for making savings diminishes. Therefore the designer must employ the available tools at the earliest possible moment. The stage of the design must have reached the level of detail appropriate for the particular tool otherwise the results may not be applicable. Detailed simulations are not usually worthwhile in the initial planning phases as the number of design options is still high and many parameters have yet to be established. Using complex tools too early leads to high design costs and in any case there is no time to use them in the initial planning phases.

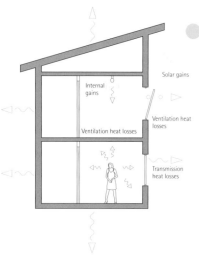

Fig. 6.2.3 **Energy system of a building**

Static design method

Static design methods are the most popular because they are quick, simple and inexpensive to use. They are particularly useful in the early planning stages. Equations, graphs or simple computer programs are used for many construction design tasks, including the calculation of the heating heat demand, cooling load, the required lighting levels or air changes. They are usually based on equations or correlations established from experience, measurement or parametric studies. Static methods describe relationships with respect to energy without taking into account the dynamic of time; in other words, the values of physical parameters cannot be determined for a particular point in time.

Potential studies Potential studies estimate the feasibility in principle of preliminary energy room climatisation concepts. Potential studies often involve drawing up an energy budget. This type of analysis sets the gains and losses of a building against one another and the results are taken into account in the required heating heat capacity or room climatisation system in summer. Further tools used in potential studies include rules of thumb for estimating the heat load, cold air drop, the amount of solar energy admitted or heat to be removed.

Design charts These charts find many uses in design, where they can be made to represent complex processes in a simple way. DIN standards frequently contain design charts. They are also used to show the performance of building energy components, e.g. passive cooling systems. A decision diagram is a special form of design chart that depicts decision making paths for the general selection of

concepts for and the areas and limits of use of building energy systems.

Simplified calculation methods Simplified calculation methods can be used for the design of conventional building and energy concepts. The most popular are used to calculate the annual heating heat demand and the cooling load or as a means of assessing the room climate in summer (Tab. 6.2.3). These simplified methods can also be applied in appropriate circumstances to provide various levels of detailed information for the energy balance over a heating period, monthly or for a day-night cycle.

Requirement	$S \leq S_{all}$	S S_{all}	Calculated solar gain coefficient [-] Allowable highest value [-]
Calculated solar gain coefficient S	$S = \sum (A_{Window} \cdot g_{total})/A_G$	A_{Window} g_{total} A_G	Window area (clear opening size) [m²] g-value glazing incl. shading (g · F_c) [-] Net area of room or part of room [m²]
Allowable highest value S_{all}	$S_{all} = \sum S_x$	S	Proportionally adjusted solar gain coefficient taking into account climatic region, building type, night ventilation, solar control glazing, window inclination, orientation [-]

Tab. 6.2.3 **Procedure for the simplified certification of the summer heat insulation**

Daylighting simulation

Daylighting simulation programs are used to predict and analyse illumination scenarios. Typical uses include the analysis of daylight distribution, the luminance, the efficiency of light deflection systems and the optimisation of the interaction between artificial and natural light. There are two main calculation techniques: radiosity and ray tracing. The radiosity process calculates the distribution of illuminance in the room using the distribution of diffuse light (Fig. 6.2.5). The basic principle equates the introduced radiated energy from light sources to the radiation energy absorbed by all surfaces. The required illuminance is calculated for every surface. Advantages include rapid modelling and short calculation times. The effects of direct light such as shadows and reflections or mirroring cannot be displayed. The results are presented as two- or three-dimensional graphs showing the distribution of illuminance or luminance.

Calculation techniques In the ray tracing process the individual light rays are tracked as they are reflected from the surfaces. The results are realistic three-dimensional images of the rooms being investigated. The lighting data for all surfaces can be mapped using false colour images. Ray tracing allows shading and light deflection elements to be modelled and accurate representation of shadows and reflection or mirroring. Modelling is very expensive and involves long calculations, depending on the level of detail required.

Programs The most popular program for ray tracing is "Radiance", and for radiosity "Superlite". Both programs are included in the integrated software package "Adeline". Various user interfaces are available to generate the input data for "Radiance". The programs can import geometric data exported from CAD programs.

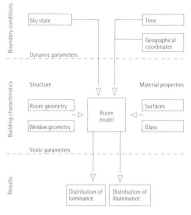

Fig. 6.2.4 **Data flow chart for daylighting simulation**

  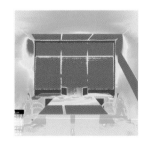

a

b

c

Fig. 6.2.5 **Results of daylighting simulation using the radiosity technique for a 70% glazed south-facing room at noon**
a *overcast sky*
b *summer day with sunshine and shading*
c *summer day with sunshine and light deflection*

Thermal simulation

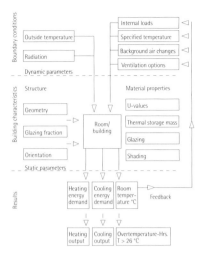

Fig. 6.2.6 **Data flow chart for a thermal simulation**

Thermal and energy-related processes in buildings are highly dynamic, especially if they are coupled with complex energy generation and transfer systems. Detailed estimates of heating and cooling loads, loads plotted against time, or room air and operating temperatures require dynamic analysis procedures that take into account the time components of building climate, internal loads and thermal storage. This involves the recalculation of the system states (temperatures, outputs) at regular time intervals. The results of one calculation stage give the starting values for the calculation for the next time interval.

Programs The most used programs in practice are "Trnsys" and "Tass". The modularity and flexibility of "Trnsys" make it a good tool for solving detailed problems. "Tass" has an input structure that makes it suitable for the simulation of whole buildings. Flow processes are analysed and data transfer for lighting simulation is possible.

Modelling In modelling a building, heat balances for each room are created in which all incoming and outgoing heat flows are input. The computer idealisations are designed as "single node models" because they assume that all heat flows act on a single ideal homogeneous volume of air.

To achieve highly accurate results the boundary conditions of the computer model must be in as close agreement as possible with those of the proposed building. This applies for climatic data, user profiles, building geometry and component characteristics. A dynamic building simulation requires that walls be defined not by their U-values but by the physical characteristics of each of their layers. The use of the building must be specified with respect to time in terms of their occupancy density, internal loads etc. Representative data sets with average hourly values from the German meteorological office must be used for the weather information.

The room model calculates the energy exchange between the surface and an air node. For this reason only an average air temperature is calculated. This is adequate for small rooms. For larger rooms, e.g. atria or halls, thermal layering or flows can create different local temperatures. Room models with an air node have a limited output. This can be overcome to some extent by splitting the room into more than one zone. If this is not successful a detailed calculation using flow simulation is required.

Results The results are a dynamic time-related thermal model of the building showing, e.g. room temperature, or cooling and heating loads relating to the specific building characteristics and conditions of use. The results are output for each time interval. The data can be converted into charts by a spreadsheet program for ease of interpretation (Figs. 6.2.7 and 6.2.8).

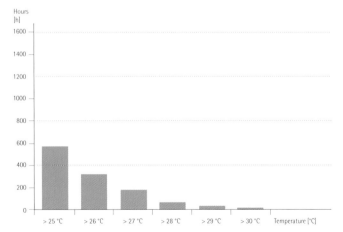

Fig. 6.2.7 **Temperature profile for the same room over the whole year**
Overtemperatures in a 70% glazed south-facing room with external shading and window ventilation over the whole year. The graph shows approximately 350 hours at a temperature above 26 °C.

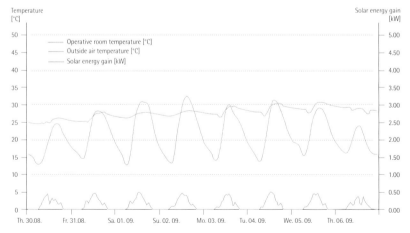

Fig. 6.2.8 **Temperature graph for the same room during a hot summer week**

Flow simulation

In simulating flows for a building, the flows in rooms are handled separately to through-air flows. Room flow simulation can model the flow within a room in great detail. Through-air flow simulation considers the exchange of air between the building and its surroundings and between individual rooms.

Room flow simulation This type of flow simulation calculates room temperature conditions within individual rooms. The technique is frequently used for thermal comfort analysis and for the investigation of smoke propagation in the event of fire. A flow simulation is therefore required when various effects relevant to rooms have to be investigated that cannot be modelled with a thermal simulation program, e.g. temperature layering in atria, aspects of supply air introduction into rooms or the propagation of pollutants.

Flow simulation is based on the finite element method (FEM), which divides the room to be investigated into small volumes using a virtual narrow mesh grillage, e.g. 5 x 5 x 5 cm. The technique models the energy and mass flows between neighbouring cells to calculate local temperatures, pressures and air velocities in the room. These calculations can be carried out for steady state or dynamic conditions. The computing time may be considerable depending on the size of the room involved, the fineness of the grid used and whether a steady or dynamic state is being investigated. Calculations may take anything from one hour to several days.

The physical parameters are output for each cell. This information can be post-processed to yield graphical output for easier interpretation of the results. Typical forms of output include sections showing temperatures or airflow velocities in one plane of a room (Fig. 6.2.11). If a dynamic simulation is carried out the processes can be displayed as a movie.

One popular flow simulation program is "Fluent". Based on "Fluent", "Airpak" is a program package specially designed for use with buildings. A room flow module is available for the program package "Tass".

Through-flow simulation Through-flow simulation is used to model air changes in individual rooms or through-flow processes in buildings. The results can show whether there are adequate air changes in individual rooms and allow flow directions and air exchanges within a building to be analysed so that undesirable odour transmission, draughts or return air flows of heated air can be avoided. Through-flow simulation is an important tool in the planning and design of natural and hybrid (combinations of natural and mechanical) ventilation systems.

The various rooms are modelled in a network of nodes and the air mass and volume flows are balanced. Pressure differences caused by thermal currents, wind or fans provide the driving force. Openings between rooms, windows, overflow openings or leakage are input in terms of their flow resistances.

Through-flow simulations show the sequence of air changes with respect to time. The results are output in tables and can be converted into charts for easier interpretation. Air changes for the whole room are given. Local air velocities cannot be calculated. Air changes driven by wind conditions must avoid being affected by gusts.

The simulation program in most widespread use is "Comis", which is also available as "Trnflow" to interface with "Trnsys". In conjunction with "Tass", the program can be used to calculate air flow through buildings.

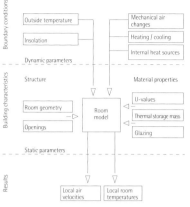

Fig. 6.2.9 **Data flow chart for flow simulation**

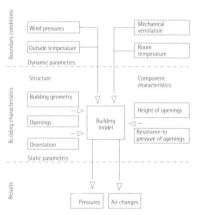

Fig. 6.2.10 **Data flow chart for through-flow simulation**

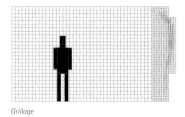

Grillage

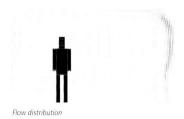

Flow distribution

Temperature distribution

Fig. 6.2.11 **Results of room flow simulation shown as a section**

In situ measurements

Measurements in completed buildings are used to check the proper functioning and quality of a system. These investigations may be necessary following complaints by building users. Another application is the optimisation of building services during the commissioning phase.

Blower door test As heat energy is lost through uncontrolled air changes in winter and there is the danger of damage to the building fabric occurring, it should be possible to make the building substantially air tight. This state can be checked with the blower door test (Fig. 6.2.12). The n_{50}-value is a measure of this air tightness. The measurement system consists of a fan, which is mounted at an opening in the building envelope, normally an entrance door, a pressure difference gauge and a volume flow meter. The volume flow necessary to keep the pressure difference constant is measured and used to calculate the n_{50}-value. The measurements are made with positive and negative pressures to test the efficiency of sealing strips or window seals in both directions. Smoke can be used to locate leaks. In winter the areas of incoming cold air can be located by combining blower door measurements with thermography whilst creating a negative pressure in the building and recording images with an infrared camera.

Thermography An infrared camera can take the temperature of a surface without touching it. Different temperatures are shown in different colours (Fig. 6.2.13). The higher the heat loss through the building envelope, the hotter is the outside surface temperature. Areas with increased heat losses, e.g. heat bridges or construction faults in the insulation, can be located. Thermographic photographs are normally taken when outside temperatures are low.

Room climate measurements Room climate measurement involves the collection of comfort-related data such as air velocity, operative room temperature or air humidity at different places, possibly over an extended period. Low air velocities mean that thermal anemometers are normally used. Globe thermometers measure the air temperature at a point in the room and the radiation temperature of all the surfaces enclosing the room. This enables the operative room temperature to be determined. This temperature offers the best correlation with human sensitivity to heat. Moisture sensors are used to measure relative air humidity.

Tracer gas analysis The exchange of air that takes place naturally or by means of a ventilation system in a room can be measured using a tracer gas analysis. A tracer gas, usually CO_2 or N_2O, is introduced into the room and its concentration monitored over time to determine the rate of air change. There are a number of measurement strategies: the tracer gas can be used once and the decay time determined. Another option is to keep the concentration of the gas constant. The amount of gas introduced then gives the reference value. Several measuring locations may be necessary depending on the room size. Another area for investigation is the exchange of air inside buildings. For this the tracer gas is introduced into one room and its concentration measured in other areas of the building.

Luminance camera The lighting of rooms using natural light is becoming increasingly important, especially in offices. There must be adequate light without glare. A luminance camera can be used to measure the luminance, the physical measure of brightness in candela per square metre (cd/m^2) and determine contrast (Fig. 6.2.14). It is beneficial when doing this to model the whole situation and hence avoid distortions from changing light conditions outside the room. The influence of degrees of cloud cover, the efficiency of natural light deflection systems and the effectiveness of solar or antiglare devices can be checked using a luminance camera.

Hourly air changes n_{50} [–]
This value indicates the hourly air changes due to leaks at a pressure difference of 50 Pa ($n_{50} = V_{50} / V_{Building}$).

Fig. 6.2.12 **Blower door test**

Fig. 6.2.13 **Thermographic image**

Fig. 6.2.14 **Luminance measurement**

Climate laboratory

Using numerical analyses, predictions can be made about room climate, even in complex projects. In some cases it is nevertheless required or desirable to carry out a full-scale experimental verification of the computer analysis.

This type of investigation is mainly performed in a climate laboratory (Fig. 6.2.16). The set-up must model the geometry of the room and the climatic influences to an adequate accuracy. To make the room as dimensionally accurate as possible, it may be necessary to vary the room height or depth. Climate laboratories are therefore often erected in modules so that they can be combined and extended as required. This faithfulness to room geometry is only required if rooms that will be actually built are to be investigated.

Two main methods are used to model the outside climatic conditions. The first is to set the internal surface temperature of the walls by means of heat plates through which water is circulating to a value which is in balance with the U-value of the wall and the specified outside temperature. The second method is to attach a room on the outside facade of the test room. The specified outside climatic conditions are created in this extra room. Typical properties measured in a climate laboratory include air velocity, operative room temperature and relative air humidity (Fig. 6.2.17). Numerous other parameters relevant to energy, acoustics and lighting can also be measured as required. Different visualisation techniques can be used to be able to make accurate estimates of airflows. The simplest way is to release theatrical smoke (Fig. 6.2.15). The light sheet process is a more expensive technique in which particles, often helium-filled glycerin bubbles, are introduced into the room. Sheets of light are created with beams of light or lasers to illuminate the particles in a plane. These sections are photographed and analysed by software.

Fig. 6.2.15 **Flow visualisation with theatrical smoke**

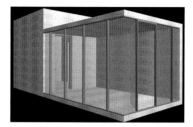

Fig. 6.2.16 **Climate laboratory at the Lehrstuhl für Bauklimatik und Haustechnik, TU Munich** *(in construction)*

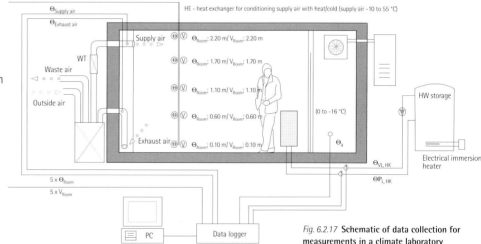

Fig. 6.2.17 **Schematic of data collection for measurements in a climate laboratory**

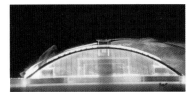

Fig. 6.2.18 **Wind tunnel investigation of the Design Centre Linz at TU Munich**

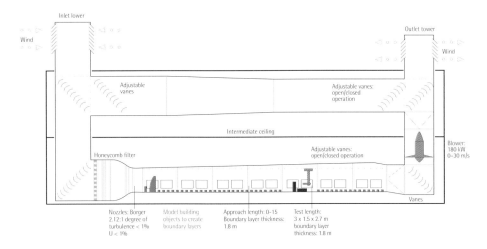

Fig. 6.2.19 **Schematic showing functional components of the boundary layer wind tunnel at TU Munich**

Fig. 6.2.20 **Building model in the test area of the wind tunnel at TU Munich**
(All Figs. Dr.-Ing. Pernpeintner, TU Munich)

Wind tunnel

The effect of the wind on the building skin and the flow of wind through the building play a major role in the development of the facade concept. An understanding of the aerodynamic conditions is important in the positioning of supply and exhaust air openings (Fig. 6.2.18). The values of positive and negative pressures and their fluctuation over time are particularly important. Recontamination is also important. This can be caused by returning flows of exhaust air. Another area of investigation is the flow velocities outside the building. High wind velocities at the corners of the building can reduce comfort, too little exchange of air can delay the removal of pollutants.

Wind tunnel tests are required especially where the design is beyond the current state of the art and existing standards are not relevant. The effect of wind cannot yet be modelled on the computer without a great deal of work. A wind tunnel investigation allows wind flows including gusts to be modelled up to a height of about 300 m. To correctly reproduce wind flows the wind tunnel requires a long approach length (Fig. 6.2.20). The wind boundary layer can be faithfully reproduced by building in eddy generators and creating a suitable roughness to the floor.

On reduced scale models the wind pressures and suctions can be measured and conclusions drawn on the real situation. The wind pressures are sampled by means of holes drilled into the model and fed through flexible tubes to a pressure sensor. The pressure distribution over the whole surface of the building can be calculated by interpolation between the measurement points. The transfer of the pressures measured in the wind tunnel (Fig. 6.2.19) on to the proposed building is by means of the aerodynamic pressure coefficient (c_p) measured on the model. The building model is assembled on a turntable so that different wind directions can be investigated. To take into account wind currents through the surrounding buildings and the topography, it is usual for the adjacent buildings be modelled as well.

Threads or smoke can be used for visualising the flow directions and turbulence. The distribution of wind velocities on the scale of the building's urban surroundings is generally investigated using the sand erosion process. To do this an even layer of sand is applied to a model of the surrounding topography. Zones of high wind velocity exhibit greater erosion of the sand.

Artificial sky

The artificial sky is a visualisation and measuring tool used as a means of decision making about the lighting of the real project. The larger the scale of a model, the better the effects of light on the materials can be assessed. The people responsible for the project can feel confident about the effect of their building at an early stage.

Individual luminaires are arranged in a hemisphere to form the concave sphere of the artificial sky. A total of 393 individual luminaires are arranged in 12 circles at different levels (Figs. 6.2.21 and 6.2.22). Each luminaire is fitted with an opalescent high voltage halogen incandescent lamp and a parabolic aluminium reflector. To match the colour temperature of natural light a colour filter is fitted at each light aperture. An artificial sun is added for an almost natural simulation of the sky on the model (Fig. 6.2.23). All states of the sky at any geographic location can be simulated by intelligent switching and regulation of individual or groups of luminaires. The horizontal and vertical progress of illuminance is measured at several levels. The maximum achievable levels of illuminance and the relationship between horizontal and vertical illuminance can be determined. These values are used to define the spatial milieu.

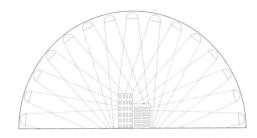

Fig. 6.2.21 **The principles of model testing under an artificial sky**

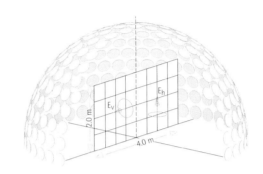

Fig. 6.2.22 **Test zone under an artificial sky**
Horizontal illuminance E_h [lx]
Vertical illuminance E_v [lx]

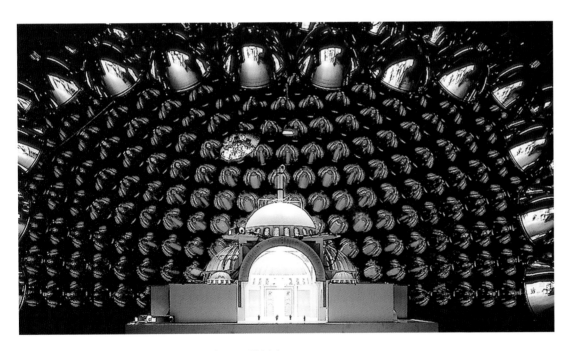

Fig. 6.2.23 **Model of the mosque in Kuala Lumpur under an artificial sky**
The artificial sky in the Bartenbach lighting laboratory has been in use for 25 years and is employed as a testing, presentation and simulation tool. It is regarded as one of the largest and most up-to-date facilities in the world. (All Figs. Bartenbach light laboratory.)

General literature

Daniels, K.: Advanced Building Systems. A Technical Guide for Architects and Engineers. Basel/Boston/Berlin 2003

Daniels, K.: Low-Tech Light-Tech High-Tech. Building in the Information Age. Basel/Boston/Berlin 2000

Hausladen, G., de Saldanha, M., Liedl, P.: Bauklimatik und Energietechnik für hohe Häuser. In: Bergmeister, Konrad, Wörner, Johann-Dietrich: Betonkalender. Berlin 2003

Hausladen, G., de Saldanha, M., Liedl, P., Meindl, H.: Climadesign. Strategien für die ganzheitliche Gebäudeplanung. In: Cziesielski, E.: Bauphysik Kalender. Berlin 2004

Herzog, T., Krippner, R., Lang, W.: Facade Construction Manual. Basel/Boston/Berlin 2004

Herzog, T. Hrsg.; Solar Energy in Architecture and Urban Planning op.cit.

Neufert, E. und P.: Architects' Data. Oxford 2002, 3rd edition

Schittich, C., Staib, G., Balkow, D., Schuler, M., Sobek, W.: Glass Construction Manual. Basel/Boston/Berlin 1999

Tischner, U., Schmincke, E., Rubik, F., Prösler, M.: How to do EcoDesign? Basel/Boston/Berlin 2000

Climate design

Fathy, H.: Natural Energy and Vernacular Architecture. Principles and Examples with Reference to Hot Arid Climates. Chicago 1986

Hausladen, G. (Ed.): Innovative Gebäude-, Technik- und Energiekonzepte. Munich 2001

Hausladen, G., de Saldanha, M., Nowak, W., Liedl, P.: Einführung in die Bauklimatik. Klima und Energiekonzepte für Gebäude. Munich 2003

Hausladen, G., Saldanha, de M., Sager, Ch., Liedl, P.: ClimaDesign. Munich 2003

www.climadesign.de

Man

Bartenbach, C.: Tagesbelichtung von Arbeitsräumen. Lichttechnische und wahrnehmungspsychologische Aspekte. Munich 2002

Birbaumer, N., Schmidt, R.: Biologische Psychologie. Berlin/ Heidelberg 1999

Brandi, U., Geissmar-Brandi, C.: Lightbook. Basel/Boston/Berlin 2001

Fanger, P. O.: Mensch und Raumklima. In: Rietschel, H., Esdorn, H.: Raumklimatechnik, Band 1. Grundlagen. Berlin 1994, 16. Auflage

Fasold, W., Veres, W.: Schallschutz + Raumakustik in der Praxis. Planungsbeispiele und konstruktive Lösungen. Berlin 1998

Schricker, R.: Kreative Raum-Akustik für Architekten und Designer. Stuttgart/ Munich 2001

bph.hbt.arch.ethz.de

http://www.hunecke.de

Systems

Compagno, A.: Intelligente Glasfassaden/Intelligent Glass Facades. Basel/Boston/Berlin 2002

Daniels, K.: Skin Technology; Werkbericht 10, HL-Technik AG, Munich/Zürich, March 1992

Danner, D., Dassler, F. H., Krause, J. R. (Ed.): Die klima-aktive Fassade. Leinfelden-Echterdingen 1999

Hindrichs, D. U., Heusler, W.: Fassaden/Facades. Basel/Boston/Berlin 2004

Köster, H.: Dynamic Daylighting Architecture. Basel/Boston/Berlin 2004

Lieb, R. –D.: Double-Skin Facades. Basel/Boston/Berlin 2001

Schittich, C.: In Detail: Solar Architecture. Basel/Boston/Berlin 2003

Schneider, A. (Ed.): Solar Architektur für Europa. Basel/ Boston/ Berlin 1996

Szermann, M., Gertis, K., Kaase, H.: Auswirkung der Tageslichtnutzung auf das energetische Verhalten von Bürogebäuden. Stuttgart 1994

Watts, A.: Modern Construction Facades. Basel/Boston/Berlin 2005

Zimmermann, M.: Handbuch der passiven Kühlung. Dübendorf 1999

Typologies

Ambrozy, H. G., Giertlová, Z.: Planungshandbuch Holzwerkstoffe. Technologie – Konstruktion – Anwendung. Vienna 2004

Bednar, M.J.: The New Atrium. New York 1986

Bundesamt für Energie, Bern (Ed.): Lüftung von großen Räumen – Handbuch für Planer. Dübendorf 1998, 2. Auflage

Eisele, J., Kloft, E. (Ed.): High-Rise Manual. Typology and Design, Construction and Technology. Basel/Boston/Berlin 2003

Pültz, G.: Bauklimatischer Entwurf für moderne Glasarchitektur. Passive Maßnahmen der Energieeinsparung. Angewandte Bauphysik. Berlin 2002

Saxon, R.: Atrium Buildings. Development and Design. London 1986
Stewart, M.: The Other Office, 2004

Herzog, T.: Nachhaltige Höhe / Sustainable Height, Munich/London/ New York, 2000

Technologies

Braun, H., Grömling, D.: Research and Technology Buildings. Basel/Boston/Berlin 2005

Bubenzer, A., Luther, J.: Photovoltaics Guidebook for Decision-Makers. Basel/Boston/Berlin 2003

Goldblatt, D. L.: Sustainable Energy Consumption and Society. Basel/Boston/Berlin 2005

Henning, H. M.: Solar-Assisted Air-Conditioning of Buildings. Basel/Boston/Berlin 2004

Humm, O., Toggweiler, P: Photovoltaics and Architecture. Photovoltaik und Architektur. Basel/Boston/Berlin 1993

Interpane Glas Industrie AG: Gestalten mit Glas. Lauenförde 2002, 6. Auflage

Lieb, R.-D.: Double-Skin Facades. Basel/Boston/Berlin 2001

Marshall, J. M., Dimova-Malinovska, D.: Photovoltaic and Photoactive Materials – Properties, Technology and Applications. Basel/Boston/Berlin 2002

Richardson, J., Björheden, R., Hakkila, P., Lowe, A. T., Smith, C. T.: Bioenergy from Sustainable Forestry. Basel/Boston/Berlin 2002

Wellpott E.: Technischer Ausbau von Gebäuden. Stuttgart 1979, 8. Auflage 2000

Wilson, H. R.: Potential of thermotropic layers to prevent overheating; SPIE 2255, 1994

http://www.bine.fiz-karlsruhe.de
Fachinformationszentrum Karlsruhe

Planning

Erhorn, H., Stoffel, J.: ADELINE 3.0. Building Energy Analysis and Design Tools for Solar Applications. Stuttgart 2002

Gauzin-Müller, D.: Sustainable Architecture. Basel/Boston/Berlin 2002

Harlow, W. M.: Art Forms from Plantlife. NewHarlow, W. M.: Art Forms from Plantlife. New York 1976 Klima, die Kraft mit der wir leben, hrsg. vom WWF und Pro Futura. Munich 1994

Hauser, G., Hausladen, G.: Energiebilanzierung von Gebäuden. Stuttgart 1998

Lam, W.: Sunlight as a Formgiver for Architecture. Atlanta 1986

Patterson, W.: The Energy Alternative. Changing the Way the World Works. London 1990

Standards

Man

EN 12464-1 Lighting of work places, Brussels 2002

DIN EN 12464-2 Lighting of work places, Berlin 2003 (Draft)

DIN EN 12665 Basic terms and criteria for specifying lighting requirements. Berlin 2002

DIN EN ISO 7730 Analytical determination and interpretation of thermal comfort using calculation of the PMV and PPD indices and local thermal comfort. Berlin 2003 (Draft)

Typologies

DIN EN ISO 7730 Analytical determination and interpretation of thermal comfort using calculation of the PMV and PPD indices and local thermal comfort. Berlin 2003 (Draft)

Index

Authors

**Prof. Dr.-Ing.
Gerhard Hausladen**
07.10.1947
Mechanical
Engineering,
TU Munich

Moritz Selinger
26.11.1979
Architecture,
TU Munich
Facade concepts,
room conditioning

Martin Ehlers
Dipl.-Ing.,
Dipl.-Ing. (FH)
19.05.1965
Mechanical
Engineering,
TU Dresden
Supply Engineering,
FH Munich
Room climate

Josef Bauer
14.04.1965
Technician,
Regensburg
Room climate,
energy concept
development

Michael de Saldanha
Dipl.-Ing.
05.04.1966
Architecture,
GH Kassel,
Energy systems
electronics engineer,
Climate Design

Fabian Ghazai
Dipl.-Ing.
28.06.1977
Architecture,
TU Munich
Technologies,
IT Administration

Dr. Helge Hartwig
Dipl.-Phys.
02.11.1961
Physics, TU Munich
Windows, facades,
natural light systems,
shading,
switchable glass

Cornelia Jacobsen
Dipl.-Ing. (FH)
19.06.1970
Physical Technology,
FH Munich
Energy concepts,
facade advice

Petra Liedl
Dipl.-Ing.
21.07.1976
Architecture,
TU Munich
Climate Design

Barbara Hausmann
11.11.1980
Architecture,
TU Munich
Building climatics

Alexandra Liedl
07.09.1979
Psychology,
University of Jena
Man,
intercultural matters

Martin Bauer
Dipl.-Ing. (FH)
27.11.1975
Supply Engineering,
Munich
Sanitary engineering,
fire protection
systems

Christina Sager
Dipl.-Ing.
24.06.1975
Architecture,
GH Kassel
Climate Design,
facade planning,
energy concept
development

Hannah Lippert
08.09.1979
Architecture,
TU Munich
Building climatics

Christian Zacherl
Dipl.-Ing.
18.05.1977
Architecture,
TU Munich
Atria

Oliver Trieb
Dipl.-Ing. (FH)
24.06.1965
Mechanical
Engineering,
Neubiberg
Supply engineering,
building
technical services

Hana Meindl
Dipl.-Ing.
22.12.1975
Architecture,
TU Munich
Building typology,
sound insulation,
residential buildings

Antonia Schaller
05.07.1979
Architecture,
TU Munich
Building climatics

Simone Steiger
Dipl.-Ing.
11.09.1978
Architecture,
TU Munich
Building climatics

Martin Kirschner
Dipl.-Ing. (FH)
16.03.1973
Supply Engineering,
Munich
Heating and
climate technology

Christiane Kirschbaum
17.12.1979
Architecture,
TU Munich
Man, lighting
concepts,
illustration
coordination

Wolfgang Nowak
Dipl.-Ing.
01.11.1969
Mechanical
Engineering,
TU Munich
Climate laboratory

Rainer Sonntag
Dipl.-Ing.
29.05.1960
Mining Engineering,
TU Clausthal
Fire protection,
Lecturer
TU Munich

Christian Klein
Dipl.-Ing. (FH)
20.11.1971
Supply Engineering,
Munich
Heating and
climate
technology, I&C

Michael Smola
20.01.1979
Architecture,
TU Munich
Facade concepts,
Climate Design

Ulla Feinweber
Dipl.-Ing.
27.10.1963
Architecture,
TU Munich
Building typology

**Dr.-Ing.
Christoph Meyer**
03.12.1961
Mechanical
Engineering,
TH Karlsruhe,
Promotion Uni Kassel
Technical
building services

Stefan Löbe
Dipl.-Ing. (FH)
22.03.1977
Supply Engineering,
Munich
Heating and
climate technology

The authors in the first three rows work at the Lehrstuhl für Bauklimatik und Haustechnik, TU Munich.
The authors in the bottom row work at Ingenieurbüro Hausladen in Kirchheim, Munich

Illustration credits

Illustrations

The authors and publisher would like to thank all those who have contributed to the publishing of this book by providing their illustrations, granting permission for their reproduction or giving advice. All the drawings in this book have been produced in-house. Photographs for which no photographer is named have been obtained from the departmental library. Despite intensive efforts we were not able to determine the owners of some of the illustrations. The copyrights of these images are nevertheless preserved. Where this has occurred we would welcome the relevant information. The numbering refers to the number of the figure in the book or the page number.

Climate design

Man
Klaus Schweiger: page 15

Systems
Auer + Weber + Architekten: 3.3.10, 3.3.12, 3.3.13
Bernhardt und Partner: 3.2.20
Bieling & Bieling: 3.2.22
Herzog + Partner: page 38 second column, second illustration
Meyer, Constantin: page 38 first column, first illustration, page 38 first column, third illustration, page 38 second column, first illustration, page 38 third column, second illustration
Gebr. Trox GmbH: page 60 all

Typologies
Auer + Weber + Architekten: 4.1.20, 4.1.21, 4.1.22, 4.1.23, 4.1.24, 4.1.25, 4.1.27, 4.2.8, 4.2.9, 4.2.10
Bauer, Josef: 4.4.7
Beishuizen, Wim: page 131 bottom
Görner, Reinhard/ Artur: page 121 top
GWG: 4.4.8 and page 126 bottom
Halbe, Roland: page 101 top
Henn Architekten: page 116
Huthmacher, Werner/ Artur: page 121 bottom
Kunz, Edwin: page 131 centre
Lange, Jörg: page 131 top
Lehrstuhl Huse, TUM: page 111 bottom
Lehrstuhl Königs, TUM: page 100 (from: Glässel, J.: Städtische Sonnenräume, Karlsruhe 1985)

Korn, Moritz/ Herzog + Partner: 4.1.29
Klomfar, Bruno: page 81 bottom
Kunnert, Stefan: 4.2.9
Lanz Architekten: 4.1.17
Leistner, Dieter/ Artur: page 98, 4.4.4, 4.4.6 and page 110
Meyer, Constantin: 4.2.4, 4.2.5, 4.4.11, 4.6.6, 4.6.10 and page 129 bottom, page 138 bottom
Riehle, Thomas/ Artur: page 81 centre
Schiebel, Christian: page 94 bottom
Weiß, Gerhardt: page 80, page 101 top, page 120
Wormbs, Valentin: 4.3.4 and page 111 centre, page 121 centre

Technologies
Bartenbach Lichtlabor: page 149 right top
Dr. Hartwig, Helge: page 147 right top
Meyer, Constantin: page 148 left top, page 151 right top, page 159 right top, page 160 left top, page 161 right top, page 171 right top, page 176 left top, page 177 right top
Minimax GmbH & Co.KG: page 157 right top
Schweiger, Klaus: page 146 left top
Gebr. Trox GmbH: page 153 right top

Planning
Auer + Weber Architekten: page 179
Bartenbach Lichtlabor: page 186 second column, first illustration, third line, first illustration Bild, 6.2.23
fechner media: page 186 second column, sixth illustration
Dr. Hartwig, Helge: page 186 second column, second illustration
Nowak, Wolfgang and Meindl, Hana: 6.2.16
Dr.-Ing. Pernpeintner, Albert: page 186 first column, fourth illustration, 6.2.18, 6.2.20

All drawings have been created based on the documents made available by the participating architectural offices. All the graphics in the chapter Man and some graphics in the chapter Typologies were created by Andreas Kretzer, Munich.

This book was prepared at the Institut für Entwerfen und Bautechnik, Fakultät für Architektur, Lehrstuhl für Bauklimatik und Haustechnik, Technische Universität Munich.

Translation into English: Raymond Peat, Aberdeenshire UK
English Copy editing: John O'Toole, New York

A CIP catalogue record for this book is available from the Library of Congress, Washington D.C., USA

Bibliographic information published by Die Deutsche Bibliothek.
Die Deutsche Bibliothek lists this publication in the Deutsche
Nationalbibliografie; detailed bibliographic data is available in the
Internet at http://dnb.ddb.de.

© German edition 2005 ClimaDesign by Verlag Georg D.W. Callwey GmbH & Co.KG Munich.
2005 Licence granted to Birkhäuser –Publishers for Architecture, P.O. Box 133, CH-4010 Basel, Switzerland
Part of Springer Science + Business Media

Printed on acid-free paper produced from chlorine-free pulp. TCF ∞
Printed in Germany
ISBN-10: 3-7643-7244-3
ISBN-13: 978-3-7643-7244-6

9 8 7 6 5 4 3 2 1   www.birkhauser.ch